Understanding Maritime Security

Understanding Maritime Security

CHRISTIAN BUEGER
TIMOTHY EDMUNDS

Oxford University Press is a department of the University of Oxford. It furthers
the University's objective of excellence in research, scholarship, and education
by publishing worldwide. Oxford is a registered trade mark of Oxford University
Press in the UK and certain other countries.

Published in the United States of America by Oxford University Press
198 Madison Avenue, New York, NY 10016, United States of America.

© Oxford University Press 2024

All rights reserved. No part of this publication may be reproduced, stored in
a retrieval system, or transmitted, in any form or by any means, without the
prior permission in writing of Oxford University Press, or as expressly permitted
by law, by license, or under terms agreed with the appropriate reproduction
rights organization. Inquiries concerning reproduction outside the scope of the
above should be sent to the Rights Department, Oxford University Press, at the
address above.

You must not circulate this work in any other form
and you must impose this same condition on any acquirer.

Library of Congress Cataloging-in-Publication Data
Names: Bueger, Christian, 1975– author. | Edmunds, Timothy, author.
Title: Understanding maritime security / Christian Bueger, University of
Copenhagen and Timothy Edmunds, University of Bristol.
Description: New York, NY : Oxford University Press, [2024] |
Includes bibliographical references and index.
Identifiers: LCCN 2024000725 (print) | LCCN 2024000726 (ebook) |
ISBN 9780197767153 (paperback) | ISBN 9780197767146 (hardback) |
ISBN 9780197767177 (epub)
Subjects: LCSH: Sea-power. | Maritime terrorism. | National security. |
Sea control. | Piracy—Prevention. | Ships—Security measures.
Classification: LCC V185 .B84 2024 (print) | LCC V185 (ebook) |
DDC 359/.03—dc23/eng/20240304
LC record available at https://lccn.loc.gov/2024000725
LC ebook record available at https://lccn.loc.gov/2024000726

DOI: 10.1093/oso/9780197767146.001.0001

CONTENTS

Preface vii
List of Abbreviations xi

1. Understanding Maritime Security 1
   1.1 WHY MARITIME SECURITY MATTERS 1
   1.2 WHAT IS MARITIME SECURITY? 2
   1.3 THE KEY CHARACTERISTICS OF MARITIME SECURITY 3
   1.4 THE OPPORTUNITIES OF MARITIME SECURITY 5
   1.5 HOW TO READ THIS BOOK 6

2. A Short History of Security at Sea 11
   2.1 OCEAN HISTORY AND THE EVOLUTION OF MARITIME SECURITY 11
   2.2 FOUR STRUGGLES THAT SHAPE SECURITY AT SEA 12
   2.3 THE RISE OF THE MARITIME SECURITY AGENDA 21
   2.4 THE CONTEXT FOR MARITIME SECURITY 28

3. Frameworks for Maritime Security Analysis 30
   3.1 THINKING TOOLS AND ANALYTICAL FRAMEWORKS 30
   3.2 THE LAW OF THE SEA AND LAW-CENTRIC FRAMEWORKS 31
   3.3 STATE-CENTRIC FRAMEWORKS: INTERESTS AND INSTITUTIONS 38
   3.4 INTERPRETIVE APPROACHES: MAKING MEANING, UNDERSTANDING PRACTICE 45
   3.5 THE ROOT CAUSES OF MARITIME INSECURITY 52
   3.6 USING ANALYTICAL FRAMEWORKS 58

4. Interstate Conflicts, Terrorism, and Grey Zones 60
   4.1 POLITICAL CONFLICT IN THE MARITIME DOMAIN 60
   4.2 INTERSTATE CONFLICTS AND DISPUTES 60

4.3 MARITIME TERRORISM AND EXTREMIST VIOLENCE 70

4.4 GREY ZONES 77

4.5 UNDERSTANDING CONFLICT AND TERRORISM AT SEA 84

5. Blue Crime: Pirates, Smugglers, and Ecocriminals 86

5.1 THE VARIETY OF CRIME AT SEA 86

5.2 WHAT IS BLUE CRIME? 87

5.3 THE PERILS OF PIRACY 91

5.4 SMUGGLING BY SEA 98

5.5 ILLICIT FISHING AND OTHER ENVIRONMENTAL CRIMES 110

5.6 INTERLINKAGES 118

6. The Who's Who of Maritime Security 119

6.1 ACTORS IN MARITIME SECURITY 119

6.2 WHAT'S IN A STATE? NAVIES, COAST GUARDS, AND OTHER AGENCIES 120

6.3 A GLOBAL FIELD: INTERNATIONAL AND REGIONAL ORGANIZATIONS 128

6.4 PROFIT: THE INDUSTRY AND PRIVATE SECURITY PROVIDERS 137

6.5 MORE THAN PROTEST? NONGOVERNMENTAL ORGANIZATIONS AND ACTIVISTS 145

6.6 INTEGRATING MARITIME SECURITY ACTORS 151

7. The Toolbox of Maritime Security Solutions 153

7.1 IDENTIFYING SOLUTIONS 153

7.2 INFORMALITY AND EXPERIMENTALISM 154

7.3 OPERATIONS AT SEA 160

7.4 MARITIME SECURITY STRATEGIES 165

7.5 MARITIME DOMAIN AWARENESS 171

7.6 CAPACITY-BUILDING 180

7.7 USING AND IMPROVING THE TOOLBOX 188

8. New Challenges and a Look to the Future 190

8.1 THE EVOLVING MARITIME SECURITY ENVIRONMENT 190

8.2 AUTOMATION AND CYBER SECURITY 191

8.3 CRITICAL INFRASTRUCTURE PROTECTION: PORTS, CABLES, AND PIPELINES 197

8.4 CLIMATE CHANGE AND BIODIVERSITY LOSS 204

8.5 BETWEEN PLANETARY THINKING AND GEOPOLITICS 209

8.6 FIFTH WAVE OR NEW ERA? 215

Index 219

PREFACE

Understanding Maritime Security provides the first coherent and concise introduction to the complex field of maritime security. The book synthesizes a decade of scholarship, research, teaching, talking, and thinking about maritime security. It evolved from conversations with people engaged in the diverse spectrum of maritime tasks in different part of the world. It aims to make intricate matters digestible, to connect the dots between different issues and disciplinary approaches, and to take a global view.

This book could not have been written without the feedback received from colleagues in academia, policy, planning, and out at sea, the participants in training courses that we taught in Bangkok, Geneva, Malta, Rome, Singapore, Stellenbosch, and Monterrey, as well as the students of the University of Copenhagen Department of Political Science's Security and Risk Masters Programme. Our experiences from teaching maritime security and exploring issues together in such settings has profoundly influenced this book.

We are grateful to the numerous colleagues who agreed to review sections of the manuscript. Specifically, we would like to thank Sean Andrews, Sir Anthony Dymock, Douglas Guilfoyle, John Huggins, Emiliano Magnalardo, Andrew Mallia, Sara McLaughlin Mitchell, Marianne Perondoise, Jan Stockbruegger, Bec Strating, and the anonymous reviewers from Oxford University Press, who all provided invaluable and detailed comments, suggestions, and advice. We are also grateful to Scott Edwards for research assistance that has informed Chapter 5.

In addition, we are indebted to friends and colleagues for numerous insightful conversations and engagements over the years that have influenced our thinking on maritime security. They include Felicity Attard, Matthias Albert, Johnathan Luke Austin, Darshana Baruah, Bob Beckman, Curtis Bell, Anthony Bergin, Siri Bjune, Mark Blaine, Henrik Breitenbauch, David Brewster, Malcolm Brown, Sebastian Bruns, Andrea Calderaro, Bruno de Seixas Carvalho, Allan Cole,

Edward Chan, Chris Chant, Jane Chan Git Yin, Caroline Cowen, Elizabeth DeSombre, Klaus Dodds, James Driver, Sir Malcolm Evans, Jonas Franken, Brendan Flynn, Basil Germond, Sofia Galani, Dennis Hardy, Justin Hastings, Marcus Houben, Shanaka Jayasekara, Lydelle Joubert, Natalie Klein, Collin Koh Swee Lean, Axel Klein, James Kraska, Kristian Søby Kristensen, Steve Lalande, Jessica Larsen, Tobias Liebetrau, Anna Leander, Philippe Le Billon, Felix Mallin, Robert McCabe, Elizabeth Mendenhall, Kaitlin Meredith, Raj Mohabeer, Giulia Nicoloso, Dan O'Mahoney, Matthew Parker, Jeffrey Payne, Kimberley Peters, Kerstin Petretto, Vonintsoa Rafaly, Ian Ralby, Dennis Riva, Sanjeet Ruhal, Barry Ryan, Nilanthi Samaranayake, Antje Scharenberg, Anna Sergi, Anja Shortland, Joshua Tallis, Simone Tholens, Geoffrey Till, Clive Schofield, Licinia Simao, Michelle Stallone, Francois Vrey, Timothy Walker, Brian Wilson, Anders Wivel, the staff of the Information Fusion Center in Singapore, the Danish Ministry of Foreign Affairs, the United Kingdom Department for Transport, the European External Action Servies, the European Commission, Indian Ocean Commission, the United Kingdom Joint Maritime Security Centre, University of Coventry, Atlantic Center of the Portuguese Ministry of Defense, and colleagues from the Global Insecurities Centre at the University of Bristol and the Department of Political Science of the University of Copenhagen, as well as those who have attended events organized by the SafeSeas network.

Research for this book has benefitted from grants and institutional support from the British Academy (GF160017); the UK Economic and Social Research Council (ES/S008810/1; ES/T501840/1); the Danish Ministry of Foreign Affairs, administered by DANIDA; the Velux Foundation; Geneva Graduate Institute; Indian Ocean Commission; University of Copenhagen; University of Bristol; University of Malta; and University of Seychelles.

The book draws on and extends ideas published in earlier articles.

We draw throughout on ideas first discussed in Christian Bueger and Timothy Edmunds, "Beyond Seablindness: A New Agenda for Maritime Security Studies," *International Affairs* 93, no. 6 (2017): 1293–1311.

Chapter 3 draws on Christian Bueger, "What is Maritime Security?," *Marine Policy* 53 (2015): 159–164, and Christian Bueger, "Learning from Piracy: Future Challenges of Maritime Security Governance," *Global Affairs* 1, no. 1 (2015): 33–42.

Chapter 5 synthesizes arguments presented in Christian Bueger and Timothy Edmunds, "Blue Crime: Conceptualising Transnational Organised Crime at Sea," *Marine Policy* 119 (2020): 1–8.

Chapter 7 develops ideas first presented in Christian Bueger and Timothy Edmunds, *Mastering Maritime Security: Reflexive Capacity Building and the Western Indian Ocean Experience. A Best Practice Toolkit* (Cardiff: SafeSeas, February 2018).

Chapter 7 also draws on ideas presented in Christian Bueger, "From Dusk to Dawn? Maritime Domain Awareness in Southeast Asia," *Contemporary Southeast Asia* 17, no. 2 (2015): 157–182, and Christian Bueger, "Effective Maritime Domain Awareness in the Western Indian Ocean," Policy Brief 104, June 2017, Institute for Security Studies: Pretoria, Copenhagen and Bristol, October 2023.

LIST OF ABBREVIATIONS

ASEAN	Association of Southeast Asian States
BBNJ	Biodiversity Beyond Areas of National Jurisdiction
CGPCS	Contact Group on Piracy off the Coast of Somalia
CMF	Combined Maritime Forces
DcoC	Djibouti Code of Conduct
EEZ	Exclusive Economic Zone
EU	European Union
FAO	Food and Agriculture Organization
G20	Group of 20
G7	Group of 7
GFW	Global Fishing Watch
GMCP	Global Maritime Crime Programme of the United Nations Office on Drugs and Crime
ICJ	International Court of Justice
IFC	Information Fusion Centre of the Singapore navy
IHO	International Hydrographic Organization
ILO	International Labour Organization
IMO	International Maritime Organization
IO	International Organizations
IOM	International Organization for Migration
ISA	International Seabed Authority
ISPS	International Ship and Port Facility Security Code
ITLOS	International Tribunal for the Law of the Sea
IUU	fishing Illegal, Unregulated and Underreported fishing
MARPOL	International Convention for the Prevention of Pollution from Ships
MDA	Maritime Domain Awareness
MSA	Maritime Situational Awareness

MSCHoA	Maritime Security Centre Horn of Africa of the European Union
MSO	Maritime Security Operations
NAFO	Northwest Atlantic Fishery Organization
NATO	North Atlantic Treaty Organization
NGO	Non-Governmental Organization
ReCAAP	Regional Cooperation Agreement on Combating Piracy and Armed Robbery against Ships in Asia
RFMO	Regional Fisheries Management Organization
SHADE	Shared Awareness and Deconfliction meeting
SUA	Convention for the Suppression of Unlawful Acts against the Safety of Maritime Navigation
UKMTO	United Kingdom Maritime Trade Operations
UN	United Nations
UNCLOS	United Nations Convention on the Law of the Sea
UNCTAD	United Nations Conference on Trade and Development
UNDP	United Nations Development Programme
UNEP	United Nations Environment Programme
UNESCO	United Nations Educational, Scientific, and Cultural Organization
UNHCR	United Nations High Commissioner for Refugees
UNODC	United Nations Office on Drugs and Crime
UNWTO	World Tourism Organization of the United Nations
WMO	World Meteorological Organization

1
Understanding Maritime Security

1.1 Why Maritime Security Matters

The oceans are the lifeblood of the global economy. Over 80% of the volume of all global trade is transported by sea. Ninety-nine percent of transcontinental communications transit through data cables that lie on the ocean floor. The oceans are a source of food for large parts of the global population. A significant proportion of the world's energy supply is either directly derived from the sea through oil and gas platforms or wind farms, or is transported by ships and pipelines. Yet the sea can also be a site of danger and harm.

Maritime security is a concept that addresses the diverse threats, risks, challenges, and opportunities of the maritime space. It presents a way of understanding and responding to issues of insecurity and crime at sea as well as enhancing the governance of the sea and the welfare of people dependent on it.

In the popular image, piracy is the main problem on this agenda. And indeed, piracy is one of the most prevalent issues that maritime security operations deal with today. However, maritime security addresses a wide range of challenges. These include serious crimes at sea, such as the smuggling of narcotics, weapons, or people, and illicit fishing that harms the marine environment. Militarized disputes between states, maritime terrorism, and other forms of violence at sea are also important concerns.

The agenda of maritime security was first introduced in the late 1990s as part of a wider trend toward rethinking security beyond military threats and the state—a development known as the widening and deepening of security.[1] In this sense, maritime security provides a new outlook on which problems of security at sea require attention. These are not limited to questions of war and peace between states, but also relate to the fight against maritime crime, and the need

---

[1] Barry Buzan and Lene Hansen, *The Evolution of International Security Studies* (Cambridge: Cambridge University Press, 2009), 187–225.

Understanding Maritime Security. Christian Bueger and Timothy Edmunds, Oxford University Press.
© Oxford University Press 2024. DOI: 10.1093/oso/9780197767146.003.0001

to safeguard shipping, ensure sustainable resource exploitation, and protect the marine environment. Maritime security thinking draws on and advances older and more established discourses, including sea power, marine safety, and the law of the sea, but interprets and complements them in new ways.

Maritime security is a complex challenge. It incorporates a multitude of threats and risks, and the wide range of actors and organizations that are implicated in addressing them. These include government entities—navies, coast guards, maritime police, fisheries agencies, and so on—but also international and regional organizations, private companies, and civil society actors. The number of agencies, ministries, and nonstate actors involved in maritime security is thus substantial.

The goal of this book is to provide an overview of the main challenges and issues on the maritime security agenda, and to acquaint professionals and analysts with the repertoire of major maritime security solutions. The book provides you with frameworks for analyzing issues, countries, and regions in depth. It also introduces you to the most important tools that have been developed to deal with maritime security in practice.

1.2 What Is Maritime Security?

There is no one universally agreed definition of maritime security. Various actors interpret and prioritize maritime security differently, reflecting distinct interests, values, and concerns. In this respect, it is a contested concept and there is often significant divergence on the specific issues that should be included and excluded from it (see Chapter 3, Section 3.4). However, there is broad agreement on the core components of the maritime security agenda.

As a starting point, the core of maritime security can be considered to consist of three dimensions of challenge, which we illustrate in Figure 1.1.

The first is an *interstate dimension*. It concerns the security issues that arise between states. These include disputes and conflicts over boundaries, territory, or resources, and provocations or violations of international law, for example through so-called grey-zone activities at sea. As we discuss in Chapter 4, Section 4.4, grey-zone activities are coercive actions by states or their proxies which avoid the overt or attributable use of military force and therefore fall below the threshold of outright war. Examples include the aggressive use of coast guards and fishing fleets in maritime disputes, as has been the case in the South China Sea, the use of proxy forces or drones to threaten shipping in the Strait of Hormuz and Red Sea and attempts to covertly sabotage undersea maritime infrastructures such as cables and pipelines in the Baltic Sea and elsewhere.

A second dimension concerns *maritime terrorism and extremist violence* at or from the maritime domain. Extremist organizations have attacked ships and used

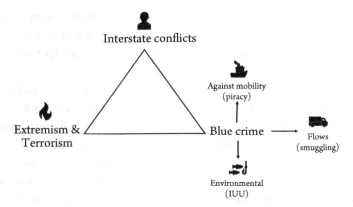

Figure 1.1 The three dimensions of maritime security

the sea as conduits for their activities. As we discuss in Chapter 4, Section 4.3, extremist attacks at sea occur much less frequently than on land, though large-scale incidents have taken place in the Western Indian Ocean and Southeast Asia. Extremist groups such as Abu Sayyaf in Southeast Asia or Al-Shabaab in Somalia also engage in maritime crimes to fund their activities. Violence on land can also spill over into the maritime domain, as has been the case with attacks on shipping off the coast of Yemen.

A third dimension is *blue crime*; that is, different expressions of transnational organized crime at sea. We identify three forms of blue crimes based on the harms they cause. These comprise, first, crimes against maritime mobility such as when pirates attack ships; second, criminal flows, such as smuggling activities that move people or illicit goods across the sea; and finally, those crimes that cause substantial harm to the marine environment such as illicit fishing or pollution at sea.

1.3 The Key Characteristics of Maritime Security

These three dimensions of maritime security (interstate conflict, extremist violence, blue crime) are distinguished from each other by the legal rules they operate under, the actors that are involved, and the kinds of legitimate responses they engender. However, they are also bound together by a series of cross-cutting characteristics that bring them together under the maritime security agenda and make it a distinct problem of international security.

The first characteristic is rather obvious. Maritime security challenges manifest on, in, or across the maritime domain, the features of which shape all three dimensions. The global ocean is vast in size, covering more than 70% of the earth's surface. It presents a unique kind of physical environment, comprising water, waves, ice, rocks, islands, and archipelagos. It is easy to hide in, and difficult to police and surveil. This can make it an attractive space for those wanting to stay hidden, such as terrorists or criminals.

The maritime space is also subject to a different legal regime to that of the land, as we explore in Chapters 2 and 3. Under the United Nations Convention on the Law of the Sea (UNCLOS), the main international treaty governing the oceans, only the first 12 nautical miles out from a state's coastline—what is known as its "territorial sea"—is controlled by states and subject to their laws. Beyond that, out to a maximum distance of 200 nautical miles from the coast is the exclusive economic zone (EEZ), in which states have special rights to explore, exploit, and manage marine resources such as fisheries or undersea oil or gas deposits. Beyond the EEZ is a unique ocean zone known as the high seas, in which no single state has jurisdiction, but international regulations apply. Ships, for instance, are governed under the laws of their designated flag states. Maritime security problems often cross between these zones and legal regimes. They thus imply complex and overlapping constellations of governmental control and responsibility, and often shared jurisdictional authority.

It is also important to recognize that few maritime security issues are problems of the sea alone. For example, organized crime in the maritime domain will be planned and funded by networks based on land, and its profits laundered and spent on land too. Many of the root causes of maritime insecurity are to be found on land, whether they be conflict and instability or economic dislocation in coastal communities. For this reason, many maritime security challenges have a liminal character, in that they take place over and across the boundary between land and sea. We explore these issues further in Chapters 3 and 5.

The second shared characteristic of maritime security is the *interconnected and interdependent* nature of challenges it presents. These interconnections are present between each of the three dimensions we outline above. For example, violent extremism and blue crimes are often closely interlinked, with political extremist groups sometimes engaging in crime at sea to help fund their activities. Interstate disputes often include aspects of blue crime. The South China Sea dispute, for instance, is driven in part by conflicts over fisheries and contestations over state-sponsored illicit fishing activities. As we discuss in Chapter 5, similar observations can be made across and between different types of blue crime, which often have significant intersections with each other.

Third, maritime security is complex in terms of the *actors* involved, as we show in detail in Chapter 6. A broad range of government agencies, industries, civil society organizations, and communities have a role to play in addressing maritime security issues or are impacted by them. Navies and coast guards are the most obvious actors. But maritime security is also a concern for border guards, fisheries control, or environmental management agencies too. In most cases, a surprisingly wide array of government agencies and departments are involved, and the number of users of the sea that have a stake in maritime security is extraordinarily high. The transnational nature of the maritime space means that multiple different states (and their agencies) commonly need to work together to solve maritime security problems.

A whole range of private actors are important for maritime security, too. Depending on the issue, these may include coastal communities and fishers, seafarers, shipping, fishing, resource extraction, and tourist industries, as well as sometimes private military and security companies. It follows that maritime security in practice requires cooperation and coordination between states, agencies, and public and private actors.

These challenges have triggered an innovative set of responses and solutions. Many states and regional organizations have produced dedicated strategies for maritime security. Novel and experimental practices have been developed to deal with the problem of actor complexity, including mechanisms for interagency coordination and the use of informal governance arrangements. New means of surveillance and information sharing, known as maritime domain awareness, have been created to better understand what is happening at sea, and to ensure rapid, sometimes multinational responses to incidents. International actors have also launched an impressive range of capacity-building and security assistance programs to support states with weak capabilities or institutions to implement these solutions. We explore this repertoire of maritime security solutions in Chapter 7.

1.4 The Opportunities of Maritime Security

Maritime security is about more than dealing with an evolving and interconnected landscape of threat and risk. It is also an opportunity to rethink how the oceans should be governed and how the diverse agendas that deal with different aspects of security at sea can be brought together. As a concept and agenda, maritime security invites us to recognize and utilize the relations between related ideas and agendas, many of which are predecessors to maritime security thinking. As shown in Figure 1.2, maritime security relates and embeds several of these in new ways.

Debates on national security, sea power, and naval strategy have long dominated security thinking at sea and remain important to the maritime security agenda today. Equally, maritime security is coupled with the marine safety agenda, where the goal is to prevent accidents, the loss of life at sea, and pollution from marine activity. Maritime security also invites us to consider how

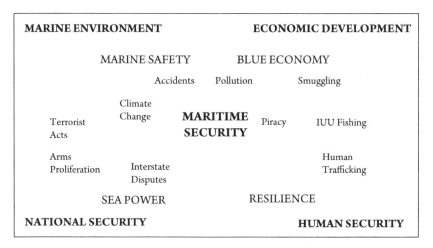

Figure 1.2 The scope of maritime security. Source: Christian Bueger, "What Is Maritime Security?," *Marine Policy* 53 (March 2015): 161.

security is related to and shapes sustainable economic development, marine environmental protection, and the concerns of the people living by and from the sea. These issues are known as the blue economy, environmental security, and human security agendas. They are vital in conceptualizing the meaning and practice of maritime security, since they tell us what is at stake in the debate: the welfare of states, coastal communities, people, and the health of the marine environment. Maritime security is hence a connector, weaving together different challenges, opportunities, and agendas, and providing new solutions to address these issues productively and cooperatively.

1.5 How to Read This Book

The aim of this book is to introduce the maritime security analyst and professional, as well as the general reader, to what they need to know about maritime security. Our focus is on introducing you to the most important frameworks for analyzing maritime security (Chapters 2 and 3) and the main issues on the maritime security agenda (Chapters 4 and 5), as well as the practical tools that have been developed to deal with maritime security (Chapters 6 and 7). We conclude the book with an outlook of where the maritime security agenda is heading in the future (Chapter 8).

The maritime security analyst and professional is often confronted with a fragmented and complex picture. Much of the current literature and analysis is spread across regions and academic disciplines and is often hard to access. Our goal is to bring these issues together and connect the dots. By showing how things hang together, we bring different lines of discussion in maritime security together in a coherent picture. This includes the diverse ideas and arguments developed in debates on the law of the sea, sea power, naval strategy, coast guard functions, marine safety, transnational crime, surveillance, marine protection, blue economy, blue justice, or capacity-building. This allows for a better understanding how maritime security links issues, actors, and opportunities in theory and practice.

While our focus is on exploring linkages and underlying principles, we will also introduce you to a series of cases and incidents that have influenced maritime security globally. We draw particularly on examples from Europe, the Mediterranean, the Gulf of Guinea, the Western Indian Ocean, and Southeast Asia, because these regions have been the primary focus of many maritime security activities. We will often refer to developments in these regions, since many of the tools for responding to maritime security have been developed in these contexts. Yet they are relevant for other regions and situations as well and speak to maritime security globally, including in the Atlantic, the Caribbean, South Pacific, the Arctic, and Antarctica.

This approach also has some limitations. Since we focus on awareness, context, and understanding, we will not provide you with deep dives into empirical cases or investigate technical standards or legal treaties in detail. The goal of *Understanding Maritime Security* is less to explore the various important discussions related to the use of naval forces or the organization of naval operations, marine safety standards, or debates on how to interpret UNCLOS and related treaties or principles of litigation. Very good introductions to these subject matters already exist, and we will guide you to these throughout this book. Here we focus on how maritime security as a concept and agenda integrates and relates to these specific issue areas.

In introducing you to the essence of maritime security, we are foregrounding connections and providing frameworks for thinking. This implies that we do not take a strong stance on what works and what does not, for example, or what should or should not be prioritized. Indeed, how solutions play out is highly dependent on context, and our discussion is meant to inform good choices of priorities and solutions, rather than to prescribe them.

Our survey of maritime security starts out from a discussion of historical context in Chapter 2. This is important because it allows us to understand where the maritime security concept and agenda has come from, how it relates to wider debates and contentions on ocean governance, the international system and global political economy, and how it has evolved since its inception. We argue that the maritime security agenda represents a distinct way of understanding the problem of insecurity at sea. However, we also suggest that it has a backdrop in earlier ways of thinking, in particular the work on sea power, the law of the sea, and marine safety. The chapter explores these connections and the broader themes that condition the nature of the maritime security challenge today. We also introduce the evolution of maritime security thinking in a series of distinct waves which take us up until the present day.

Chapter 3 introduces four analytical frameworks for the study of maritime security. These frameworks provide us with an initial showcase of what is at stake in the maritime security agenda, and why it is so complex and difficult to deal with. Drawing on research from a range of academic disciplines, including law, security studies, international relations, criminology, and development studies, we provide different perspectives on the maritime security problematic. Each of the frameworks we outline has its own strengths and weaknesses. The analyst and practitioner hence needs to have a comprehensive understanding of how and where the different frameworks can be useful. We discuss international legal analysis, state-centric approaches that focus on power and institutions, and interpretive approaches that focus on meaning making, and analyze the practical challenges that maritime security gives rise to. We also explore the factors that give rise to maritime insecurities in the first place, often known as the root causes. Taken together, these frameworks provide a grounding in how to go about analyzing maritime security challenges and solutions.

In Chapters 4 and 5 we draw on the triangle of maritime security challenges introduced above. We explore each of the dimensions of maritime security in depth. Chapter 4 addresses politically motivated maritime security challenges. We consider interstate conflicts and terrorism, before discussing a series of recent practices that have become known as grey-zone or hybrid warfare. These introduce new ambiguities and uncertainties into the state/nonstate divide and pose difficult challenges for maritime security forces and international law.

Chapter 5 investigates blue crime, which is often considered to lie at the heart of the maritime security agenda. Blue crime is an important concept for grasping the different facets and relations of transnational crime at sea, and we provide a more detailed discussion of the benefits of the term. This provides the basis from which we then explore concrete expressions of blue crime. We first focus on piracy off the coast of Somalia, in Southeast Asia, and in the Gulf of Guinea to show how this crime harms marine transport. We then show how criminals use the sea for various types of trafficking activities which cause harms on land, focusing on the smuggling of narcotics and people. Finally, we discuss environmental crimes at sea. These are illicit activities that harm the maritime environment in various ways. We focus particularly on illicit fishing as an emblematic example of this kind of crime.

What ways and means are available to address these maritime security challenges? Chapters 6 and 7 focus on responses and solutions. To understand solutions, we require a good sense of which actors are part of maritime security, what kinds of logics drive them, and what their capabilities and limits are. In Chapter 6, we first explore states as the pivotal actors of maritime security. We investigate how countries organize their responses across multiple different government departments and agencies and discuss issues of civil–military relations and coordination between them. Next, we look at international and regional organizations. These provide platforms for coordination, the development of rules, monitoring at sea, and capacity-building. From there, we turn to the role of the commercial sector in maritime security, including the shipping industry and private security providers. These are actors whose activities are driven primarily by profit rather than general interests. Finally, we address civil society and nongovernmental organizations. These often challenge state and industry activities through their political activism but can also provide important expertise and sometimes even direct capability support to these same actors.

Chapter 7 introduces the practical instruments that form the repertoire of maritime security solutions. We first discuss informal and experimental governance approaches. These include a variety of important mechanisms that are used at national and regional levels for coordination and cooperation. From there we turn to maritime security strategies as a tool for prioritizing, organizing, and coordinating maritime security responses, before introducing the concept and practice of maritime domain awareness. This comprises a series of information sharing and surveillance activities, the goal of which is to provide accurate knowledge of what is going on at sea, and to coordinate responses to it. Finally, we investigate capacity-building and security assistance projects which aim to assist states which lack the resources and capacities to secure their maritime zones, and which serve to promulgate the maritime security agenda globally. Each of these solutions faces challenges of implementation, and we investigate these thoroughly throughout the chapter.

What is the future of maritime security? In Chapter 8 we zoom out by looking at newly emerging challenges in maritime security. We first discuss the expansion of automation and digitalization, and the growing importance of cyber security in the maritime domain. Next, we turn to the increasing convergence between debates on maritime security and critical infrastructure protection at sea. We focus on the need to protect subsea critical infrastructures such as data cables as a key driver in this debate. From there, we discuss the impact of climate change and biodiversity loss on the maritime security agenda, including the range of new challenges and tasks these issues are likely to present. Finally, we address two paradoxical shifts in global politics that are influencing the evolution of security at sea. These comprise, on the one hand, a shift toward planetary and holistic thinking in relation to ecosystems and sustainable development in ocean governance, and, on the other, a resurgence of geopolitical thinking and strategic competition in the maritime domain.

While we recommend that the book chapters be read in progression, we equally invite you to just straightforwardly dive into the chapter that interests you the most. We also recommend that the chapters be read in pairs. If you are interested in context and frameworks of analysis, you will find this covered in Chapters 2 and 3. For those most interested in the problems and issues of the triangle of maritime security, we address these in Chapters 4 and 5. If you are working on solutions to maritime security, for instance, in the field of strategy, operations or capacity-building projects, it is best to read Chapters 6 and 7 together. Chapter 6 will provide you with an overview of the actors that you need to consider, while Chapter 7 offers important thinking on the implications and challenges of more hands-on solutions. For those interested in the future of maritime security, including what challenges need to be anticipated and require strategic planning, Chapter 8 is a must-read.

Whether you read individual chapters or the entire book, you will gain an in-depth understanding of what is at stake in maritime security. You will learn what the key issues of security at sea are, and what effective responses and solutions to these issues might look like in practice. Whether you want to generally expand your knowledge in the area, seek a new career, or handle a specific professional task, the book provides you with the essential knowledge you require.

2

A Short History of Security at Sea

2.1 Ocean History and the Evolution of Maritime Security

Security challenges at sea have been present throughout history. For centuries, states and colonial empires have engaged in conflicts to establish maritime dominance. They have also confronted threats posed by pirates, smugglers, and various criminals operating in the maritime domain. The contemporary maritime security agenda traces its roots to a series of earlier debates, controversies, and ways of thinking about the oceans. This chapter examines the rise of maritime security as a discernible concept and political agenda and reviews the historical context in which this evolution took place. The purpose of this historical account is to provide a deeper understanding of the origins of the maritime security agenda, and to identify its continuities and relationships with earlier concerns.

We begin by discussing four historical struggles that characterize security at sea. The first of these struggles is between competing grand visions of how the oceans should be governed. The second concerns naval dominance and control of the sea between states. A third relates to capitalist expansion and its limits, while a fourth encompasses issues of legality, justice, and representation. We trace the development of these struggles over time and show how, from the 1950s to the 1990s, the main elements of the present international order at sea took shape. These four struggles prefigure but also set the conditions for the rise of the maritime security agenda from the early 2000s onward.

We go on to identify five subsequent waves of maritime security thinking. During the first wave, the primary focus is on maritime terrorism. It is followed by a second wave that develops in response to the problem of piracy off the coast of Somalia. A third wave is characterized by the rise of holistic thinking, which acknowledges the interconnections between maritime security issues and the need for integrated solutions. This is followed by a fourth wave, marked by the further expansion of the agenda, and strong emphasis on capacity-building to promote this understanding globally. Finally, we suggest that a fifth wave is emerging, characterized by geopolitical competition on the one hand and the rise of planetary thinking to address the impacts of climate change and biodiversity loss on the other.

2.2 Four Struggles That Shape Security at Sea

Nearly two-thirds of the Earth's surface is covered by water. In the common imagination, the geographical, political, and social space of the sea is set against that of the land. The land is characterized by patterns of law, order, and control. It can be occupied, settled, and inhabited. In contrast, the sea appears inhospitable to human life and affairs. It is a constantly shifting environment, wracked by storms, and devoid of solid ground to walk on or drinkable water to sustain oneself. For these reasons, the oceans have often been understood as a "space beyond geography,"[1] or as a "space beyond society."[2]

Yet the oceans have always played a critical role in human society and relations.[3] In prehistory they provided the highways that allowed human populations to settle the globe. Since antiquity, commerce and communication have been conducted across seas and along riverine systems. Fishing has provided a critical source of protein for societies worldwide, with fishers venturing ever farther from their own coastlines. Throughout this time, the oceans have allowed exchange and connection between societies that were geographically distant on land. They played a pivotal role in enabling trade and warfare between states and empires, and later enabled the rise of the European colonialism.

In fact, contrary to being an empty space devoid of human politics and society, the seas have been the battleground for intense political rivalries and a hub of social activity for many centuries. In the following sections, we explore these struggles and consider how they established the conditions for the rise of the maritime security agenda as we see it today.

---

[1] Philip Steinberg, "Free Sea," in *Spatiality, Sovereignty and Carl Schmitt: Geographies of the Nomos*, ed. Legg Stephen (Abingdon: Routledge, 2011), 268–275.

[2] Kimberley Peters, "Future Promises for Contemporary Social and Cultural Geographies of the Sea," *Geography Compass* 4, no. 9 (2010): 268–275.

[3] David Armitage, Alison Bashford, and Sujit Sivasundaram, eds., *Oceanic Histories* (Cambridge: Cambridge University Press, 2017).

Grand Ocean Visions

Perhaps the most foundational of the struggles revolves around three competing grand visions of ocean governance and control.[4]

The first is the view that seas can be claimed and territorialized in the same way as the land. In law, this position is often referred to by the Latin term *mare clausum*, which means "closed sea." The idea of closed seas was formalized in the 1494 Treaty of Tordesillas, when Portugal and Spain divided the then-known global ocean between them as their sovereign domains. More recently, the issue has been discussed as a question over who has control over and access to ocean resources, including fisheries and oil and gas reserves, but also who should have responsibility for search and rescue, marine safety, and environmental protection. The key anchoring concept of this vision is *territory*. Much of the debate concerns the extent to which the oceans should be territorialized and subjected to sovereign control.[5]

A contrasting, and second, position is that of a "free sea" (*mare liberum*), which posits that the ocean is a space beyond human ownership and control. This position is often seen as the opposite of territorialization in that it holds that the ocean should not be owned or controlled by any political power. The idea is historically linked to the Dutch scholar Hugo Grotius and his 1609 essay "*Mare Liberum*," in which he stressed the importance of open seas for trade. As Zoltán Glück notes, *mare liberum* implies an ideal-type maritime environment as a "a frictionless, obstacle free space of circulation."[6] The key organizing concept in this line of thought is *freedom*, both in terms of freedom of navigation and movement for ships, and the freedom to exploit ocean resources in an unrestricted manner. This issue is particularly important in narrow straits or chokepoints, such as the Suez Canal or the Strait of Malacca, through which the free movement of ships is necessary for global trade.

Though enduring, the notion of free seas has always been contested, whether through historical piracy, commerce raiding during wartime, or debates over the territorialization of home waters. In the contemporary context, the focus is on the issue of freedom of navigation, and the extent to which this should be

---

[4] David Bosco, *The Poseidon Project: The Struggle to Govern the World's Oceans* (Oxford: Oxford University Press, 2022).

[5] For the debate, see Daniel Lambach, "The Territorialization of the Global Commons: Evidence From Ocean Governance," *Politics and Governance* 10, no. 3 (July 2022): 41–50; Christian Bueger, "Pragmatic Spaces and the Maritime Security Agenda," in *The Routledge Handbook of Ocean Space*, ed. Kimberley Peters, Jon Anderson, Andrew Davies, and Philip Steinberg (London: Routledge, 2022), 179–189.

[6] Zoltán Glück, "Piracy and the Production of Security Space," *Environment and Planning D: Society and Space* 33, no. 4 (August 2015): 645.

restricted or controlled by states according to their political, strategic, or economic interests.

Finally, a third vision sees the maritime domain as a global commons and part of the shared heritage of humankind. This is a more recent position. It was outlined most prominently by Arvid Pardo and Elisabeth Mann Borgese during the law of the sea negotiations of the 1970s and 1980s. Contrary to the concept of freedom, where no one is in charge, this position suggests that everyone should have responsibility for the stewardship and conservation of the ocean. Accordingly, ocean governance should be carried out by international organizations to which states would delegate this authority. The key concept is here that of the *common*. Much of the debate concerns how the income from ocean resource exploitation can be distributed equitably.[7]

These three visions present competing understandings of what kind of space the ocean is, and who should be responsible for its governance, control, and stewardship. The question of how to reconcile these visions, and how to manage the tensions between them in practice, is one of the overarching themes which underpins the rise of maritime security thinking.

Naval Dominance and Sea Control

One of the implications of thinking of the seas either as closed territories subject to the sovereignty of states (*mare clausum*) or as free seas lying beyond individual state control (*mare liberum*) is that they become the object of political and military competition between states. In the closed seas formulation, states must defend and protect their maritime territories from encroachment or predation by rival powers. In contrast, the free seas position sees the oceans as largely unrestricted spaces, in which geopolitical struggles can be played out and maritime trade depends on protection through the application of naval power.

As Alfred Thayer Mahan argued in his classic text *The Influence of Sea Power upon History*, mastery of the sea through naval supremacy was the key to the geopolitical, military, and economic rise of maritime powers such as the United Kingdom and United States.[8] It enabled them to secure their own borders, dominate global trade, and project military power abroad. Certainly naval power was critical to the rise of the European empires from the late 1400s onward. In the fifteenth century, navigation and shipbuilding technologies, alongside military innovations such as the development of cannon and other firearms, enabled

---

[7] Elisabeth Mann Borgese, *The Oceanic Circle: Governing the Seas as a Global Resource* (Washington, DC: Brookings Institution, 1999).

[8] A. T. Mahan, *The Influence of Sea Power upon History, 1660–1783* (Cambridge: Cambridge University Press, 2010 [1890]).

Portugal and Spain to form colonial empires in South America and Asia.[9] The later rise of England, France, and the Netherlands as naval and maritime trading powers allowed them to embark on colonial enterprises of their own. Control of the seas facilitated vast global networks of colonial extraction, exploitation, and trade; the creation of settler states in the Americas, Southern Africa, and Australasia; and the rise, and eventually the demise, of the transatlantic slave trade.

Naval power has also been critical to the conduct of war between states. Sea battles such as Lepanto (1571), between the Catholic states of Europe and the Ottoman Empire; Trafalgar (1805), between Britain and France; Tsushima (1905), between Russia and Japan; and Midway (1942), between the United States and Japan were all inflection points in the geopolitical landscape of their times. Naval dominance at sea was key to the allied victories in both the First and Second World Wars, enabling strategies of blockade and global power projection. The two world wars also saw major shifts in weapons technology that extended the reach of naval power above and below the water, rendering the ocean an increasingly three-dimensional space for military forces. The development of submarine technology provided new tools for commerce raiding and naval blockade. Naval aviation and aircraft carriers allowed the extension of naval power far into the land, and well beyond the firing range of even the largest battleships.

Technological advancements, particularly the advent of nuclear weapons, also shaped the Cold War at sea.[10] The oceans provided a hiding place for both side's nuclear missile submarines, while radar, sonar, aviation, and missile technologies increased the range and lethality of warships. This period also saw the maintenance of overseas naval bases for the projection of power and influence at distance, a new interest in small island states as nuclear weapons testing sites as well as countermoves such as the creation of nuclear weapons free zones at sea, and new security partnerships and assistance programs with allied states.

The end of the Cold War and the collapse of the Soviet Union ended this period of superpower rivalry at sea. In its wake, the United States was able to establish a largely unchallenged geopolitical and naval hegemony at sea, with no real comparator adversary either extant or imminently rising. This situation is now changing (see Chapter 4, Section 4.4 and Chapter 8, Section 8.5). However, by

---

[9] It also led to the major global transformation known as the Columbian Exchange, whereby diseases, food, animals, plants, and populations were rapidly circulated between Europe and the America. Alfred W. Crosby Jr., *The Columbian Exchange: Biological and Cultural Consequences of 1492* (Westport, CT: Greenwood Press, 1973).

[10] Steven T. Wills, *Strategy Shelved: The Collapse of Cold War Naval Strategic Planning* (Annapolis, MD: Naval Institute Press, 2021).

the early 1990s, and in common with other areas of global politics at the time, the struggle for naval dominance appeared to have been settled in favor of the West.

Capitalist Expansion and the Limits of Growth

We have already seen the important historical role the seas have played in global commerce and trade. The principle of a free sea is derived at least in part from a desire to preserve the oceans as a conduit for unobstructed trade, a construction that favors the interests of maritime powers and the commercial shipping industry.[11]

However, the period since the end of the Second World War has seen an unprecedented expansion in the use of the ocean for commercial purposes, as both a cause and consequence of wider processes of globalization. This is a phenomenon that Jean-Baptiste Jouffray and his colleagues have called the "blue acceleration."[12] The blue acceleration is visible in all areas of maritime commercial activity, including shipping, fisheries and aquaculture, oil and gas exploitation, offshore energy production, submarine cables, and tourism and recreation. In 1980, for example, around 102 million metric tons of containerized cargo were shipped by sea. By 2017, this figure had grown to 1.83 billion metric tons.[13] Similarly, in 1950, fisheries and aquaculture production amounted to just under 20 million metric tons a year. By 2020, this figure had risen to just under 180 million metric tons, excluding illicit fishing.[14] Oil and gas drilling at sea, mass tourism in coastal regions and on cruise ships, and the growth of offshore wind energy installations are all entirely products of the postwar period.

This expansion of maritime commercial activity is a consequence of a series of transformative technological developments. In shipping, containerization—that is, the widespread adoption of standardized shipping boxes and corresponding infrastructure—allowed for the swifter and more efficient transportation of cargoes by sea, at ever-increasing scales.[15] In fisheries, developments in

---

[11] Liam Campling and Alejandro Colás, *Capitalism and the Sea: The Maritime Factor in the Making of the Modern World* (London: Verso, 2021).

[12] Jean-Baptiste Jouffray, Robert Blasiak, Albert V. Norström, Henrik Österblom, and Magnus Nyström, "The Blue Acceleration: The Trajectory of Human Expansion into the Ocean," *One Earth* 2, no. 1 (January 2020): 43–54.

[13] Anna Nagurney, "A Brief History of the Shipping Container," *The Maritime Executive*, September 2021, https://maritime-executive.com/editorials/a-brief-history-of-the-shipping-container.

[14] FAO, *The State of World Fisheries and Aquaculture 2022* (Rome: Food and Agriculture Organization, 2022), 4.

[15] Marc Levinson, *The Box: How the Shipping Container Made the World Smaller and the World Economy Bigger* (Princeton, NJ: Princeton University Press, 2016).

navigation technologies, vessel size, fishing methods, and the processing of fish at sea have enabled long distance fishing at an industrial scale. Fishing boats are now larger, can stay at sea longer, bring home larger catches, and operate in waters far from home.[16] The subsidization of fishing in some countries has also led to an overproduction of vessels, and enabled fishing to continue even in circumstances where it might otherwise be unprofitable. Oil rigs and deep-water drilling technologies allow access to previously inaccessible seabed marine hydrocarbon resources, and in the future seem likely to open deep seabed minerals to commercial exploitation too. Communications technologies and affordable air travel have enabled populations to take holidays at beach resorts or on cruise ships the world over.

The blue acceleration has seen a massive intensification of human activities at sea and opened new opportunities for economic development and growth. However, the intensity of this expansion is such that it has led not only to the oceans becoming congested, but also to a deepening ecological crisis in the marine environment. The expansion of shipping, for example, is now seen as a major cause of marine pollution and biodiversity loss.[17] Marine transport is responsible for up to 3% of global greenhouse gas emissions.[18] The rise of industrial fishing has led to a precipitous collapse or decline of fish stocks. The Food and Agriculture Organization of the United Nations, for example, estimates that close to 90% of the worlds marine fish stocks are fully exploited, overexploited, or depleted, with the observable collapse or near collapse of some fish species.[19] The extraction and transportation of oil by sea has led to major spills and environmental disasters.

These pressures point to an increasing awareness of the limits of capitalist expansion at sea. While on the one hand, the oceans are seen as a source of economic growth and development, on the other the detrimental environmental consequences and decline of ocean health puts future development at risk. This

---

[16] Elizabeth R. DeSombre and Jeffrey S. Barkin, *Fish* (Cambridge: Polity, 2011).

[17] Tony R. Walker, Olubukola Adebambo, Monica C. Del Aguila Feijoo, Elias Elhaimer, Tahazzud Hossain, Stuart Johnston Edwards, Courtney E. Morrison, Jessica Romo, Nameeta Sharma, Stephanie Taylor, and Sanam Zomorodi, "Environmental Effects of Marine Transportation," in *World Seas: An Environmental Evaluation (Second Edition)*, ed. Charles Sheppard (Cambridge, MA: Academic Press, 2019), 505–530.

[18] It should be noted that some argue that shipping remains a clean form of transport compared to other methods due to its relative efficiency in moving large cargos across long distances. While shipping carries 80 to 90% of global trade by weight, for example, it is road transport that produces 65% of global freight emissions.

[19] Mukhisa Kituyi and Peter Thomson, "90% of Fish Stocks Are Used Up—Fisheries Subsidies Must Stop," United Nations Conference on Trade and Development, July 2018, https://unctad.org/news/90-fish-stocks-are-used-fisheries-subsidies-must-stop.

tension sets the scene for the fourth of the struggles that shapes security at sea. This concerns the question of how the oceans should be governed, and by whom.

Legalization and Decolonization

The question of how far international treaties and public international law should bind states and establish rules for the oceans is a debate that is as old as the idea of international law itself.[20] It lies at the heart of the three grand ocean visions we outline above and has precedent in some of the earliest attempts at international law-making. The 1494 Treaty of Tordesillas was the first bilateral treaty of the oceans, for example, while the 1856 Paris Declaration Respecting Maritime Law, which outlawed privateering, has sometimes been hailed as the birthplace of universal international law.[21]

Some of the first efforts to establish more complex international treaty frameworks and international institutions also relate to the oceans. The International Telegraph Union, established in 1865 (later renamed the International Telecommunication Union), is the oldest international organization still in existence. It was established to regulate international standards in telegraph communication, and to provide rules for the use of the seabed for laying international cables.[22] The Titanic disaster of 1912, which resulted in the deaths of some 1,500 passengers and attracted widespread international media attention, led to the adoption of the first International Convention for the Safety of Life at Sea (SOLAS) in London in 1914. SOLAS established new international rules for shipping, such as the need to carry sufficient lifeboats and to train crews in evacuation. While it has been revised several times since its creation, the convention still governs maritime safety today.

Since the end of the Second World War and the creation of the United Nations (UN) system, the formulation of rules for the oceans and the instalment of international institutions has accelerated significantly. In 1948, the UN created the Inter-Governmental Maritime Consultative Organization (renamed as the International Maritime Organization, IMO, in 1982) primarily to ensure common standards for shipping. The Food and Agriculture Organization (FAO) was formed even earlier, in 1945, with the aim of eliminating world

---

[20] David J. Bederman, "The Sea," in *The Oxford Handbook of the History of International Law*, ed. Bardo Fassbender, Anne Peters, and Simone Peter (Oxford: Oxford University Press, 2014), 361–373.

[21] Daniel Hellar-Roazen, *The Enemy of All: Piracy and the Law of Nations* (Princeton, NJ: Princeton University Press, 2009).

[22] Simone M. Müller, *Wiring the World: The Social and Cultural Creation of Global Telegraph Networks* (New York: Columbia University Press, 2016).

hunger, and included a mandate to develop new rules for international fishing. Between them, the IMO and FAO became the primary vehicles for advancing international technical standards for the maritime domain. They have since been complemented by a range of other international organizations with maritime responsibilities (see Chapter 6, Section 6.3).

The need to agree more general rules and norms for the oceans was also recognized early in the post–World War II period and was dealt with through the UN Conference on the law of the sea process. The first conference (UNCLOS I) was held in in 1956 and led to a series of new conventions—on the territorial sea, on the continental shelf, on the high seas—that came into force in the early 1960s. However, it failed to resolve key questions around the delimitation of territorial waters and the rules that should be applied to them. In the meantime, states began to take unilateral action to extend their territorial waters, in some cases claiming as much as 200 nautical miles from their coastlines.

A second UN conference was convened in 1960 to resolve the matter but failed to reach a conclusion. Another attempt was made in 1973 when a third UN conference (UNCLOS III) was convened. Some 160 states participated, including many recently decolonized and newly formed states. UNCLOS III took nine years to negotiate, but eventually a new overarching treaty—the UN Convention on the Law of the Sea (UNCLOS)—was agreed in 1982. We explore the provisions and implications of UNCLOS in the following chapter, when we investigate how international legal scholars approach maritime security.

The difficulties in agreeing a shared legally binding treaty related in part to longstanding contentions around freedom of the seas and territorialization. However, two other issues were also at stake. One was the question of whether rules for the oceans should be formulated through a single holistic regime or through various devolved specialized agencies and regional bodies.[23] The issue was settled when UNCLOS agreed on a one ocean principle, which implied that the holistic view should prevail. However, in practice some rules do differ between regional seas, and there continue to be contentions over the relations between issue specific institutions such as the FAO and IMO.

A second issue was the question of how to respond to the large number of new states that were created by the decolonization of European empires after the Second World War.[24] Many of the core principles of the UN system had been agreed prior to decolonization, and at time when the UN itself had far fewer members than it does today. By the time the UNCLOS III negotiations started,

---

[23] Ernst B. Haas, "Why Collaborate? Issue-Linkage and International Regimes," *World Politics* 32, no. 3 (April 1980): 357–405.

[24] J. S. Nye, "Ocean Rule Making from a World Politics Perspective," *Ocean Development & International Law* 3, no. 1 (January 1975): 29–52.

the situation had changed significantly. Dozens of newly independent states had come onto the world stage and were asserting an increasingly independent voice in international politics. Many also had long coastlines and strong maritime interests, including as small island states or archipelagic nations.

In consequence, the stakes of the UNCLOS III negotiations for the newly independent states were very high. They demanded the right to share in the wealth being generated from the ocean economy, which for the most part remained in the hands of the former colonial powers. This debate brought important questions of justice and equity into the UNCLOS process. These questions continue to be a key area of struggle today, both in terms of how the costs and benefits of capitalist expansion are distributed, but also the division of responsibility for ensuring security at sea and protecting the marine environment.

This struggle was influenced by practical and sometimes even logistical issues. Many of the new states came to the negotiation table without fully clarified positions and may also have lacked the expertise and technical capabilities to fully represent their interests. While the UNCLOS negotiations were led by decolonized states, such as Malta and Singapore, many participants were dissatisfied about the outcomes of the treaty. This dissatisfaction has led to ongoing calls to revise UNCLOS to better reflect the interests of postcolonial states today, but also to strengthen the capacities of weaker states.

The legacy of UNCLOS III, and the question of how small states with strong maritime interests but weak capacities can participate in negotiating treaties and complying with the rights and obligations established by them, remains an animating question in maritime security today. The struggle over whether the oceans are best governed through further treaties and new international organizations, as discussed in Chapter 3, Section 3.2 and Chapter 8, Section 8.5, equally continues.

Summary

These four struggles provide us with a grand reconstruction of what is at stake in the history of security at sea. They highlight the tensions and forces that underpin ocean governance and establish the context for the emergence of maritime security as a distinct body of thought and practice.

By the early 1990s, the political order at sea seemed to have settled. The finalization of UNCLOS represented an accommodation of sorts between the three grand ocean visions of territory, freedom, and the global common. The specter of naval contestation at sea appeared to have dissipated with the end of the Cold War, piracy was seen as a primarily historical phenomenon, and the management of territorial disputes at sea had become increasingly regulated and institutionalized through international law procedures installed by UNCLOS. The legal regime dealing with the maritime domain had strengthened significantly. These changes implied an understanding of the ocean as a space that requires management, governance, and policing rather than a site of pure circulation, limitless resource extraction, and imminent military confrontation.

2.3 The Rise of the Maritime Security Agenda

Let us now look at how maritime security developed against the background of the four struggles and the settlements of the immediate post–Cold War period. We focus here on broader trends to give a sense of how the maritime security agenda has evolved. This will provide us with a starting point from which to explore these issues and developments in more depth in subsequent chapters.

To structure our discussion, we use the metaphor of waves. Telling the history in this way is helpful because it gives us a sense that there are recognizable and changing trends in maritime security thinking, but no strict dividing lines or periods. While the waves are situated in time and to some degree follow one another sequentially, they also overlap and have no clear breaking points. Each wave has a different problem as its focus, leading to a specific set of practical responses and solutions. As shown in Figure 2.1, we introduce four waves that encompass the period from the later 1990s to the early 2020s and end with the question of whether a fifth wave is on the horizon. We return to this question in further detail when we discuss the future of maritime security in Chapter 8.

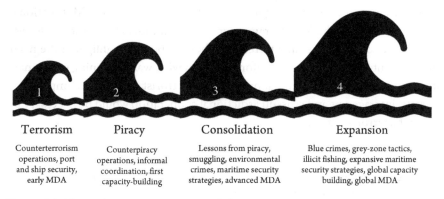

Figure 2.1 The evolving maritime security debate

Wave 1: Maritime Terrorism

The first direct references to the concept of maritime security can be found in the 1990s. In this early discussion, the term is used in a rather loose and ad hoc way, with little to suggest a coherent agenda or distinct body of thought. For example, one early study uses it to refer to the naval aspects of peacekeeping operations.[25]

The evolution of the maritime security concept as an identifiable way of thinking about security at sea only really began to gather pace in the late 1990s and early 2000s. Two core developments spurred this rise. The first was a wider rethinking of the security concept to encompass issues beyond those directly associated with the military and war, and to consider the role of actors other than the state. This change has become known as the "widening and deepening" of security.[26]

Second, this wider shift in security thinking was accompanied by a growing recognition of the threat posed by nonstate actors in the maritime domain specifically. This included the newly resurgent threat of piracy, initially in Southeast Asia, but also increased concerns about the risk of maritime terrorism. These concerns intensified after an attack on a US warship—the *USS Cole*—by an extremist group in 2000 and assumed critical significance in the wake of the attacks on the United States of September 11, 2001. The United States and its allies focused unprecedented attention on how extremist groups could use the sea to facilitate their activities, as well as the potential vulnerability of ships and ports to terrorist attacks.

Security at sea was rethought through a counterterrorism lens. As we show in Chapter 4, Section 4.3, this new approach led to some remarkable consequences. Because terrorist organizations could potentially exploit vulnerabilities in maritime transport systems, all kinds of previously benign civil activities, especially those associated with shipping and ports, were drawn into the counterterrorism response and subject to new regulations and inspection regimes. Multinational naval operations in the Mediterranean and Western Indian Ocean were also established to combat maritime terrorism. These responses highlighted the need for better intelligence and more information on what was happening in the maritime domain. The transnational nature of the terrorist threat at sea implied interstate, interagency, and cross-jurisdictional cooperation would be necessary to prevent a terrorist attack.

---

[25] Michael Pugh, *Maritime Security and Peacekeeping: A Framework for United Nations Operations* (Manchester: Manchester University Press, 1994).

[26] Barry Buzan and Lene Hansen, *The Evolution of International Security Studies* (Cambridge: Cambridge University Press, 2009), 187–225.

This first wave of thinking set the tone for the maritime security agenda and led to the development of many of the principles and tools that have since come to characterize it in subsequent years. These include measures to enhance port and ship security and for the inspection of cargoes, multinational naval operations, and the first generation of maritime domain awareness programs (see Chapter 7, Section 7.5).

Wave 2: Piracy and the First Expansion of Maritime Security Thinking

A second wave of maritime security thinking began to emerge around 2008, largely in response to an escalation of pirate activities off the coast of Somalia (see Chapter 5, Section 5.3). Piracy in Southeast Asia had been recognized as an issue in the first wave of maritime security thinking, and before. However, it was primarily seen as a local or regional problem that did not require a global response.[27]

Piracy off the coast of Somalia was different, both because of its intensity, but also because regional states lacked the capacity to address the threat. Somali pirate gangs adopted a highly lucrative kidnap for ransom model, with ships and crews being hijacked and then detained for months or even years at a time until a ransom was paid.[28] The frequency and nature of these attacks caused major disruption to global transport and trade, as well as significant costs to the shipping industry.

It quickly became apparent that piracy off the coast of Somalia was a serious problem requiring international action. In 2008, the UN Security Council issued Resolution 1816, which called for a concerted international response to address the piracy threat. The resulting activities at sea and on land were unprecedented and served to refocus and accelerate the development of maritime security thinking and practice. They comprised several distinct multinational naval missions, the creation of novel arrangements for operational coordination between actors, new diplomatic fora to coordinate action, the development of regional maritime domain awareness and information sharing mechanisms, the formation of a new legal system to facilitate the prosecution of pirate suspects, and the establishment of the first maritime security capacity-building projects with regional states. This period also saw close collaboration between maritime security actors and the shipping industry, including the introduction of best

---

[27] For a good indication of the debate around this time, see the contributions in Peter Lehr, ed., *Violence at Sea: Piracy in the Age of Global Terrorism* (Abingdon: Routledge, 2007).

[28] Sarah Percy and Anja Shortland, "The Business of Piracy in Somalia," *Journal of Strategic Studies* 36, no. 4 (August 2013): 541–578.

practices for transiting pirate-infested waters, and the widespread use of private armed guards on ships (see Chapter 6, Section 6.4).

Due to these measures, Somali piracy was contained to manageable levels in a relatively short time period of less than four years.[29] This second wave of maritime security thinking thus represented a major success story of global cooperation to address problems of insecurity at sea. It established a repertoire of maritime security responses that to a great extent have endured to this day. Indeed, it is notable that much of the toolbox of maritime security, as we discuss in Chapter 7, was first laid out during this wave. It also brought new challenges to the maritime security debate, in particular the question of how to address the root causes of piracy, and how best to assist local actors in developing their own capacities for maritime security and law enforcement at sea over the long term.

Wave 3: Lessons Learned and the Rise of Holistic Maritime Security Approaches

A third wave of maritime security has its origins in the lessons learned from counterpiracy responses off the coast of Somalia. These included a recognition of the importance of other types of maritime crime and insecurity, both in terms of their relation to piracy and also as security problems in their own right. Illegal fishing, for example, had played a key role in exacerbating the rise of piracy off the coast of Somalia.[30] Similarly, evidence suggested that Somali pirate networks had not disappeared, but transferred their activities into other forms of maritime crime such as arms and people smuggling.[31]

As more was understood about piracy and its consequences, security in the maritime domain came to be seen as an interlinked complex of threats, rather than as a series of discreet challenges. A range of other maritime insecurities beyond piracy, including irregular migration by sea, smuggling of various types, and illegal fishing began to feature more strongly in maritime security discussions.

In Europe and North Africa, the unfolding "migration crisis" in the Mediterranean Sea and the growth of people smuggling in the region was one of the core developments in this shift (see Chapter 5, Section 5.4). The European

---

[29] At the time of writing, there had been no successful large-scale piracy attack off the coast of Somalia since 2012, although smaller incidents involving regionally operating dhows and fishing vessels were reported pointing to the risk of a return of piracy.

[30] Abdi Ismail Samatar, Mark Lindberg, and Basil Mahayni, "The Dialectics of Piracy in Somalia: The Rich versus the Poor," *Third World Quarterly* 31, no. 8 (December 2010): 1377–1394.

[31] Katja Lindskov Jacobsen, "Poly-Criminal Pirates and Ballooning Effects: Implications for International Counter-Piracy," *Global Policy* 10, no. 1 (2019): 52–59.

Union states asked how the lessons from piracy could be used to address this problem and some of the tools developed in counterpiracy were adopted.

Many of the organizations and arrangements that were initially established to combat piracy in the Western Indian Ocean shifted their attention to these other maritime crimes as well. This pattern was visible in other piracy hotspots too such as Southeast Asia and the Gulf of Guinea. Lessons learned and best practices were also shared between regions, in areas including diplomatic and operational coordination, maritime domain awareness, and information sharing (see Chapter 7, Section 7.5).

This turn to a holistic approach highlighted the need for more focused strategic thinking about maritime security at both state and regional levels. It required a better understanding of the nature of different maritime security challenges, including their modus operandi, root causes and interconnections. It also suggested the importance of better mechanisms for interagency coordination and collaboration between states and with other actors such as the shipping industry. In addition, it highlighted the difficulty of mobilizing action across a more diverse set of issue-areas, not all of which carried the same level of collective priority as piracy had. In consequence, many states and regional organizations initiated maritime security strategy processes to order and organize their responses more effectively. It is notable, for example, that the European Union (EU), France, India, Spain, and the United Kingdom all published dedicated maritime security strategies between 2014 and 2015. Many of these strategies proposed new governance systems and coordination mechanisms for maritime security agencies and activities (see Chapter 7, Section 7.4).

In many respects, it is this third wave that settled the maritime security agenda as we know it today. This period saw the consolidation of maritime security as a holistic concept that links together different threats and challenges at sea, and the emergence of a shared repertoire of policy and operational solutions.

Wave 4: Global Expansion and Capacity-Building

If the third wave of maritime security thinking saw the consolidation of the maritime security agenda, the fourth wave is characterized by its global expansion. The spread of maritime security thinking during this time has been such that it now structures strategic and operational practices across the world. Tools including maritime domain awareness, maritime security strategies, and interagency coordination are in common usage with many different countries and regional organizations. An illustration of this phenomena is the introduction and strengthening of maritime domain awareness mechanisms across regions, drawing on the example of pioneering initiatives such as the Information Fusion

Centre in Singapore.[32] The drafting of maritime security strategies has also become a global practice, with states in Europe, Africa, Southeast Asia, and elsewhere embarking on such processes.

A watershed moment came in August 2021 when the UN Security Council held an open debate on maritime security at the level of heads of state and ministers.[33] While in previous years the Council had discussed specific problems in maritime security, such as piracy of the coast of Somalia or transnational organized crime at sea, this was the first time it had approached the issue as a holistic challenge to be addressed collectively. While the debate was unable to reach a formal conclusion, it is a measure of the seriousness with which the issue was considered was that the discussion included proposals to establish a permanent institution for maritime security within the UN wider structure.

A key driver for this global expansion of maritime security thinking has been the proliferation of ambitious capacity-building projects.[34] Numerous international actors, in particular Australia, the EU, Japan, the United Kingdom, and the United States, and a range of UN bodies and agencies, have initiated major regional and national programs to help countries strengthen their maritime law enforcement capacities and enable them to police their own waters effectively (see Chapter 7, Section 7.6). These programs have also played a critical role in propagating the maritime security agenda across the world. The growth of the UN Office on Drugs and Crime's Global Maritime Crime Programme is a key example of this expansion. What began as a small-scale prison support program in Kenya quickly became a global enterprise with hundreds of staff providing capacity-building projects around the world.[35]

A second factor influencing this expansion has been a recognition of the importance of what is often called the blue economy—that is, the potential of the maritime domain to provide economic growth and employment opportunities. For many countries, particularly in the Global South, investing in maritime security only made sense when they realized that there were substantial economic development and employment opportunities at stake. They recognized that economic investments depended on a safe, secure, and well-regulated maritime

---

[32] Christian Bueger and Jane Chan, eds., *Paving the Way for Regional Maritime Domain Awareness* (Singapore: S. Rajaratnam School of International Studies, 2019).

[33] United Nations Security Council, "Issuing Presidential Statement, Security Council Underlines Importance of Maritime Safety, Safeguarding Oceans for Legitimate Use," August 9, 2021, https://press.un.org/en/2021/sc14598.doc.htm.

[34] Christian Bueger, Timothy Edmunds, and Robert McCabe, "Into the Sea: Capacity-Building Innovations and the Maritime Security Challenge," *Third World Quarterly* 41, no. 2 (February 2020): 228–246.

[35] "Global Maritime Crime Programme," United Nations Office on Drugs and Crime, accessed June 2, 2023, www.unodc.org/unodc/en/piracy/index.html.

environment that would allow industries such as tourism or sustainable fishing to flourish.[36] For these reasons, the maritime security agenda has been adopted by many coastal states who see protecting their ocean territories as an important requirement for economic growth.

This merger of maritime security and the blue economy has focused attention on the environmental impacts of human activity at sea, including the tensions between capitalist expansion, economic development, and marine environmental sustainability (see Chapter 8, Section 8.4). It also highlights the harms caused by global maritime economic activities. For example, accidents and oil spills associated with the global shipping industry have caused major environmental damage to marine ecosystems. Industrial-scale fishing, both legal and illegal, has contributed to the depletion of fish stocks and the decline of coastal livelihoods, especially in the Global South. These issues have important implications for global justice, with controversies over how far states and other actors should be held accountable for the environmental harms of their activities and if existing legal regimes are sufficient.[37]

The fourth wave thus not only stands for the global expansion of the maritime security agenda, but also the recognition of how maritime security is related to other contemporary ocean governance concerns related to blue economy, ocean health, and blue justice.

A Fifth Wave on the Horizon?

While the third and fourth waves continue to shape how maritime security is understood and conceptualized today, it is also apparent that a fifth wave of maritime security thinking may now be emerging. Maritime security is increasingly discussed as an interstate problem that needs to be addressed through military and naval means, rather than as a collective issue of (civil) maritime law enforcement. This development is, in large part, a consequence of the return of geopolitical competition to international politics, in which maritime security issues play a significant part.

At the same time, and perhaps conversely, concerns about climate change, biodiversity loss, sustainable development, and marine protection are shaping the maritime security agenda more extensively. These have the effect of pulling the

---

[36] Michelle Voyer, Clive Schofield, Kamal Azmi, Robin Warner, Alistair McIlgorm, and Genevieve Quirk, "Maritime Security and the Blue Economy: Intersections and Interdependencies in the Indian Ocean," *Journal of the Indian Ocean Region* 14, no. 1 (January 2018): 28–48.

[37] Ifesinachi Okafor-Yarwood and Dyhia Belhabib, "The Duplicity of the European Union Common Fisheries Policy in Third Countries: Evidence from the Gulf of Guinea," *Ocean & Coastal Management* 184 (February 2020): 104953.

maritime security debate toward large-scale planetary and ecosystem thinking and the need for a collective global response.

Maritime security strategies issued in 2022 and 2023 by the United Kingdom and the EU are telling in that they straddle this conundrum and aim to integrate both concerns. Understanding how these two countervailing trends in maritime security are likely to play out in the future is a question we address in the concluding Chapter 8.

2.4 The Context for Maritime Security

As we have shown in this chapter, the contemporary maritime security agenda traces its origins to the late 1990s. Yet it has its roots in a series of older and more enduring struggles around the status and significance of the ocean in global affairs. This history is characterized by four major struggles: over grand ocean visions, over naval dominance and control of the sea, over capitalist expansion and its limits, and over law and representation. These struggles prefigure some of the key debates and contentions in maritime security today, but also establish the wider context and parameters within which its evolution has taken place.

Four distinct waves of thinking have shaped the contemporary maritime security agenda, with a fifth wave currently on the horizon. Initially, the main concern was with maritime terrorism, particularly in the wake of the 9/11 attacks of 2001. This period saw new interventions around ship and port security for counterterrorism purposes. A second wave emerged in 2008 in response to the rise of piracy off the coast of Somalia. This was the point at which many of the main tools of maritime security were first put into practice, in areas including operational coordination, information sharing, and capacity-building. The decline of Somali piracy from 2012 ushered in a third wave of maritime security thinking. This wave was characterized by a broadening of the agenda to include maritime crimes beyond piracy, including smuggling and illicit fishing, and a consolidation of the maritime security toolbox. A subsequent fourth wave has seen the global expansion of maritime security through capacity-building and the proliferation of a standardized repertoire of solutions. A new fifth wave is still taking shape and appears to engage two countervailing trends comprising a return to geopolitics and interstate competition on the one hand, and the rise of planetary scale thinking to deal with environmental pressures at sea on the other.

The maritime security agenda represents a fundamental rethinking of security at sea. Over the years it has become more complex and multifaceted, as new problems have come to international attention and more actors have become involved. The major components of the maritime security thinking had been largely settled by the end of the 2010. However, it has continued to evolve as lessons from past practices are absorbed, political priorities change, and new challenges emerge. In the following chapters we dive deeper into the specificities of maritime security.

3
Frameworks for Maritime Security Analysis

3.1 Thinking Tools and Analytical Frameworks

Maritime security thinking has developed against the background of a particular global political and economic context. However, it also has historical antecedents in earlier debates, controversies, and ways of thinking about the oceans. This was the key argument of the last chapter. It already provides the maritime security professional and analyst with an important analytical framework in the form of historical reconstruction. It asks what influences the evolution of maritime security and how problems and priorities change over time. In this chapter we explore four other frameworks for understanding maritime security.

The term "framework" refers to a more or less coherent body of thoughts, assumptions, priorities, and terms that facilitate analysis of particular aspects of maritime security. A framework draws on a specific set of concepts. In the previous chapter, we singled out the concepts of problems and of time—the domain of history. The following four frameworks foreground others. The first concentrates on law and the importance of regulation and treaties. The second prioritizes the state and its interests, and how these can be coordinated and contained through institutions. The third emphasizes meanings and how they are made in discourse and practice. The fourth investigates causes and the underlying drivers of maritime insecurity. These frameworks derive from, and are often specific and practical reformulations of, more general approaches in academic disciplines such as international law, international relations, security studies, and criminology.

Our ambition in this chapter is twofold. First, we want to provide the maritime security analyst and professional with a better understanding of the rich portfolio of analytical frameworks through which to understand maritime security. Second, we demonstrate that each of the frameworks has analytical value

Understanding Maritime Security. Christian Bueger and Timothy Edmunds, Oxford University Press.
© Oxford University Press 2024. DOI: 10.1093/oso/9780197767146.003.0003

and strengths but also weaknesses, oversights, and gaps. It is important to be familiar with the entire repertoire to make informed choices, and to understand which questions might benefit the most from a particular approach.

3.2 The Law of the Sea and Law-Centric Frameworks

The study of ocean governance is often considered to be the dominion of legal scholarship. Indeed, since the conclusion of the UN Convention on the Law of the Sea (UNCLOS) in 1982, legal analysis and interpretation of the implication and use of the treaty has been a key path for understanding maritime security. To explain how legal analyses contribute to understanding maritime security, we first need to introduce the essential principles of UNCLOS and how it presents answers to some of the struggles we described in Chapter 2. This is also an important backdrop for our entire discussion since these principles provide the key legal parameters of maritime security. After this introduction, we lay out how legal frameworks contribute to the discussion. We briefly detail the maritime security challenges that evolved after UNCLOS was adopted before discussing the strengths and limits of legal analyses.

The Law of the Sea

As we discussed in Chapter 2, one of the key struggles of security at sea was between different grand ocean visions of what the role of states should be in ocean governance. We distinguished between the idea of a closed sea, under the sovereign control of states; a free sea, to be ruled by no one; and the sea as a global common, governed by international organizations.

Reconciling these three positions in one overarching treaty was the primary goal of the UNCLOS negotiations. The ambition of this goal also explains why the negotiations took over 30 years to complete. Interpreting this complex treaty, with its 320 articles and nine annexes, including implementing agreements dealing with issues such as seabed mining, high seas fishing, and port state measures, is the domain of an entire legal subdiscipline to which excellent introductions are available.[1] Here we focus on the basics of the treaty that

---

[1] See for an introduction Yoshifumi Tanaka, *The International Law of Sea* (Cambridge: Cambridge University Press, 2019), and more specifically to maritime security James Kraska and Raul Pedrozo, *International Maritime Security Law* (Leiden: Brill Nijhoff, 2013); Natalie Klein, *Maritime Security and the Law of the Sea* (Oxford: Oxford University Press, 2011); Sofia Galani and Malcolm D. Evans, "The Interplay Between Maritime Security and the 1982 United Nations Convention on the Law

every practitioner and analyst needs to know, which can be condensed to two key issues: the spatial regime and the flag state principle.

A Spatial Regime

UNCLOS is widely considered to be the "constitution" of the ocean, providing the foundational principles of oceanic use. It represents an important compromise between the three grand ocean visions that is most apparent in the way that UNCLOS introduces a particular spatial regime. States are given rights and obligations in specified maritime zones, as shown in figure 3.1. These zones are measured in nautical miles.[2] Their starting point is the so-called baseline, which is the coastline of a country. Within each zone a different balance of rights and duties prevails between the coastal state and other users of the ocean ("flag states" or "navigating states"). This variable allocation of legal power reflects the two fundamental pressures on rulemaking in ocean space: the desire for flag states to have maximum freedom of navigation, and coastal states' desire to have maximum authority to regulate.

The first zone comprises territorial waters, which extend to 12 nautical miles from the baseline. Here states have full jurisdiction and sovereignty subject only to limited exceptions dealing with innocent passage for foreign flagged vessels. They can enforce their national laws and exploit resources according to their own preferences. A zone stretching 200 nautical miles from the baseline is identified as the exclusive economic zone (EEZ). Here coastal states have exclusive sovereign rights to the exploration and exploitation of marine resources, and responsibilities for environmental protection. Coastal states have no express authority to take action in this zone with respect to other issues. However, a contiguous zone extends from the end of territorial waters into the EEZ to a point no further than 24 nautical miles from the baseline, in which states can enforce laws on some specific matters such as migration, customs, and quarantine. Beyond the EEZ are the high seas, where no state has formal jurisdiction, but a range of provisions regulate behavior in this space. About two-thirds of the ocean is considered to fall into this category. Some maritime areas, such as the North Sea, are semienclosed and only comprised of territorial waters and EEZs.

---

of the Sea: Help or Hindrance?," in *Maritime Security and the Law of the Sea: Help of Hinderance?*, ed. Malcolm D. Evans and Sofia Galani (Cheltenham: Edward Elgar, 2020), 1–24; as well as more encompassing Donald R. Rothwell, Alex G. Oude Elferink, Karen N. Scott, and Tim Stephens, eds., *The Oxford Handbook of the Law of the Sea* (Oxford: Oxford University Press, 2015). A useful hands-on introduction is also available in UNODC, *Maritime Crime: A Manual for Criminal Justice Practitioners, Third Edition* (Vienna: UNODC, 2020), https://www.unodc.org/documents/Maritime_crime/GMCP_Maritime_3rd_edition_Ebook.pdf.

[2] One nautical mile equates to 1,852 meters.

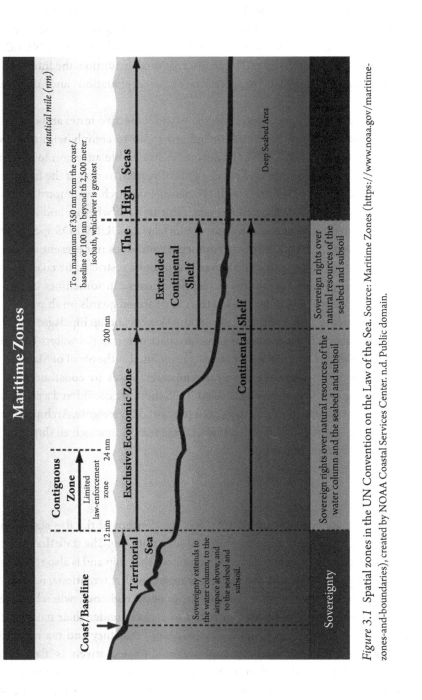

Figure 3.1 Spatial zones in the UN Convention on the Law of the Sea. Source: Maritime Zones (https://www.noaa.gov/maritime-zones-and-boundaries), created by NOAA Coastal Services Center. n.d. Public domain.

Since the ocean is a three-dimensional space, UNCLOS also makes special provisions for the seabed. On the ocean floor states can claim a continental shelf in addition to the EEZ, in which they have sovereign rights to resource extraction. Everything on the seabed outside these zones, is defined by UNCLOS as "the Area." The Area is managed by an international institution, the International Seabed Authority, which regulates resource exploitation and distributes revenues.

Rules and regulations differ according to the respective zones and define and delimit what states are permitted or obliged to do to comply with the law of the sea. In this respect, UNCLOS devotes considerable attention to rules and regulations that determine the transit rights of vessels, as well as the freedom to lay cables and pipelines or to conduct scientific research. An important provision is the concept of "innocent passage." This lays out whether and how states have rights to limit navigation in their territorial waters. UNCLOS specifies that if passage is for peaceful purposes (innocent) and does not present a threat in another way (e.g., from pollution), then it cannot be restricted by coastal states. The question of what constitutes peaceful purposes can sometimes be controversial, for example when it comes to the use of armed guards on ships.

A provision is also made for international straits and archipelagic sea lands. International straits are waterways that are part of territorial waters but are of special importance for international navigation, such as the Strait of Malacca, the Suez Canal, or the Strait of Hormuz. Archipelagic states are constituted wholly by one or a group of islands. Under UNCLOS these are considered a single unit, with the waters between them subject to territorial sovereignty. Archipelagic sea lands are designated sea lanes that transit these waters, in which all ships and aircraft enjoy the right of passage.

Flag States

The second key principle of UNCLOS is the concept of the flag state. Under UNCLOS every ship is required to sail under a state flag. The state that provides the flag (the flag state) has jurisdiction on board that ship and is also responsible for ensuring that the vessel and its crew complies with international regulations.

Some states operate what are known as open registries, whereby foreign owned or operated vessels are permitted to register under their national flag. Many open registry flags generally offer looser regulatory and tax regimes to ship owners, and as such are sometimes referred to pejoratively as "flags of convenience." They are also often located in countries with limited enforcement capacities or will to exercise them. Some have even outsourced their flag state responsibilities to private companies, which handle the registration of ships and compliance. Others, such as Mongolia, are landlocked. This has led to a situation in which countries with some of the weakest regulatory regimes are responsible for large number of vessels in the global merchant fleet. Weak, ineffective, or even negligent flag state regulation may thus contribute to exploitation of seafarers and breach of safety or environmental standards.

Importantly, flag state rules imply that if a state wants to stop, interdict, or board a vessel, for instance to inspect it for narcotics, it requires the consent of the flag state to do so.[3] Gaining flag state permissions can be a time-consuming process. It is often a severe practical hurdle in law enforcement at sea, not least because some flag state authorities are run more diligently and professionally than others. When the nationality of a vessel is unknown or indeterminate, states have the authority to board, and similar "rights to visit" also apply in the case of international sanctions.[4]

After UNCLOS

UNCLOS entered into force in 1994 and has been ratified by 168 parties. States that have not ratified the convention include the United States, Colombia, Israel, Iran, Peru, Türkiye, and Venezuela. However, many of these states, including the United States and Türkiye, recognize the provisions of UNCLOS as customary law and have introduced national laws that adhere to the key principles of the treaty. Others, such as Iran, have signed the Convention but have not ratified it. UNCLOS provides the key foundational legal principles that underpin maritime security. However, since it entered into force in 1994, several important legal challenges have come to the fore.

A first challenge relates to ambiguities in the legal text. For example, there is an ongoing debate over the precise meaning of freedom of navigation and innocent passage, and whether coastal states are allowed to limit the passage of particular vessels, such as warships or those which carry dangerous goods in their territorial waters.[5] The concept of the EEZ equally raises ongoing questions of interpretation, such as under which conditions foreign military actors are allowed to carry out naval exercises or intelligence gathering operations.[6]

---

[3] Douglas Guilfoyle, *Shipping Interdiction and the Law of the Sea* (Cambridge: Cambridge University Press, 2009), 1–20.

[4] Efthymios Papastavridis, *The Interception of Vessels on the High Seas: Contemporary Challenges to the Legal Order of the Oceans* (Oxford: Hart, 2013).

[5] Klein, *Maritime Security and the Law of the Sea*, 25–43, 74–84.

[6] Klein, *Maritime Security and the Law of the Sea*, 46–54, and Sienho Yee, "Sketching the Debate on Military Activities in the EEZ: An Editorial," *Chinese Journal of International Law* 9, no.1 (2010): 1–7.

The question of enforcement—that is, how to ensure that the provisions of the treaty are followed and noncompliance addressed—is also problematic. For example, the piracy provisions in UNCLOS give each country the right to intercept, arrest, and prosecute pirates, but no state has the explicit obligation to do so.[7] Overcoming the limitations imposed by flag state regulations, especially the open registries with lax compliance systems, represents another vital concern.[8]

An additional range of issues arises from the fact that UNCLOS is not the sole source of international public law addressing oceans and maritime security. Surveys of the international law relevant to maritime security show how enormous this body of law is.[9] It includes, for example, conventions by the International Maritime Organization (IMO), but also treaties and legal regimes in the fields of human rights, labor rights, and environmental protection. Legal analysts have argued that this might lead to a problem of fragmentation in international law,[10] where it is unclear how these diverse treaties should relate to each other and under which conditions one should take precedence over another. It might also produce the problem that states selectively choose which rules to follow and which ones to ignore, or even argue against the universal applicability of UNCLOS.

Subsequent treaties have also been concluded to more detail to general provisions of UNCLOS. The 1995 United Nations Fish Stock Agreement, for example, was expressly designed to add further detail to UNCLOS regarding regulation of high seas fishing beyond national jurisdiction and has 96 parties.[11] The same problems of fragmentation may arise, however, when not all UNCLOS parties join such implementing agreements.

A third set of challenges is linked to the fact that UNCLOS and its related legal agreements are peacetime treaties. They are not applicable under conditions of interstate war. A different set of laws is required for these situations. These are summarized in the 1994 San Remo Manual on Armed Conflict at Sea, which was revised in the 2023 Newport Manual.[12] Contrary to UNCLOS, these are not

---

[7] Guilfoyle, *Shipping Interdiction and the Law of the Sea*; Douglas Guilfoyle, *Modern Piracy: Legal Challenges and Responses* (Cheltenham: Edward Elgar, 2013).

[8] North Atlantic Fisheries Intelligence Group, *Chasing Red Herrings: Flags of Convenience, Secrecy and the Impact on Fisheries Crime Law Enforcement* (Copenhagen: Nordic Council of Ministers, 2018).

[9] Kraska and Pedrozo, *International Maritime Security Law*; Klein, *Maritime Security and the Law of the Sea*.

[10] Margaret A. Young, *Trading Fish, Saving Fish: The Interaction between Regimes in International Law* (Cambridge: Cambridge University Press, 2011).

[11] David A. Balton and Holly R. Koehler, "Reviewing the United Nations Fish Stocks Treaty," *Sustainable Development Law and Policy* 7, no. 1 (2006): 5–9, 75.

[12] James Kraska, Raul "Pete" Pedrozo, David Letts, Wolff Heintschel von Heinegg, Rob McLaughlin, James Farrant, Yurika Ishii, Gurpreet S. Khurana, and Koki Sato, "The Newport Manual

legally binding treaties adopted and ratified by states, but advisory documents agreed upon by a group of international legal experts. While legal expert opinion is considered a subsidiary source of international law, these documents have limited legal force but may point to an emerging consensus on key issues.

Finally, UNCLOS is a treaty of its time. A series of currently emerging issues—including technological developments such as floating energy platforms, automation and artificial intelligence, or sea-level rise caused by climate change—were not envisaged during the drafting process, and today create potential gaps in the law of the sea. This has spurred growing discomfort with UNCLOS among some countries. In 2022, for example, a committee of the United Kingdom House of Lords engaged in a thorough review of whether the treaty should be renegotiated.[13]

The Focus of Legal Analysis: Strengths and Weaknesses

UNCLOS and the related body of international law provides a framework for legal analyses of maritime security. These analyses revolve around questions of what actions are permissible at sea, and the obligations and responsibilities of states in this regard. They are especially useful for understanding specific maritime security problems, such combatting piracy, or the use of armed guards on commercial vessels. Legal analyses interpret real-world situations in the context of legal documents. They aim to show which articles of UNCLOS are applicable in the light of other treaties, consider what actions states should take on this basis, and ask whether additional policies or laws are required for them to do so.

Legal analyses have some limitations. One of their limits can be described as "solutionism"; that is, analysts sometimes assume that there is only one accurate, or at least preferable, interpretation of the law once all arguments have been heard. There can also be a tendency to assume that states want to follow the law and want to be guided by legal experts. Legal analysts thus risk neglecting the possibility that states may sometimes prefer situations of legal ambiguity or may even manipulate the law in their own interest; a phenomenon that has been described as "lawfare" or "legal statecraft."[14] Similar to the framework we introduce in the next section, law of the sea analyses are also often inherently

on the Law of Naval Warfare," *International Law Studies* 101 (May 2023), https://digital-commons.usnwc.edu/ils/vol101/iss1/1.

[13] Mariam Mgeladze, "UK House of Lords Inquiry: Is the UN Convention on the Law of the Sea Still Fit for Purpose?," *Journal of Territorial and Maritime Studies* 10, no. 1 (2023): 79–91.

[14] Orde F. Kittrie, *Lawfare: Law as a Weapon of War* (Oxford: Oxford University Press, 2016); Douglas Guilfoyle, "Litigation as Statecraft: Small States and the Law of the Sea," *British Yearbook of International Law*, May 2023, brad009, doi:10.1093/bybil/brad009.

state-centric. They tend to limit their focus to states as the key actors in making and enforcing international law. This focus can leave little room for analysis of other kinds of political actors, such as companies or social movements.

Finally, legal approaches have been criticized for ignoring or playing down the role of power politics in both the historical creation and application of international law. Cases of maritime interstate conflict, such as over the Chagos Islands and in South China Sea (see Chapter 4, Section 4.2), show that larger state powers can ignore or sideline international law. A growing movement of postcolonial scholars are also reconsidering the history and development of international law, with particular attention to colonial legacies.[15]

3.3 State-Centric Frameworks: Interests and Institutions

A second set of frameworks starts out from the premise that it is the responsibility of states to ensure maritime security. This means that analysts focus on the activities and interactions of states, while paying less attention to the role of other actors or factors that shape maritime security. These are frameworks that are most frequently associated with research conducted in international relations, security studies, and strategic studies, but are not limited to these disciplines.

We introduce two frameworks which analysts use to make sense of state behavior. The first foregrounds competition between states. It posits that even with a major treaty governing the seas, and the existence of several important international organizations with responsibility for ocean issues, states act in selfish ways and the international system remains at heart anarchic in nature. By way of contrast, the second emphasizes cooperation and holds that international rules, identities, and networks bind states together. Accordingly, analyses should focus on the work of international organizations and how states form communities and networks.

Interests and Competition

The first framework takes power and national interests as core categories and emphasizes competition. Despite institutions such as UNCLOS, they interpret the ocean as an arena of contestation and competition over territory, resources,

---

[15] See for example Prabhakar Singh and Benoît Mayer, eds., *Critical International Law: Postrealism, Postcolonialism, and Transnationalism* (Oxford: Oxford University Press, 2014).

and access to them. In other words, and according to this this line of thinking, international norms and rules cannot bound the struggle for dominance that we discussed in Chapter 2.

In this understanding, the primary objective of states is survival. They strive to directly and indirectly control territory to secure their interests and gain advantage over competitors. Great powers will largely do so by expanding their influence and power, while smaller powers will seek shelter in forming alliances and coalitions. Studies drawing on this framework are often labeled in security debates as "realist"[16] or "geopolitical."[17]

Two central assumptions underpin such analyses. The first is that states are the main actors in international politics. A second is the concept of international anarchy, in the sense that there is no one single global authority or sovereign power that can govern the affairs of states. This does not mean that the international system is without order or rules. Organizations such as the United Nations and treaties such as UNCLOS can provide ways of managing state interactions and constraining state behavior. However, in an anarchic international system they do so only under certain conditions, and with the acquiescence of the state actors with whom sovereignty ultimately lies. Rules can be broken if states chose to exercise their power to do so, in ways that can only be countered by the opposing power of other states, up to and including violent conflict between them.

States pursue a variety of strategies to deal with the problem of international anarchy, in ways that shape their interactions with each other at sea. Some states chose to increase their power resources, both to pursue their own interests and make them less vulnerable to pressure or predation by other states. The maritime domain has a critical role to play in these struggles because it enables states to trade and project military power at a potentially global scale. Strategic theorists highlight the importance of sea power in this respect; that is, the capacity of a state to utilize the seas for commercial and military purposes or to prevent others from doing so.[18] Accordingly, defense technologies and naval capacities are often key issues for analysts.

Other states might form coalitions and alliances with the aim of pooling their resources to counteract a powerful or threatening competitor. In the maritime domain, we see this strategy at work in the formation of military alliances with

---

[16] For an introduction, see William C. Wohlforth, "Realism," in *The Oxford Handbook of International Relations*, ed. Christian Reus-Smit and Duncan Snidal (Oxford: Oxford University Press, 2008), 131–149.

[17] A useful overview of the debates under this label is provided in Klaus Dodds, *Geopolitics: A Very Short Introduction*, 3rd ed. (Oxford: Oxford University Press, 2019).

[18] Andrew Lambert, *Seapower States: Maritime Culture, Continental Empires and the Conflict That Made the Modern World* (New Haven, CT: Yale University Press, 2018); Geoffrey Till, *Seapower: A Guide for the Twenty-First Century*, 4th ed. (London: Routledge, 2018).

strong naval components such as North Atlantic Treaty Organization (NATO). More limited security agreements, such as the AUKUS security pact between Australia, the United Kingdom, and the United States or the Quadrilateral Security Dialogue between Australia, Indian, Japan, and the United States, also belong to such strategies (see Chapter 6, Section 6.3). These latter agreements are both explicitly maritime in nature and focus on counteracting Chinese influence in the Indo-Pacific region.

States might also pursue strategies to strengthen international regulation and rules with the goal of constraining the actions of powerful states and potential competitors. This strategy has often been linked to small states in acting as entrepreneurs for global rules and norms.[19] International treaties show the strength and limits of these strategies. As we explore in Chapter 4, UNCLOS has enabled unprecedented cooperation over the management of maritime interstate disputes at sea. However, judgments of its dispute settlement mechanisms have also sometimes been ignored by powerful states (see Chapter 4, Section 4.2).

By this reading, interstate competition is baked into the international system, in the maritime domain and elsewhere. As new powers arise the status quo will be challenged, new interests and configurations of power will emerge, and countermoves will be made by other states to secure their own interests against powerful competitors. These changes can lead to new patterns of interstate competition at sea, as rising powers see new opportunities for advantage and others seek to defend their interests. While treaties such as UNCLOS can constrain and regulate these behaviors, they do so only under certain conditions, and may even themselves act as a vehicle through which interstate competition is played out.

Issues in Interstate Competition

In the previous section we argued that changes in the balance of power can lead to new dynamics of competition at sea. However, given that the oceans cannot be settled or occupied, what do states compete over in the maritime domain? As recent research has argued, there are three key issues at stake: functional value, institutionalization and territorialization, and symbolic status.[20]

Functional value refers to the physical properties and resources of the sea, and the various political, economic, and strategic functions these can serve. For example, much of the literature on sea power is concerned with control over,

---

[19] See for example the essays in Jessica L. Beyer, Iver B. Neumann, and Sieglinde Gstohl, eds., *Small States in International Relations* (Seattle: University of Washington Press, 2006).

[20] Andreas Østhagen, "Troubled Seas? The Changing Politics of Maritime Boundary Disputes," *Ocean & Coastal Management* 205 (May 2021): 105535.

protection of, or access to key maritime strategic spaces such as chokepoints, seabed infrastructures such as submarine cables, and sea lanes of communication, including trade routes. These allow states to use the seas to freely pursue economic interests such as maritime trade. They are also important for military purposes, for example to restrict the movements of enemy warships, allow freedom of action for friendly forces, or ensure resupply and assistance from allied states. These things can be of critical importance during times of conflict and war.

Competition over functional issues also takes place over who has the right to exploit ocean resources for economic purposes, whether those be fisheries, oil and gas, or seabed minerals. The potential for such competition has increased with the capitalist expansion of maritime activities that we discussed in Chapter 2, Section 2.2. The limits of that expansion, for example the decline in fish stocks, may also create new tensions between states over access to—or stewardship of—these resources.

The second kind of contention revolves around the ways that institutions allocate jurisdictional rights to states. As we have seen, the period since the Second World War has seen a growth of legal regimes that give states the rights to govern and exploit ocean space, culminating in the finalization of UNCLOS in 1982. UNCLOS established clear rules for determining how state jurisdiction at sea, alongside formal mechanisms for the settlement of competing claims or disputes. However, UNCLOS created new challenges of interstate competition too, albeit in ways that to date at least have largely been contained by the rules it put into place. This is both because of ongoing technical disagreements over the way that maritime boundaries should be calculated, but also because the new maritime zones it established created additional friction points and zones of functional interest for states. In addition, it lent new significance to previously unimportant geographical features such as uninhabited islands and rocks, the status and ownership of which could potentially anchor huge new areas of ocean space into a state's EEZ.

Finally, the salience of both functional and institutional competition can be increased by their symbolic importance. As Andreas Østhagen notes, one of the implications of the zones established by UNCLOS is that they assign higher symbolic value to ocean space as national territory, rather than as purely functional areas of economic activity or strategic importance.[21] This national symbolism can imbue interstate disputes at sea with significant domestic political meaning, particularly if there is a sense that national sovereignty is threatened in some way. It can also make them more difficult to resolve if issues of national

[21] Østhagen, "Troubled Seas?," 7–8.

pride and identity become bound to the outcome of any settlement process. Indeed, some scholars suggest that disputes with such intangible qualities are more likely to lead to the use of force than functional or institutional competition on their own.[22]

Rules, Norms, Identities, and Cooperation

A second kind of state-centric framework argues that anarchy and competition can be overcome through mutual interdependence and institutions, and hence stresses cooperation. Studies drawing on this framework often go by terms such as "institutionalism"[23] and "constructivism."[24]

In this argumentation, international treaties, such as UNCLOS or the conventions of the IMO, establish rules, norms, and expectations, which allow states to predict each other's behavior and intentions and realize collective gains, such as through free and open trade. These rules and norms allow states to move beyond competition to establish cooperative security solutions that work to the benefit of all. The analyst thus needs to investigate how far states have internalized the agreed shared rules and norms, how they influence their development and evolutions, and how far these things condition their actions and behaviors.

States delegate many ocean governance issues to international organizations, such as the IMO, to manage on their behalf. International organizations play an important role in ensuring transparency between states and monitoring their compliance with rules.[25] They can help to ensure that states understand what kinds of behavior they can expect from each other. In these ways, international organizations have emerged as key forums for state interactions. This is an issue we explore further in Chapter 6, where we discuss the specific role of international organizations in the maritime domain.

A related line of analysis focuses on how government types and constitutions influence state relations in international politics. For example, some research

---

[22] Sara McLaughlin Mitchell, "Clashes at Sea: Explaining the Onset, Militarization, and Resolution of Diplomatic Maritime Claims," *Security Studies* 29, no. 4 (August 2020): 637–670.

[23] See the introductory text by Arthur A. Stein, "Neoliberal Institutionalism," in *The Oxford Handbook of International Relations*, ed. Christian Reus-Smit and Duncan Snidal (Oxford University Press, 2008), xx–xx.

[24] For an introduction to the debates under this label, see Emmanuel Adler, "Constructivism in International Relations: Sources, Contributions and Debates," in *Handbook of International Relations, Second Edition*, ed. Walter Carlsnaes, Thomas Risse, and Beth A. Simmons (London: Sage, 2012), xx–xx.

[25] A good overview and introduction is provided in J. Samuel Barkin, *International Organization: Theories and Institutions* (Basingstoke: Palgrave Macmillan, 2006).

suggests that states with democratic governments rarely, if ever, engage in wars with each or interpret other democracies as threats. This has become known as the democratic peace thesis.[26] It implies that democracies have special relations with each other, and that the form of government system a country has influences its relations with other states of the same type. In the maritime domain, it might imply that some states are more inclined to work together, for example in capacity-building or coordinated maritime security operations. It also suggests that competing territorial claims between such states are unlikely to lead to armed conflict. They might, however, reach the level of a militarized dispute, as the example of the fish wars between democracies we discuss in Chapter 4 illustrates.

Other strands of analysis aim to understand the circumstances under which states can form strong bonds with each other. These bonds can then lead to shared identities and trust relations, which in turn determine how national interests are defined, and what foreign and maritime security policies are considered acceptable. The concept of a "security community," for example, describes a group of countries among which nonviolent dispute resolution is the norm, hostile activities are unthinkable, and states instead approach problems through collective enterprises.[27] The transatlantic community and its institutional form (NATO), the European Union (EU), and the Association of Southeast Asian States (ASEAN), are often seen as examples of security communities. They are all cases in which states have shown a strong preference to work together through shared maritime security initiatives such as joint operations at sea (see Chapter 7, Section 7.3).

These forms of analysis thus suggests that the preferences and interests of states might vary considerably in terms of whether they are democracies, or members of an existing or developing security community.

Closely related frameworks rely on concepts such as networks or "assemblages" to describe forms of cooperation.[28] The outlook and styles of analysis here are similar to those of the security community: analysts study the various ties and connections that exist between states. The concept of the Global Network of

---

[26] See for example: Christopher Layne, "Kant or Cant: The Myth of the Democratic Peace," *International Security* 19, no. 2 (1994): 5–49; John M. Owen, "How Liberalism Produces Democratic Peace," *International Security* 19, no. 2 (1994): 87–125.

[27] Emanuel Adler and Patricia Greve, "When Security Community Meets Balance of Power: Overlapping Regional Mechanisms of Security Governance," *Review of International Studies* 35, no. S1 (February 2009): 59–84.

[28] Avant, Deborah D. "Pragmatic Networks and Transnational Governance of Private Military and Security Services," *International Studies Quarterly* 60, no. 2 (2016): 330–342; and Christian Bueger, "Territory, Authority, Expertise: Global Governance and the Counter-Piracy Assemblage," *European Journal of International Relations* 24, no. 3 (2018): 614–637.

Navies developed by United States navy strategists in the mid-2000s is a good example of this kind of thinking in action. Introduced in 2005 as the idea of a "1000 ship navy," then as the Global Maritime Partnership Initiative, it suggested that global navies should work toward interoperability, shared surveillance, and information sharing for maritime security purposes. As a global network, this collective structure would provide a flexible means to form ad hoc coalitions to address maritime security threats around the world.[29] Such network thinking underpins many aspects of the toolbox of maritime security we go on to discuss in Chapter 7.

Strengths and Weaknesses

For frameworks which emphasizes competition, maritime security will always be in the hands of, and to some degree dependent on, the activities of powerful states. It is these states who decide which issues are addressed, and which not. In consequence, analysts need to identify what the interests of the great powers are, how they interact with each other in the maritime domain, and what action space is left for smaller powers.

Those that foreground cooperation instead argue that international treaties and organizations introduce new obligations and responsibilities for states in maritime security that condition their freedom of action. They also recognize that many maritime security tasks, such as information sharing and capacity-building, have been delegated to international organizations. Hence, analysis focuses on how institutions and cooperation work in concept and practice, but also how agreed norms and rules shape the activities of states, including their national interests and maritime security policies, and how states form closer forms of cooperation as communities or networks.

State-centric approaches are most useful for understanding competition and cooperation between states and the role of international organizations in maritime security. However, they can risk overvaluing the importance of states and often conceptualize them as unitary actors, without paying attention to their internal relations, structures, and political processes. This can lead analysts to rely on a high level of abstraction and aggregation, with a lack of attention to how maritime security problems are dealt with in detail or in practice. These approaches can also bias toward analyses that draw on a relatively static picture, with less focus on short time shifts and changing prioritizations.

---

[29] Jason Dittmer, "The State, All at Sea: Interoperability and the Global Network of Navies," *Environment and Planning C: Politics and Space* 39, no. 7 (November 2021): 1389–1406.

3.4 Interpretive Approaches: Making Meaning, Understanding Practice

A third set of frameworks for maritime security analysis are derived from interpretive styles of research. These forms of analysis do not start out from the premise that states automatically have priority. Instead, they are interested in the underlying logics that make a broader set of (state and nonstate) actors in maritime security think and act the way they do. They investigate how problems become construed as maritime security issues and why they are prioritized. They also try to understand what actors say and do when they claim to be acting in the name of maritime security.

Interpretive approaches are more open than state-centric frameworks in that they routinely consider a wider variety of actors than states alone. These might include, for example, experts that conduct threat assessments, nongovernmental organizations that raise awareness of maritime security issues, the news media reporting on a particular case, or industry associations campaigning to take a problem more seriously.

Interpretive approaches provide accounts of how and why understandings of security at sea shift over time and how actors respond to these. Chapter 2 has already shown how such changes shaped the rise and evolution of the maritime security agenda. Understanding these changes and their consequences is a priority of interpretive analysis. This is especially useful for understanding the rise and decline of particular issues as security priorities but also for explaining key controversies in maritime security, its boundaries, and its relations with other agendas such as marine safety, the blue economy, and national security. Interpretive approaches also provide insight into why sometimes quite different understandings of what maritime security entails persist between different actors. In the following sections, we highlight three major interpretivist approaches: concept analysis, securitization, and security-as-practice.

Concept Analysis

The first approach focuses on the language used to grasp maritime security. It starts out from the observation that categories and concepts in use often lack clear definition and are inherently contested. Political actors and scholars alike disagree over what maritime security entails and what kinds of issues (e.g., interstate conflict at sea, or marine environmental degradation) should be included in it.

Concept analysis is grounded in the idea that if we can understand why and where particular concepts are controversial, we can map their core components,

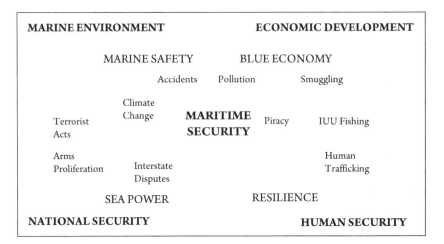

Figure 3.2 Maritime security matrix. Source: Christian Bueger, "What Is Maritime Security?," *Marine Policy* 53 (March 2015): 161.

boundaries, interconnections, and relations.[30] This in turn allows us to understand the variety of meanings they may have for different actors, and to identify tensions and intersections between these.

All concepts are to some degree contested because they depend on different normative assumptions about which issues should be valued and which not. Moreover, concepts like maritime security do not operate in a vacuum. They relate to other similar concepts and counterconcepts in what is sometimes called a "conceptual architecture."[31] Think, for example, about how the two concepts of war and peace are related to each other. Each, to some degree, derives its meaning from the other, and peace is often defined as the absence of war. Studying these relations is at the heart of concept analysis. In our context, it means understanding the boundaries and potential scope of the maritime security concept itself, but also how it relates to other concepts (such as marine safety), and how distinct issues, for example piracy, are placed in these relationships.

Figure 3.2 that we have already introduced in the introduction provides a tool for maritime security analysis in the form of a matrix with four corners of related concepts: 1) national security and sea power; 2) environmental concerns and marine safety, including measures to reduce the harm caused by maritime activities; 3) economic and development concerns, as expressed in the idea of the blue economy, and 4) human security and resilience.

---

[30] Felix Berenskoetter, "Approaches to Concept Analysis," *Millennium* 45, no. 2 (January 2017): 151–173.

[31] Peter de Bolla, *The Architecture of Concepts: The Historical Formation of Human Rights* (New York: Fordham University Press, 2013).

The usefulness of the matrix lies in mapping out how different actors position issues against its various conceptual components. It does not provide a conclusive answer to the question of what maritime security is, but offers a tool for grasping divergences and similarities, and where and why these occur. For example, for some countries, maritime security is closely linked to the blue economy and is prioritized because insecurity at sea hinders investments in economic development. This is the case for many African states today, for whom the motivation to engage in maritime security derives primarily from blue economy concerns. For others, maritime security is mainly about interstate threats and closely linked to national security concerns. This is currently the case for many countries in the region of the South China Sea.

Different actors might also evaluate issues in radically different ways. For small island states, for example, climate change might be interpreted as a national security problem rather than an environmental issue, because of the potential threat it poses to their national way of life and even existence.

The matrix above is an invitation to think creatively about how actors relate concepts, issues, and concerns to each other. Since security discourses evolve over time, tomorrow's matrix of the maritime security concept and how it relates to others might look different from the one outlined here.

Securitization

Securitization is one of the best-known frameworks in interpretive security debates. It is best described as an analysis of the processes through which threats are constructed and become accepted as security issues requiring extraordinary, often militarized responses.[32] Securitization implies that we need to follow closely how actors come to understand and present issues in the maritime domain as threats, and how these constructions condition certain types of security response.

Securitization analysts contend that issues become constructed as threats not necessarily because of the objective dangers that they pose to specific actors and objects, but because they are constructed as such through discourse and representations, and in ways that become widely accepted by key political, bureaucratic, and public audiences. To do so they work with a distinct analytical framework. As outlined in Figure 3.3, this consists of a grammar of 1) the threat

---

[32] Securitization theory as an approach was first outlined in Barry Buzan, Ole Waever, and Jaap de Wilde, *Security: A New Framework for Analysis* (London: Lynne Rienner, 1998). A concise and useful introduction to securitization analysis is provided in Thierry Balzacq, Sarah Léonard, and Jan Ruzicka, "'Securitization' Revisited: Theory and Cases," *International Relations* 30, no. 4 (December 2016): 494–531.

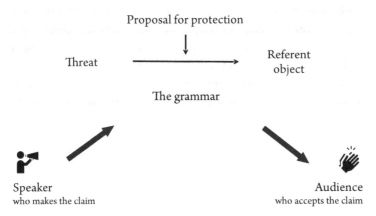

Figure 3.3 The securitization framework

that is identified, 2) the referent object that is threatened, and 3) a proposal for measures to take, as well as 4) a speaker that makes a securitization claim, and 5) an audience that accepts or rejects that claim.

The evolution of the maritime security agenda which we set out in Chapter 2 can in many ways be understood as a series of such securitization processes. We can see this clearly if we look at the issue maritime terrorism.

Terrorism was at the core of the first maritime security debates of the early 2000s (see Chapter 4, Section 4.3). In part, this was a consequence of the wider discourse around terrorism that emerged in the wake of the 9/11 attacks on the United States in 2001, though the issue has antecedents dating back to the Cold War period and before (see Chapter 4, Section 4.3).[33] The United States government became concerned that radical Islamist groups might try to use the sea to stage an attack, for example by crashing or blowing up an oil tanker in a port. Another fear was that extremist groups could use maritime routes to smuggle arms of or weapons of mass destruction into a target state. In response to these threat scenarios the United States government established an international port security program, with the aim of reducing the risk to its national maritime interests globally. It also strengthened security measures in its own ports.

The underlying securitization logic in this process is striking. The United States identified terrorism as a particular threat to key referent objects, such as its maritime economy, populations in vicinities of ports, and the overall society which could be harmed by a terrorist attack. This threat was widely accepted and prioritized by the domestic political elite and wider population. Because any

---

[33] Buzan Barry, "Will the 'Global War on Terrorism' be the New Cold War?," *International Affairs* 82, no. 6 (2006): 1101–1118.

ship could potentially be used for a terrorist act, all civilian maritime transport came to be seen as a potential threat, leading to much closer monitoring of international maritime activities, ports, and movements. Effectively, ports and the international transport industry became securitized.

Another good example of securitization is migration to Europe. Migration at sea between countries was long considered as an issue of economic or humanitarian concern, rather than a security problem. In Europe this position changed gradually in the 1990s, with an increasing politicization of migration issues that led to them being presented as a threat to social coherence and values.[34] However, at this time, this was not a specifically maritime discourse. It was the escalating so-called migration crisis of the 2010s and the growth in people smuggling networks to facilitate these movements that led to maritime migration specifically being presented as a threat. Because much of the irregular migration into Europe takes place across the Mediterranean Sea by boat, this securitization process focused particularly on the maritime aspects of the issue. In response, states across Europe initiated an extensive security response, including naval patrols; strengthened border security; and in some cases the use of aggressive pushback tactics to turn back migrant boats at sea (see Chapter 5, Section 5.4).

Practice

Another major form of interpretive analysis is known as the "security as practice" approach.[35] Practice thinking is related to securitization analysis in that it is concerned with how issues come to be understood as security problems. However, analysts working in this tradition focus more on the everyday activities that sustain and maintain security issues through practical action. In essence, these approaches are interested in how security issues are produced through different activities, such as strategy-making, program development, reporting, or operations.

A diverse range of practices inform maritime security. For example, processes of strategy formulation play an important role in ordering maritime security thinking for states and international organizations (see Chapter 7, Section 7.4). In writing strategic documents, representatives of different actors come together to review statistics and data to establish what maritime security means in a given national or organizational context, and to define priorities and threats, but also

[34] Jef Huysmans, *The Politics of Insecurity: Fear, Migration and Asylum in the EU* (London: Routledge, 2006).
[35] Christian Bueger, "Security as Practice," in *Handbook of Security Studies*, ed. Thierry Balzacq and Myriam Dunn Cavelty, 2nd ed. (London: Routledge, 2016).

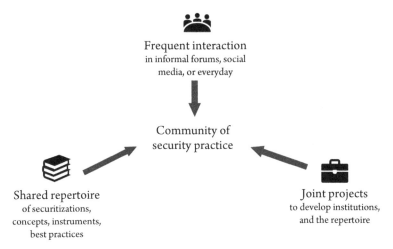

Figure 3.4 The three dimensions of communities of security practice

to determine what responses are appropriate and which agencies should play what roles in delivering them.[36]

Similarly, the programming and implementation of maritime security operations, such as coordinated coast guard patrols or naval missions, are practical activities through which specific threats are identified and mandates developed to enable a coordinated response to them. Surveillance activities aimed at gathering information on maritime activities and identifying suspicious behavior are another example of a practice that plays a part in this process. All these activities help to establish the meaning, content, and boundaries of maritime security, as well as to shape its evolution and development in practical actions.

One of the key questions in the security-as-practice framework is how these practices can lead to the development of groups of actors that interact closely, share a repertoire of tools, and engage in common projects (see Figure 3.4). These are known as "communities of practice."[37] Communities of practice can cut across organizational and national boundaries and can become informal governance vehicles for maritime security through which professionals address maritime security together.[38] For example, international coast guard

---

[36] Christian Bueger and Frank Gadinger, "Making Grand Strategy in Practice," in *The Oxford Handbook of Grand Strategy*, ed. Thierry Balzacq and Ronald R. Krebs (Oxford: Oxford University Press, 2021), 142–158.

[37] Etienne Wenger, *Communities of Practice: Learning, Meaning and Identity* (Cambridge: Cambridge University Press, 1998).

[38] Christian Bueger, "Communities of Security Practice at Work? The Emerging African Maritime Security Regime," *African Security* 6, no. 3–4 (July 2013): 297–316.

function forums or forums of prosecutors might lead to frequent interaction, common understandings of problems, and a community that understands issues in particular way that is common to each other, but distinct from other agencies in their home states. Communities of practice are important because they can facilitate shared responses across otherwise diverse groups of actors and can propagate a common toolbox of maritime security approaches and solutions across boundaries (see Chapter 7). Indeed, the objective of capacity-building is often to develop and expand communities of practice in particular areas.

In summary, analysts working with the practice framework argue that it is not only threat construction processes but also a broader range of practical actions that advance the meaning of maritime security. It is therefore important to study closely how these activities are carried out and what kinds of understandings of maritime security they establish.

Strengths and Weaknesses

Asking the question "what is maritime security?" leads to a research agenda that aims to map the meaning of the concept and understand its composition in discourse and practice. Interpretive studies have direct policy implications at national and international levels. They reveal when and how actors agree and disagree, and over what issues. These insights can assist with coordination problems. They also enable a different type of interpretation of maritime disputes that does not start with the assumed interests and positions of actors, but with an analysis of the meaning they attach to the maritime domain as a security space. These kinds of studies assist in establishing the content and boundaries of maritime security analysis and help to signpost its links into other policy fields, such as economic development or environmental protection. Finally, such frameworks can be important in identifying gaps, silences, and oversights. They can, for instance, reveal which issues have been securitized and which ones are not included in the maritime security agenda, but potentially should be. Analyses can also reveal which speakers and whose practices dominate, and what actors are marginalized in debates and the response to threats.

In the way that interpretive analyses emphasize the fine-grained and detailed reconstruction of processes, they are particularly well suited to deal with complex situations. However, they are often criticized for paying insufficient attention to larger historical and systemic dynamics and transformation. They are also open to the critique that they take the claim about the political construction of threats too far, and in so doing downplay the importance of objectively given forms of danger.

3.5 The Root Causes of Maritime Insecurity

A fourth set of frameworks aims to reconstruct how and why maritime security threats develop as they do. What causes maritime insecurity? These kinds of analyses can provide important clues for policymakers about what they can do to tackle maritime security issues, and potentially prevent them from escalating or even arising in the first place. In many maritime security debates, you will find representatives arguing that the root causes of maritime security and crime should be addressed. Most often the argument is that attention should be paid to factors such as unemployment, poverty, or environmental degradation.

While the origins of interstate disputes are best explained by the state-centric frameworks we discuss above, understanding the causes of blue crime or maritime terrorism requires a different lens. Scholars have used increasingly refined datasets of incidents, but also qualitative and sometimes ethnographical methods to understand the causes of maritime insecurity. Due to data accessibility the causes of some maritime security threats are better understood than others. For example, the root causes of piracy are relatively well understood due in large part to the wealth of data that has been collected on piracy attacks and operations, but also because of the high levels of interest in this crime among analysts.

In the following section, we provide a concise synthesis of the major root causes of maritime insecurity. What constitutes a cause, rather than a correlation, a structural condition, or an enabling factor is the subject of intricate philosophical debate.[39] Here we operate with a rather loose understanding. Our goal is to outline some of the main factors that have been identified as enabling the growth of maritime insecurity, including blue crime and terrorism. We outline seven root causes with the aim of providing a comprehensive and practical understanding how and why maritime insecurity arises, and a guide against which to judge countermeasures and responses.

Seven Root Causes

As indicated in Figure 3.5, the seven root causes of maritime insecurity are 1) geography, 2) wider patterns of insecurity and violence, 3) weak law enforcement and corruption, 4) economic dislocation, 5) cultural acceptability and legitimation, 6) skills, and 7) entrepreneurs. These causes are related to and influence

---

[39] Milja Kurki, *Causation in International Relations: Reclaiming Causal Analysis* (Cambridge: Cambridge University Press, 2008).

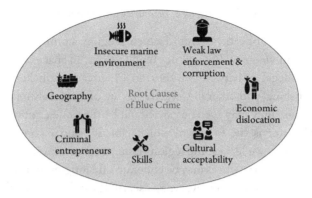

Figure 3.5 The seven root causes of maritime insecurity

each other. No one single cause on its own is likely to lead to the rise of criminal or terrorist activities at sea, and, usually, a combination of factors is at play.

Geography

Maritime insecurity is more likely in some locations rather than others. Some coastal regions and maritime spaces have geographic characteristics—physical, human, and economic—that make them especially conducive to criminal or terrorist activities. For example, major sea lanes or port facilities provide lucrative potential targets for pirates and other maritime criminals. As we show in our discussion of piracy in Chapter 5, Section 5.3, it is no coincidence that pirate activities thrive in areas with lots of high value maritime traffic.

Geography is also important for logistical and operational reasons. Coastal regions or islands that are difficult to reach or control can provide hideouts for criminal enterprises, enabling them to store, load, and distribute illicit goods. Ransom piracy requires isolated sites where vessels can be anchored and supplied with basic needs such as food, water, and fuel. In contrast, other types of crime—such as oil theft, for example—are dependent on the existence of a certain level of coastal infrastructure to allow stolen cargoes to be processed and laundered. In other areas, weather conditions, currents, or high waves, but also a lack potential of targets, might make it less likely that crimes will occur. Criminal activity can also be facilitated by geographical distribution of different enforcement regimes. What is illegal in one country may not be in an adjacent one, which can create opportunities for cross-border criminal activity and enterprise. Geographical conditions can hence play a major role in facilitating the rise of blue crime and conditioning its nature and characteristics.

Wider Patterns of Insecurity and Violence

A closely related factor is the extent to which a region is prone to wider patterns of insecurity and violence. Blue crimes tend to occur in spaces where there is a host of other illegal activity. As we show in Chapter 5, trafficking, smuggling, piracy, illicit fishing, and other illegal activities are often closely related and reinforce each other. They may even be carried out by the same criminal networks.

A crucial factor is the extent to which violence and insecurity at sea are normalized. For example, in some regions it may be a common practice to carry weapons at sea, minor offences may be endemic, and long-established smuggling routes may be in regular, even everyday use. All these factors can facilitate and encourage the rise of a diverse range of criminal activities at sea. Some studies show that even minor insecurities can increasingly spiral and escalate over time if not taken seriously and addressed.[40]

Weak Law Enforcement and Corruption

A third cause relates to the capacity of states to effectively govern and police the waters under their direct jurisdiction and nearby areas of the high seas. In essence, weak law enforcement and criminal justice capacities are conducive to higher levels of maritime security. This is the reasoning that underpins many of the maritime security capacity-building initiatives we discuss in Chapter 7, Section 7.6. The basic logic here is that the lower the risk that perpetrators will be stopped, caught, and punished for illicit activities, the higher the likelihood that they will occur.

A wide range of different law enforcement and criminal justice activities are relevant to maritime security. They include at-sea patrolling and surveillance, policing, intelligence, and investigative work on land, as well as the effectiveness of the judicial sector in prosecuting and punishing criminal activities. Official corruption can also be an important factor here. Organized criminals often do not operate fully outside the law, but in collaboration with corrupt law enforcement agencies, government officials, or port authorities.[41] Corrupt actors can facilitate blue crimes in many ways, including by passing targeting information to pirates, facilitating the movement of smuggled goods through ports, issuing unauthorized licenses to illicit fishing vessels, or by turning a blind eye or providing shelter to organized criminal activities at sea or on land. Finally, the quality of

---

[40] Joshua Tallis, *The War for Muddy Waters: Pirates, Terrorists, Traffickers and Maritime Insecurity* (Annapolis, MD: Naval Institute Press, 2019).

[41] See for example the contributions in Leslie Holmes, ed., *Terrorism, Organised Crime and Corruption: Networks and Linkages* (Cheltenham: Edward Elgar, 2010).

coordination between national law enforcement agencies within a region can also be an important consideration given that many maritime insecurities are transnational or take place in border regions.

This argument also requires some qualification. Colloquially, the rise of insecurity is often attributed to state failure or the absence of the state in particular regions. However, research has shown that crime thrives under conditions where there is a certain minimum level of state governance.[42] This is because criminals require logistics, infrastructures, and a certain degree of security or protection to run their operations. For example, studies of piracy operations in Somalia and the Gulf of Guinea demonstrate the extent to which they are dependent on working governance structures to launder their profits, to protect their operations from other criminals, and for supply lines and recruitment.[43]

Economic Dislocation

Poverty is often considered to be an important cause of maritime insecurity. Certainly economic factors matter in explaining the prevalence of crime, given that it is a fundamentally profit-driven activity. However, most scholars agree that the link between poverty and criminality is less direct than often assumed. After all, not everyone who is poor becomes a criminal.

What matters more is relative economic inequality, including relations between the rich and poor and the degree to which individuals or groups are marginalized or feel dislocated in a regional or national economy. Communities that engage in or support crime tend to have been economically marginalized, put at a disadvantage by economic development, decolonization, and globalization processes, or have been excluded from local wealth generation activities such as offshore oil exploitation or national fisheries.[44] In circumstances of high unemployment, or when legitimate coastal livelihoods such as fishing are in decline, ordinary people may also be tempted to engage in criminal activities either for profit or simply to help make ends meet.[45]

Economic dislocation in the maritime sector is often closely linked to questions of "blue justice"; that is, how the risks and revenues of the global

---

[42] Anja Shortland and Federico Varese, "State-Building, Informal Governance and Organised Crime: The Case of Somali Piracy," *Political Studies* 64, no. 4 (December 2016): 811–831.

[43] Justin V. Hastings and Sarah G. Phillips, "Maritime Piracy Business Networks and Institutions in Africa," *African Affairs* 114, no. 457 (October 2015): 555–576.

[44] J. L. Anderson, "Piracy and World History: An Economic Perspective on Maritime Predation," *Journal of World History* 6, no. 2 (1995): 175–199; Jatin Dua, *Captured at Sea: Piracy and Protection in the Indian Ocean* (Berkeley: University of California Press, 2019).

[45] Ursula Daxecker and Brandon Prins, *Pirate Lands: Governance and Maritime Piracy* (New York: Oxford University Press, 2021), 100.

ocean economy can be equally distributed.[46] This indicates that economic dislocation often concerns inequalities that are historically grown and structural in nature, concerning, for example, international fisheries markets, environmental sustainability, and the participation of communities in decision-making.

Cultural Acceptability and Legitimation

Blue crime and maritime terrorism have a significant cultural dimension in that they require legitimacy in order thrive. For example, a degree of cultural acceptability and legitimacy is necessary for the recruitment of foot soldiers to organizations and networks, and to gain the support, or at least tolerance, of illicit activities by coastal communities needed for logistical and organizational reasons.[47]

The cultural acceptability of maritime crime is often linked to the notions of blue justice and issues of inequality we discuss above. These might derive from economic dislocation within states and regions, but also from old colonial patterns of exploitation, the iniquitous distribution of capital and wealth in the global economic system, or the inclusions and exclusions of the global ocean governance system.[48] These issues are especially visible in relation to the global fishing economy, where industrial fishing practices, both legal and illegal, and sponsored by global economic actors, have depleted fish stocks and led to declining incomes for small-scale fishers, especially in the Global South. In this context, blue crime and terrorism can come to be seen as a legitimate form of resistance or adaptation to a fundamentally unjust global economic and political order.

For example, the cultural acceptability of piracy in Somali coastal communities was due in part to a perception that it was a legitimate response to illicit fishing and pollution crimes conducted in Somali waters by external actors. These had denuded local fish stocks and increased the economic hardship already being suffered by coastal communities because of the collapse of the Somali state (see Chapter 5, Section 5.3). Accordingly, piracy came to be seen as a justifiable, almost state-like practice of protecting coastal waters against outside threats and

---

[46] Nathan James Bennett, Jessica Blythe, Carole Sandrine White, and Cecilia Campero, "Blue Growth and Blue Justice: Ten Risks and Solutions for the Ocean Economy," *Marine Policy* 125 (March 2021): 104387.

[47] Jon Vagg, "Rough Seas? Contemporary Piracy in South East Asia," *British Journal of Criminology* 35, no. 1 (1995): 63–80.

[48] Chris Armstrong, *A Blue New Deal: Why We Need a New Politics for the Ocean* (New Haven, CT: Yale University Press, 2021).

predation.[49] This narrative of the protective character of piracy, while in many ways a fallacy, was for a time a crucial factor in recruitment as well as for ensuring the support of local communities.[50]

Skills

Another related cultural cause is the availability of the necessary skills to engage in criminal activity at sea. Carrying out blue crimes or acts of maritime terrorism requires, for instance, navigation and boat handling skills. Capturing ships implies boarding and weapons handling skills. Kidnap for ransom requires skills such as negotiation techniques. Smuggling operations will often need good knowledge of the inner workings of transport systems, or of how to carry out negotiations with corrupt officials. Many of these skills are often widely available in coastal communities.

To return again to the case of piracy off the coast of Somalia, where these skill sets have been well described, piracy operations drew on an existing cultural repertoire, including the centuries-old navigation knowledge of fishermen and dhow traders, and the negotiation skills prevalent in a society governed by customary law and informal governance arrangements.[51] In addition, skills such as weapons handling had also been learned during years of civil war. As a Somalia specialist remarked, "the act of piracy [was] little more than an extension of activities that armed groups [had] engaged in for years: militia roadblocks, extortion and kidnapping for ransom [were] a staple source of income for gangs and militias in Somalia."[52]

Entrepreneurs

Considering that many illicit activities are large-scale enterprises or at least require extended networks to be carried out, the role of individuals within these networks is a final factor to be considered. Entrepreneurship and the capacity for leadership and organization are necessary for criminal and extremist groups to thrive and survive. All organized crime requires planning, preparation, and investment, which in turn implies that a business plan of sorts must

---

[49] Christian Bueger, "Practice, Pirates and Coast Guards: The Grand Narrative of Somali Piracy," *Third World Quarterly* 34, no. 10 (November 2013): 1811–1827.

[50] Stig Jarle Hansen, "Debunking the Piracy Myth," *The RUSI Journal* 156, no. 6 (December 2011): 26–31.

[51] Ken Menkhaus, "Vicious Circles and the Security Development Nexus in Somalia," *Conflict, Security & Development* 4, no. 2 (August 2004): 149–165.

[52] Ken Menkhaus, "Dangerous Waters," *Survival* 51, no. 1 (March 2009): 23.

be in place. A major driving force in all such activities will be criminally minded entrepreneurs or leaders, who are sometimes described as "kingpins." Likewise, terrorist operations require significant organizational and leadership skills, which is the reason why many counterterrorism operations focus on the arrest or even targeted killing of organizational leadership cadres. When entrepreneurial criminal activities are successful, they may be emulated and replicated by others, leading to the spread of new criminal practices and business models elsewhere.

Summary

Root causes is a common term in maritime security policy debates. It is often used but tends to be underspecified. In this section, we have introduced a framework that synthesizes current research and provides a roster against which to analyze the causes of insecurity at sea. This provides a starting point from which to understand regional and local variations in particular crimes or transformations over time. In addition, it has direct policy implications because it questions the scope and effectiveness of activities that focus on law enforcement alone—which is just one of several factors.

Root cause analyses are often limited by the absence of reliable data and access to criminal operations. They can also introduce a misplaced sense of certainty in overemphasizing direct causal links, or in recognizing the amenability of these issues to simplistic or straightforward corrective interventions. Many of the root causes we discuss here, such as corruption or skills, are deeply rooted, and while they can be useful for risk analyses, cannot easily be addressed through security-orientated countermeasures. Indeed, often they are linked to much wider and more intractable questions of economic development and global justice.

For the maritime security analyst and professional, root causes frameworks are important to help identify where and when maritime insecurities may be more likely to occur and play an important role in risk assessment. However, they offer more limited guidance to maritime security actors in terms of what should be done in response, by whom, and how.

3.6 Using Analytical Frameworks

The frameworks of analysis that we have introduced in this chapter all center around a particular concept, respectively: law, state interests, institutions, meanings, practice, and causes. These provide valuable starting points for making sense of maritime security.

The frameworks are often considered to be competitors with each other because they sometimes draw on incompatible assumptions. However, each allows the analyst a mechanism through which to understand a different aspect of maritime security. In this respect, they are better approached as a repertoire of analytical tools to be developed and used as appropriate, rather than as mutually exclusive explanatory rivals.

Law-centric frameworks are particularly good at understanding and clarifying the rules that states follow in maritime security. State-centric frameworks provide an insight into the more general behavior of states in the pursuit of their maritime security interests, but also provide interpretations of the role of international law and international institutions in contributing to security at sea. Frameworks centered on meaning and practice give us a better sense of how and why actors in maritime security have diverging understandings and priorities, and favor different practical solutions. They are useful for conducting fine grained analyses of specific actors and situations, as well as to making sense of the history of maritime security thinking. Finally, research on root causes offers important insights into how and why maritime insecurities, and especially blue crimes, come into being and endure. They thus have an important role to play in assessing risk and informing holistic responses on both land and sea.

If these are the strengths of the frameworks, one needs to be equally aware of their limits. Legal analyses overestimate the power of rules to guide behavior, and underestimate the political importance of legal ambiguity. Legal and state-centric analysis remain too often abstract in not considering the intricate politics of substate actors, regional political dynamics, or the important roles of other actors than states. Interpretive analyses can have the opposite problem in that they underestimate the importance of states, or focus too much on micro-dynamics rather than larger structural forces. Root cause analyses, in turn, provide little guidance on the complex politics of designing and implementing specific maritime security solutions to deeply rooted structural problems.

In the next part of the book, we examine issues on the maritime security agenda more closely, drawing on the maritime security triangle introduced in Chapter 1. We begin by investigating interstate conflicts, maritime terrorism, and the rise in what have become known as grey-zone activities at sea. From there we move on to blue crimes, including piracy, smuggling, and environmental crimes such as illicit fishing.

4
Interstate Conflicts, Terrorism, and Grey Zones

4.1 Political Conflict in the Maritime Domain

In the previous chapters we explored the history of maritime security and introduced four frameworks for analysis. In this and the following chapter, we delve deeper into the key challenges that maritime security deals with. We draw on the three dimensions introduced in Chapter 1: 1) interstate conflict, 2) terrorism and extremist violence, and 3) blue crime. These three dimensions are a useful point of orientation to organize discussion of the complex range of challenges of maritime security. Each dimension involves particular types of actors, underlying objectives, and motives. Extremist violence and blue crimes are carried out by nonstate actors, while interstate conflicts take place between state actors. States and extremist groups have in common that they pursue political objectives. This contrasts with maritime criminals, whose actions are profit-driven, and who work for private gain rather than political goals.

In this chapter we focus on the two dimensions that involve politically motivated actions. We first explore interstate conflicts and then consider maritime terrorism and extremist violence at sea. We finish with a review of grey-zone tactics at sea. These are unconventional forms of confrontation that blur the lines between interstate conflict and extremist violence since they often involve other actors than designated military forces.

4.2 Interstate Conflicts and Disputes

Disagreements between states at sea are very common. Statistics illustrate the problem well. One study finds that of the 460 maritime boundaries between countries, fewer than of half of them (180) were formally settled in 2020.[1] Another study identified 270 competitive diplomatic maritime claims globally from 1900 to 2010.[2] It also found that such maritime disputes tend to involve the less frequent use of military force than their equivalents on land. For this reason, most interstate maritime conflicts fall into the category of maritime security issues rather than outright naval warfare and military confrontation.

Maritime conflicts vary in nature and scope. In our discussion of interstate frameworks (see Chapter 3, Section 3.3), we highlighted several important forms of contestation between states:[3] competition over the physical properties and resources of the sea (functional disputes); differences over how boundaries are drawn and managed by institutions (institutional disputes); and conflicts that derive from the intangible cultural or political values that states attach to maritime territories and issues (symbolic disputes). This categorization provides us with an understanding of what is at stake in a conflict.

Conflicts at sea vary in their severity. Some are minor in nature and have a limited potential for escalation. This might be because they concern relatively trivial matters of low political priority, or because they take place between states with otherwise friendly and cooperative relations. Other conflicts are more volatile, especially if they concern territories or issues with a significant functional or symbolic value. We can thus further categorize conflicts by investigating the political attention they receive and their potential for escalation and violence.

We identify three levels of severity of interstate conflict at sea. A first level comprises *competing territorial claims*. These relate to instances where two states make diplomatic claims over the same territory, such as the ownership of a particular island or the demarcation of an ambiguous maritime border, but decide to take no further action on the matter. Next are *nonviolent disputes* over territory. These take place when states unilaterally or bilaterally contest each other's claims, and peruse these through diplomatic negotiations, arbitration, or judgments in fora such as the International Court of Justice (ICJ) or International Tribunal for the Law of the Sea (ITLOS). Finally, and more rarely, there are *militarized disputes*, in which states resort to the use of coercion and violence to enforce their claims.

Interstate conflicts are dynamic and can escalate or deescalate between these levels. For example, the discovery of hydrocarbon resources in an area of previously ambiguous borders may lead states to solidify their claims and take

---

[1] Andreas Østhagen, "Troubled Seas? The Changing Politics of Maritime Boundary Disputes," *Ocean & Coastal Management* 205 (May 2021): 1.

[2] Sara McLaughlin Mitchell, "Clashes at Sea: Explaining the Onset, Militarization, and Resolution of Diplomatic Maritime Claims," *Security Studies* 29, no. 4 (August 2020): 645.

[3] Østhagen, "Troubled Seas?"

further action. Escalation can also take place if legal proceedings or diplomatic negotiations fail to resolve an issue to everyone's satisfaction. The boundaries between nonviolent and violent disputes at sea can also be deliberately blurred by the kinds of grey-zone activities we discuss later on in this chapter.

We illustrate these distinctions by investigating four examples of interstate disputes at sea. We start with the case of a nonviolent conflict solved through peaceful resolution: the so-called Whisky War between Canada and Denmark, which ran from 1978 to 2022. Second, we discuss the ongoing Chagos Islands dispute between the United Kingdom and Mauritius as an example of a case that was addressed in legal forums but remains unresolved. Next, we turn to conflicts over resources, focusing on the so-called fish wars between the United Kingdom and Iceland and between Canada and European Union (EU) member states, both of which were militarized but ultimately resolved through negotiations. Then we discuss the South China Sea, which comprises complex web of disputes, and has a high escalatory potential.

Peaceful Resolution: The Whisky War

What became known as the Whisky War was a dispute that took place over a tiny uninhabited island of no economic value known as Hans Island.[4] The island is located in the waters between Greenland—an autonomous region of the Kingdom of Denmark—and the Northernmost territory of Canada. The Whisky War is a case of a relatively minor dispute between two allies, both NATO members, that was largely symbolic in nature. It escalated in 2015 and was resolved peacefully in 2022.

When Canada and Denmark signed a treaty delimitating their Arctic border in 1973, they could not agree on the status of Hans Island and left it open to further negotiation. In 1984 the Canadian navy planted a flag on the island, making an explicit claim to it and the waters around it. In addition to the flag, they left a bottle of whisky. In response, the Danish Minister for Greenland flew to the island, and placed the Danish flag as well as a bottle of traditional liquor. This brought the dispute its name as the whisky or liquor war.

The Danish navy subsequently visited the islands and erected new flagpoles several times. Public awareness of the dispute increased in the 2000s in line with

---

[4] P. Whitney Lackenbauer Nielsen and Rasmus Leander Nielsen, "'Close, Like-Minded Partners Committed to Democratic Principles': Settling the Hans Island/Tartupaluk Territorial Dispute," ed. Lassi Heininen, Heather Exner-Pirot, and Justin Barnes, *2022 Arctic Yearbook*, accessed June 13, 2023, https://arcticyearbook.com/arctic-yearbook/2022/2022-briefing-notes/442-close-like-minded-partners-committed-to-democratic-principles-settling-the-hans-island-tartupaluk-territorial-dispute.

the growing strategic importance of the Arctic. In 2005, the Canadian navy and Minster of Defence visited the island to place a new flag. These actions began a new round of escalation. The Danish government decided not to replace the flag immediately, but instead directly challenged Canada's sovereignty claims and its plans for geological exploration.

The dispute had now become an issue of Arctic strategy and geopolitics, with the public in both countries opposed to the surrender of any national territory, however small. The two states agreed to restart negotiations on the matter, and, if unsuccessful, to transfer the case to an international court. Negotiations dragged on for over a decade, and it was only in 2022 that the two states finally agreed to settle on a land border which split the island in half. In the light of the war in Ukraine, this resolution was interpreted as a signal to the world that countries can settle their borders peacefully without resorting to violence.

The Whisky War illustrates how conflicts between states can arise over symbolic issues of territorial delimitation. The case also stresses how transformations in the wider geopolitical environment—in this case a re-evaluation of the strategic significance of the Arctic region—can change the symbolic value and political stakes of previously dormant disputes. Finally, it demonstrates that even minor maritime conflicts can be protracted, but also how, under the right circumstances, they can be open to peaceful resolution through direct bilateral negotiations.

Colonial Legacies and the Limits of International Law: The Chagos Islands

The colonial practice of drawing largely arbitrary boundary lines, and the way that these boundaries were established during decolonization, provides another important source for interstate conflicts.[5] Conflicts of this kind might occur between two decolonized states, or with the former colonial power. The dispute over the Chagos Islands between the United Kingdom and its former colony Mauritius is a case in point.[6] It is noteworthy because it illustrates that while international law can provide a source for resolution, it also faces limits in doing so when states consider their national security interests to be at stake.

The Chagos Islands are a remote archipelago in the Western Indian Ocean that in 1814, were made part of the British colony of Mauritius. Prior to this point,

---

[5] See for example Sandip Kumar Mishra, "The Colonial Origins of Territorial Disputes in South Asia," *Journal of Territorial and Maritime Studies (JTMS)* 3, no. 1 (2016): 5–24.

[6] An accessible reconstruction of the history of Chagos and the legal dispute is Philippe Sands, *The Last Colony: A Tale of Exile, Justice and Britain's Colonial Legacy* (London: Weidenfeld & Nicolson, 2022).

they (and Mauritius) had been administered by France, which had established plantations on the previously uninhabited islands from 1793. Following French practice, the Chagos Islands were administered from Mauritius under British suzerainty. Mauritius achieved independence from the United Kingdom as part of the decolonization process in 1968. However, in 1965 the Chagos Islands had been separated to form a new colony, the British Indian Ocean Territory, and hence remained under the control of the United Kingdom.

Between 1966 and 1971, the Chagos islanders were forcefully deported to Mauritius and Seychelles and offered some limited compensation. One of the now uninhabited islands, Diego Garcia, was then leased to the United States to construct a military base. The Naval Support Facility Diego Garcia became fully operational in 1977. It soon became a major base of military operations for United States forces, initially to counter Soviet influence in the region, and later to support military operations such as wars in Iraq and Afghanistan. The base remains of significant strategic value to the United States to this day.

While not disagreeing with the leasing arrangement with the United States, the government of Mauritius and representatives of the Chagossians have long contested the United Kingdom's claim to govern the archipelago. The Chagossians claimed a right to return home and sought further compensation for their forceful deportation. For its part, Mauritius argued that the separation of the islands and the creation of a new colony in 1965 was unlawful in the context of United Nations resolutions on decolonization which ensure territorial integrity.

When the United Kingdom declared the Chagos Islands to be a Marine Protected Area in 2010, Mauritius sought arbitration under ITLOS in a plea to clarify the sovereignty issue. The tribunal concluded that the United Kingdom had no right to govern the waters of the Chagos Islands, but also judged that it was not competent to resolve the competing territorial claims because they concerned the land rather than the sea. Mauritius hence proposed a resolution to the UN General Assembly requesting an advisory opinion from the ICJ. This was passed in 2017.

The court resolved that the separation of the Chagos Islands into a new territory was contrary to international decolonization laws, and that the islands should be returned to Mauritian control. A subsequent General Assembly resolution in 2019 confirmed this judgment and called on the United Kingdom to return the islands to Mauritius. It also requested that all international organizations treat the Chagos Islands as part of Mauritian national territory. In legal terms, therefore, the dispute was settled in favor of Mauritius. However, the United Kingdom has since refused to transfer jurisdiction of the islands on the basis that they are critical to its national security interests.

The Chagos case, in which substantial marine resources and a large exclusive economic zone (EEZ) are at stake, demonstrates how international law provides important instruments for the peaceful settlement of interstate disputes. Indeed, as research has shown a majority of these conflicts are resolved by international arbitration or judgments.[7] However, the case of Chagos differs, and shows how major powers can chose to ignore the judgments of international courts should they believe it is in their interest to do so. The Chagos case is also indicative of other unresolved disputes with their colonial origins, many of which concern islands.

Fish Wars

Competition over resources underpins many maritime interstate conflicts. Marine hydrocarbons, fisheries, and other oceanic resources offer significant economic and employment opportunities for states. While drilling for marine oil and gas requires fixed installations at sea and tends not to proceed in the absence of a prior legal boundary settlement, fish stocks are migratory and do not respect national territories and political borders. Fishing can also take place at long distances from national coastlines and far from any landing points. Fisheries in many countries are not only seen as economic or nutritional resources, but also have significant symbolic value and environmental importance.[8] For these reasons, the escalatory potential of fisheries disputes is high.

In the following we introduce a series of conflicts that have become known as "fish wars": the Cod Wars between the United Kingdom and Iceland in the 1950s, 1960s, and 1970s, and the Turbot War of 1995, a militarized dispute between Canada and Spain.[9] These are noteworthy and well-studied conflicts because they show how disputes can escalate even between democracies, close allies, and members of a well-established security community (see Chapter 3, Section 3.4).[10]

---

[7] Mitchell, "Clashes at Sea," 667.

[8] Edyta Roszko, "Spectacular Fishing: Embodying Sovereignty in the Post-Brexit Channel Islands and the South China Sea," in *Variations on Sovereignty: Contestation and Transformation from Around the World*, ed. Hannes Cerny and Janis Grzybowski (London: Routledge, 2023), 174–195.

[9] For a general discussion of the tensions brought about by fisheries, and the fish wars discussed here specifically, see Elizabeth R. DeSombre, "The Security Implications of Fisheries," *International Affairs* 95, no. 5 (September 2019): 1019–1035.

[10] Gunther Hellmann and Benjamin Herborth, "Fishing in the Mild West: Democratic Peace and Militarised Interstate Disputes in the Transatlantic Community," *Review of International Studies* 34, no. 3 (July 2008): 481–506.

The Cod Wars were a series of militarized maritime disputes between the United Kingdom and Iceland.[11] Taking place prior to the finalization of UNCLOS in 1982, the dispute centered on the question of whether Iceland could declare an exclusive fishing zone around its coast. Iceland asserted its right to do so, while the United Kingdom insisted on an open seas principle for international fisheries, giving any state the right to fish outside a narrowly defined zone of territorial waters. The United Kingdom sent naval forces to strengthen its claim and protect its fishing fleets. Iceland, which had (and has) no navy, dispatched large coast guard vessels for the same purposes. While collisions, net-cutting, the firing of warning shots and even live rounds took place, no sinkings or sustained exchanges of fire occurred. The disputes escalated several times. However, they were gradually resolved through agreements brokered through NATO, of which both states were members. They were finally settled with the conclusion of UNCLOS, which established the internationally agreed concept of EEZs (see Chapter 3, Section 3.2) and clarified rights for fisheries.

In contrast, the Turbot War of 1995 was a confrontation that escalated after UNCLOS had come into force in 1994. Two NATO allies, Spain and Canada, claimed different fishing rights for turbot in the North Atlantic. The background was a concern over the sustainability of fish stocks in the region, overfishing, and the question of how to agree on fishing quotas.[12] Canada had placed a moratorium on its own fishing activities in the region to allow stocks to recover. However, the EU's Common Fisheries Policy, under which Spain operated its fishing vessels, had granted more extensive quotas to its members. The regional management organization for migratory fish stocks, the Northwest Atlantic Fishery Organization (NAFO), noted the decline in fish stocks and settled overall quotas for protection, but it did not resolve the divergence because of EU objections.

Canada resorted to unilateral means and ordered its navy, coast guard, and fisheries agency to enforce NAFO quotas on fishing vessels in international waters. In March 1995, Canadian ships attempted to board a Spanish trawler, an action which was followed by a chase which only concluded after a patrol vessel fired a warning shot. The Spanish boat was seized, and the captain charged with fisheries offences. Spain protested and sent a naval vessel of its own to protect its fishing fleet. It also drew up plans to send a larger task force to the region, but ultimately did not do so. Canada reacted by deploying additional naval forces,

---

[11] An excellent introduction to the Cod Wars is provided in Sverrir Steinsson, "The Cod Wars: A Re-Analysis," *European Security* 25, no. 2 (April 2016): 256–275.

[12] David R. Teece, "Global Overfishing and the Spanish-Canadian Turbot War: Can International Law Protect the High-Seas Environment," *Colorado Journal of International Environmental Law and Policy* 8, no. 1 (1997): 89–126.

and two further Spanish flagged trawlers were chased out the area. A diplomatic crisis unfolded, with Canada threatening further naval action. Eventually, the EU and Canada entered negotiations which led to a compromise solution. The EU was allocated higher quotas, but in return agreed to stricter monitoring and measures against illegal fishing.

The Turbot War was ultimately resolved. However, with fish stocks continuing to decline, concerns over marine biodiversity loss, and the persistence of industrialized long-distance fishing, the potential for fisheries conflicts remains ever present. There are ongoing struggles over fisheries issues between Indian and Pakistan, for example; concerns about the activities of foreign vessels in Gulf of Guinea; and direct confrontations such as that between the United Kingdom and France, which took place off the coast of the Channel Islands in 2021.[13] Growing tensions over fisheries are also a major issue in Southeast Asia. They are a key feature of the South China Sea dispute, which we turn to next.

Disputing in the Grey Zone: The Case of the South China Sea

East and Southeast Asia are home to numerous maritime disputes between states. Many are a consequence of colonial legacies, or the failure of settlements agreed in the wake of the Second World War. Maritime disputes in the region are characterized by their intractability and tendency toward militarization.[14] They are also exacerbated by the changing geopolitics of the region, and particularly the rising economic and political influence of China and its territorial claims. The most widely known, and indeed most dangerous, maritime disputes in the region can be found in the South China Sea.[15]

Located between China, Taiwan, the Philippines, Malaysia, Brunei, Indonesia, and Vietnam, the South China Sea is a region of critical economic and strategic and importance. It is crossed by some busiest shipping lanes in the world, with

---

[13] Scott Edwards and Timothy Edmunds, "Jersey Fishing Dispute: Why the UK Sent in the Navy and How to Resolve the Spat," *The Conversation*, May 2021, http://theconversation.com/jersey-fishing-dispute-why-the-uk-sent-in-the-navy-and-how-to-resolve-the-spat-maritime-security-experts-160506.

[14] Cullen S. Hendrix, Sarah M. Glaser, Joshua E. Lambert, and Paige M. Roberts, "Global Climate, El Niño, and Militarized Fisheries Disputes in the East and South China Seas," *Marine Policy* 143 (September 2022): 105137. See also the contributions in "Hybrid Warfare in Asia," *The Pacific Review* 31, special issue no. 6 (2018).

[15] For introductions to the South China Sea dispute see Leszek Buszynski and Do Thanh Hai, eds., *The South China Sea: From a Regional Maritime Dispute to Geo-Strategic Competition* (Abingdon: Routledge, 2020); Jing Huang and Andrew Bilo, eds., *Territorial Disputes in the South China Sea: Navigating Rough Waters* (Basingstoke: Palgrave Macmillan, 2014).

a trade value estimated at 5 per cent of global gross domestic product in 2019.[16] The sea's maritime geography, which includes numerous small islands, rocks, reefs, and sandbanks, creates a complex patchwork of contested and overlapping maritime territories and EEZs. Many of the countries bordering the sea are major fishing nations and compete over access to the region's fish stocks, which are substantial but in decline, as well as to the significant untapped oil and gas reserves believed to be in the area. For the main claimant, China, regional security concerns and geopolitical ambitions are also at stake. Other regional states and their global allies, such as the United States, feel threatened by China's claims and are concerned about potential risks to freedom of navigation in the region. For all countries, these issues carry significant political and symbolic importance.

The conflict in fact comprises a series of competing disputes among the seven littoral states that surround the South China Sea, specifically China, Taiwan, Philippines, Malaysia, Brunei, Indonesia, and Vietnam. At stake is the status and ownership of various geographical features in the sea, including the Spratly and Paracel island chains. These have the potential to anchor large areas of maritime territory and resources into states' EEZs or continental shelves. The dispute is complex because of the number of disputing parties, but also the ambiguous historical and legal status of the territories concerned, and the involvement of external actors.[17] Various regional states make claim to some or all the islands, with China and Taiwan advancing the most ambitious and controversial claims. China, for example, has asserted "indisputable sovereignty" over almost the entire South China Sea, based on historical claims to sovereignty within series of maritime boundary markers known as the "nine-dash line." Other states make contested and competing claims, with control being established in practice by occupation.

There is also disagreement about the legal status of the contested territories. UNCLOS defines an island as "a naturally formed area of land, surrounded by water, which is a above water at high tide." Islands are distinguished from "rocks," which "cannot sustain human habitation or economic life of their own."[18] The distinction is important because islands have EEZs, while rocks do not. The question of whether the features of the South China Sea are islands or rocks thus has significant implications for access to marine resources in the region.

---

[16] Lincoln F. Pratson, "Assessing Impacts to Maritime Shipping from Marine Chokepoint Closures," *Communications in Transportation Research* 3 (December 2023): 4.

[17] Douglas Guilfoyle and Edward Sing Yue Chan, "Lawships or Warships? Coast Guards as Agents of (in)Stability in the Pacific and South and East China Sea," *Marine Policy* 140 (June 2022): 105048.

[18] Erik Franckx, "The Regime of Islands and Rocks," in *The IMLI Manual on International Maritime Law: Volume I: The Law of the Sea*, ed. David Attard, Malgosia Fitzmaurice, and Norman Martinez (Oxford: Oxford University Press, 2014), xx–xx.

Disputes in the South China Sea have flared at various times, up to and including armed confrontations between disputants. The conflict escalated significantly after 2010, with states pursuing provocative and coercive tactics to advance their claims. These actions have included the building of artificial islands on rocks and reefs, the construction of new military facilities, the aggressive use of coast guard and fisheries patrol vessels to harass or intimidate rival parties, and the deployment of fishing fleets and oil exploration vessels into other countries' EEZs. While several regional states, including Vietnam and the Philippines, have used such unconventional means, China has done so most extensively (see Chapter 4, Section 4.4). External navies, including from the United States, the United Kingdom, France, and India, have also conducted operations in the region to contest China's claims.

In 2013, the Philippines issued arbitration against China under UNCLOS over the nine-dash line and other issues. The case was referred to the UN's Permanent Court of Arbitration. While the Court did not address the question of island ownership of maritime boundaries, it ruled in 2016 that China had no legal basis to claim historical rights under the nine-dash line that it had breached UNCLOS by island building, that it had not exercised due diligence over the activities of its fishing fleet, that it had unlawfully hindered Philippine fishers, and that it had operated its law enforcement vessels in a dangerous manner. China did not participate in the arbitration and refused to recognize the ruling, though by 2019 it had taken steps to comply with two of the Court's 11 judgments.[19]

The South China Sea illustrates how complex and tangled interstate conflicts at sea can be. While the dispute is notionally about the possession of relatively unremarkable maritime geographic features such as small islands and reefs, control over these territories confers considerable economic and strategic advantages. The dispute also has important symbolic meaning for all states in the region, entailing historically rooted claims of ownership and patterns of geopolitical ambition and rivalry, with a strong nationalist resonance for domestic audiences. Like the Chagos case, the South China Sea conflict shows the limits of international law when major powers—in this case China—choose to contest or ignore the rulings of international tribunals and arbitration. It has also functioned as a crucible for the unconventional development and use of force, which we discuss in Section 4.4 as an example of grey-zone tactics at sea.

---

[19] Asia Maritime Transparency Initiative, "Failing or Incomplete? Grading the South China Sea Arbitration," Center for Strategic and International Studies, July 2019, https://amti.csis.org/failing-or-incomplete-grading-the-south-china-sea-arbitration/.

Summary and Challenges

Interstate conflicts are one of the major dimensions of the maritime security agenda. While UNCLOS provides an overarching legal framework, and international courts forums for conflict resolution, many maritime disputes remain unresolved. Even so, and to date at least, escalation to militarized disputes remains the exception. Indeed, most disputes between states at sea have been managed or contained peacefully, if not always amicably, and in ways which do not fundamentally challenge the international consensus around UNCLOS.

The question remains as to whether this pattern will continue in the future. The national and collective benefits of the UNCLOS framework are such that few, if any, states have been willing to contest it outright. However, several factors point to future uncertainty in this regard. Major countries, notably the United Kingdom and China, have not complied with settlements provided by the institutions of international law. Other states remain uncomfortable with certain provisions in the treaty, such as the right to conduct military exercises in another country's EEZ.[20] The hunger for resources is unabated, and with fisheries in decline, revenues from fossil fuels still promising, and new prospects of mining deep sea minerals, competing claims will continue to arise. As discussed in Section 4.4, a reliance on grey-zone tactics might also challenge current forms of dispute resolution by international institutions. Finally, climate change and sea-level rise may mean that institutional disputes intensify in the future as the coastal baselines against which maritime boundaries are calculated change.[21] This is especially so in the case of claims based on islands that face inundation if sea levels rise beyond a certain point.

4.3 Maritime Terrorism and Extremist Violence

We now investigate politically motivated violence at sea carried out by nonstate actors. Our discussion focuses on instances of terrorism and extremist violence in the maritime domain. These are terms which are often contested and lack accepted legal definitions.[22] Debate continues over the pejorative nature of these terms and the question of what constitutes legitimate political violence and what

---

[20] Keyuan Zou, "Peaceful Use of the Sea and Military Intelligence Gathering in the EEZ," in *Asian Yearbook of International Law, Volume 22 (2016)* (Leiden: Brill Nijhoff, 2018), 161–176.

[21] Jonathan Lusthaus, "Shifting Sands: Sea Level Rise, Maritime Boundaries and Inter-State Conflict," *Politics* 30, no. 2 (June 2010): 113–118.

[22] See for example Richard English, "The Future Study of Terrorism," *European Journal of International Security* 1, no. 2 (July 2016): 135–149.

not. Here we refer to nonstate violence for extremist political goals, including religious, left- or right-wing goals that challenge or undermine key accepted principles of the international order, including human rights, territorial integrity, or self-determination.

Maritime terrorism was one of the core concerns of the maritime security agenda in the 2000s. It continues to be so, albeit with somewhat less prominence, because of its potential to disrupt shipping and to harm civilian populations. Terrorism and extremist violence mainly concentrate on land rather than at sea. Maritime attacks are rare events in this sense. However, several major incidents have occurred in the maritime space. These indicate the potential severity of the issue and the various ways that extremist organizations can exploit maritime space.

We begin with a brief overview of some high-profile acts of maritime terrorism and how they have shaped the debate on maritime security.[23] We go on to identify three scenarios of how extremist organizations present an ongoing threat in the maritime domain.

Major Incidents of Maritime Terrorism

Maritime terrorism is not a new phenomenon. The Cold War period saw numerous, if sporadic, attacks on ships and ports by various extremist organizations the world over.[24] However, four incidents particularly have shaped the contemporary debate and international legal context, and are important to maritime security thinking. These are the hijacking of the *MS Achille Lauro* in 1985, which precedes the maritime security agenda as we know it today; the attack on the *USS Cole* in 2000; the bombing of the *MV Limburg* in 2002; and the sinking of the *MV SuperFerry 14* in 2004. We introduce each of these cases briefly below.

The hijacking of the cruise liner *Achille Lauro* drew global attention to the problem of terrorism at sea and led to the adoption of new international

---

[23] Useful general reviews of maritime terrorism are provided in Meghan Curran, Christopher Faulkner, Curtis Bell, Tyler Lycan, Michael Van Ginkel, and Jay Benson, "Violence at Sea: How Terrorists, Insurgents, and Other Extremists Exploit the Maritime Domain" (One Earth Future Foundation/Stable Seas, August 2020), https://www.stableseas.org/post/violence-at-sea-how-terrorists-insurgents-and-other-extremists-exploit-the-maritime-domain; Michael D. Greenberg et al., *Maritime Terrorism: Risk and Liability* (Santa Monica, CA: RAND Corporation, 2006), https://www.rand.org/content/dam/rand/pubs/monographs/2006/RAND_MG520.sum.pdf.

[24] See for example Brian Michael Jenkins with Bonnie Cordes, Karen Gardela, and Geraldine Petty, "A Chronology of Terrorist Attacks and Other Criminal Actions Against Maritime Targets," Rand Paper Series (Rand Corporation, September 1983), https://www.rand.org/content/dam/rand/pubs/papers/2006/P6906.pdf.

regulations.[25] In October 1985, four men of the Palestine Liberation Front boarded the Italian flagged and owned cruise liner. Their intention was to gain passage to Israel to conduct an attack on land. However, they were accidently discovered while the ship was at anchor off the coast of Egypt. The group changed their plans and decided to hijack the vessel instead. Taking hostages on board, they commanded the captain to sail to Syria, and demanded the release of Palestinian prisoners held in Israeli prisons. Threatening to kill the passengers, one Jewish American citizen was shot and thrown overboard.

The immediate crisis was eventually resolved through negotiation. The ship returned to Egypt, where the hijackers boarded a plane to Tunisia after having been granted free passage. However, their plane was intercepted by US navy fighter jets and forced to land in Sicily. Subsequently, a major international dispute evolved between Egypt, Italy, and the United States over who had jurisdiction to prosecute the perpetrators.

The *Achille Lauro* hijacking brought the weakness of existing international law to the fore, and, in response, a new convention was negotiated under the auspices of the International Maritime Organization. The Convention for the Suppression of Unlawful Acts against the Safety of Maritime Navigation (known as the SUA or Rome convention) was signed in 1988. It obliges signatory states to introduce appropriate laws for offenses which take place on board ships and platforms on the high seas and regulates the extradition of suspects.

The second major incident took place in October 2000. An Al Qaeda-affiliated group exploded a small boat next to the US guided missile destroyer *USS Cole*.[26] The attack in the Yemeni port of Aden caused major damage and killed 17 sailors. The strategic significance of the *USS Cole* incident—the first major terrorist attack on the United States navy—was only recognized a year later, after the 9/11 attacks of 2001. The events of 9/11 showed that terrorist groups had the capability and intent to exploit vulnerabilities in transport infrastructure to target military and civilian targets. Together with the *USS Cole* bombing, they suggested that a major terrorist attack at or from the sea was a realistic threat scenario.

In response, the SUA Convention was amended and a major new obligatory technical security standard introduced: the International Ship and Port

---

[25] Malvina Halberstam, "Terrorism on the High Seas: The Achille Lauro, Piracy and the IMO Convention on Maritime Safety," *American Journal of International Law* 82, no. 2 (April 1988): 269–310.

[26] Raphael Perl and Ronald O'Rourke, "Terrorist Attack on USS Cole: Background and Issues for Congress," CRS Report for US Congress, January 2001, https://citeseerx.ist.psu.edu/document?repid=rep1&type=pdf&doi=3dcebb0810922d4723283548da702ff30fa4569c#page=59.

Facility Security (ISPS) Code.[27] The United States initiated other responses too. Perhaps most notably, it evoked NATOs Article 5 commitment—which mandates that an attack on one member state should be considered an attack on all—to establish an Alliance naval mission aimed at countering terrorist activities in the Mediterranean. It also launched a non-NATO multinational partnership in the Western Indian Ocean, known as the Combined Maritime Forces (see Chapter 7, Section 7.3) for similar purposes, and in 2003 introduced the Proliferation Security Initiative to combat the movement of weapons of mass destruction and related materials by land, air, and sea.

An incident that took place a year after the 9/11 attacks confirmed the seriousness of the potential for maritime terrorist attacks. In October 2002, the group that was behind the bombing of the USS Cole attacked a French-flagged oil tanker, the MV Limburg, off the coast of Yemen with a small boat laden with explosives. One crew member died, and the damage resulted in a major oil spill in the Gulf of Aden. The incident highlighted that terrorist groups were actively targeting maritime transport. It also showed the environmental damage such attacks could potentially inflict.

Two years later, a fourth incident demonstrated that maritime terrorism was a global problem and not just confined to the Gulf of Aden or to Western targets. In 2004, the Philippine-flagged MV SuperFerry 14 was sunk in Manila Bay by the Abu Sayyaf group using a bomb hidden in a television set. The ferry was carrying more than 800 passengers and crew when it sank, of whom 166 died. The tragedy not only highlighted the threat of maritime terrorism in Southeast Asia, but also brought new awareness of the potential vulnerability of passenger vessels to attack.

The Post-9/11 Maritime Terrorism Agenda

Political attention to the threat posed by maritime terrorism increased following 9/11, and in the light of the four incidents discussed above. Analysts have laid out a range of scenarios of how terrorist activities could unfold in the maritime domain.

Drawing insights from the attacks on the USS Cole, MV Limburg, and MV SuperFerry 14, one major scenario concerns the potential for direct attacks on maritime targets. Such attacks might include attempts to sink military or civilian vessels using explosives, drones, or suicide craft, as well as the potential for a mass-casualty attack by gunmen on board ship. In addition to the potential for

---

[27] Natalie Klein, *Maritime Security and the Law of the Sea* (Oxford: Oxford University Press, 2011), 174–195.

casualties and damage caused to the ship itself, a direct maritime attack could have further consequences too. If carried out in a sensitive area, for example in the vicinity of a major shipping lane such as the Suez Canal, it could cause significant disruption to maritime traffic. Large oil spills could bring transit to a halt until the affected area is cleaned. Any environmental damage will also impact fishing and tourism industries. A related concern are attacks on maritime infrastructures, such as oil and gas platforms, wind farms, pipelines, or underwater cables. These could disrupt energy supplies and cause environmental damage, or, in the case of data cables, severely limit communications and internet access (see Chapter 8, Section 8.3).

A second scenario concerns attempts to take control over a vessel and use it as weapon. This scenario has parallels with the 9/11 attacks in that it entails the weaponization of commercial transport. A vessel hijacked in this way could be used to carry out an attack against another maritime target, such as a ship or port facilities. Given the amount of fuel on board ships and the size of many contemporary commercial vessels, the impact of an attack like this on trade or the environment could be substantial. Some ships also transport hazardous goods such as nitrates, chemicals, or liquified natural gas. In these cases, the potential for damage and destruction is even higher. The ammonium nitrate explosion that occurred in a warehouse in the port of Beirut in 2020 is a telling indicator in this respect. The explosion caused major blast damage to the city and led to over 200 deaths and 7,000 injuries, though in this case it was caused by an act of negligence onshore rather than a terrorist attack on a ship in port.[28]

While no incident of this type has taken place to date, there are reasons to believe in the plausibility of such a scenario. In 2014, for example, a group linked to Al-Qaeda attempted to take control of a Pakistani naval vessel, the *PNS Zulfiqar*, in the port of Karachi. While unsuccessful, the group's intention had been to use the frigate to attack other targets.

A third scenario relates to how terrorists could exploit maritime trade flows to prepare attacks on land. It includes the use of maritime routes to smuggle weapons, such as small arms or explosives, for use in an attack on land. Other materials, such as chemicals, radioactive substances, or other precursors used to manufacture weapons, could also be smuggled. Given the scale and complexity of maritime trade, illicit cargos can be hidden relatively easily within containers or on board ship and are very difficult to detect. Random security scans in ports

---

[28] "UN Experts Call for International Investigation into 2020 Beirut Explosion," OHCHR, accessed June 13, 2023, https://www.ohchr.org/en/press-releases/2022/08/un-experts-call-international-investigation-2020-beirut-explosion.

frequently detect undeclared hazardous materials, including radioactive waste in containers. These incidents are likely the tip of the iceberg.

Similar methods could also be used to move terrorist operatives across borders undetected. For example, in October 2001, Italian police discovered a man with extremist connections inside a shipping container in transit from Egypt to Canada. The container was equipped with food, water, and a power supply. Another example is the 2008 Mumbai attack. A group of militant Islamists from Pakistan arrived in the city undetected on board a hijacked fishing vessel. The gunmen subsequently killed 166 people, injuring over 300.

The Link Between Terrorism and Blue Crime

If these scenarios drive much of the terrorism debate, the connection between terrorism and blue crime (see Chapter 5) is a related major concern. It is important not to conflate terrorism and crime since the acts and motivations of terrorists and criminals differ substantially, and they are addressed by two different legal regimes. Yet they can still interlink in important ways.

Terrorist and criminal groups often exploit the same vulnerabilities and use similar tactics. Hijacking a vessel to weaponize it involves the same methods as piracy, though levels of violence may be higher. Likewise, smuggling weapons or people for terrorist purposes requires the same routes and techniques that criminal organizations use. Extremist and criminal organizations might come to arrangements whereby they explicitly support each other's activities. However, the reverse can also be the case because involvement with extremist organizations may increase the exposure of criminal groups to law enforcement and security responses.

Some extremist organizations also are known to deliberately engage in blue crimes to fund their activities. The Islamic State group, for example, generated revenues from oil smuggling and the illicit trade in narcotics.[29] The Southeast Asian Abu Sayyaf group engaged in kidnap for ransom piracy in the Sulu and Celebes seas between 2016 and 2020 for similar reasons.[30] The Al-Shabab group operating in Somalia has been implicated in the smuggling of charcoal and other illicit goods in the Western Indian Ocean.[31]

---

[29] Philippe Le Billon, "Oil and the Islamic State: Revisiting "Resource Wars" Arguments in Light of ISIS Operations and State-Making Attempts," *Studies in Conflict & Terrorism* 46, no. 8 (February 2021): 1–23.

[30] Curran et al., "Violence at Sea."

[31] Katharine Petrich, "Cows, Charcoal, and Cocaine: Al-Shabaab's Criminal Activities in the Horn of Africa," *Studies in Conflict & Terrorism* 45, no. 5–6 (June 2022): 479–500.

Spillover from Land

Extremist violence on land, such as during civil wars, can also have an impact in the maritime domain. Most civil wars and extremist activities are terrestrial in orientation. However, there are some important exceptions. During the Sri Lankan civil war from 1983 to 2009, the Liberation Tigers of Tamil Eelam, also known as Tamil Tigers, operated a separate maritime branch.[32] The so-called Sea Tigers attacked ships of the Sri Lankan navy, using speedboats to conduct suicide bombings with considerable success. The group also utilized frogmen, submersibles, and mines, and targeted merchant vessels as well as military ones.

While the Sri Lankan conflict had only a limited impact on international trade, that has not been the case for the civil war in Yemen.[33] Because of the proximity of the Yemeni coastline to major global shipping route through the Red Sea and Suez Canal, the maritime spillover effects of the conflict have significant wider ramifications. Beginning in 2014, the war initially focused on land. However, from 2016, Houthi forces—one of the warring parties—expanded their activities into the maritime domain. These included missile and drone strikes against ships in port or at sea, the capture of vessels carrying supplies to the Yemeni government and their allies, the use of fast boats to conduct rocket-propelled grenade attacks against maritime targets, and the laying of mines. The rebels also extended their area of operations to neighboring Saudi Arabia. In 2020, the Singapore-flagged oil tanker *BW Rhine* was attacked by a small boat in the port of Jeddah. In 2021 oil depots in the same port were targeted by combat drones. The Sri Lankan and Yemini conflicts show how civil war and extremist violence on land can spill over into the maritime domain, where the threat to shipping from small boats, drones, and mines can be severe. Civil wars and insurgencies can also undermine the capacity of countries to police their maritime territories and contribute to the rise of blue crime.

Summary

While most terrorist incidents take place on land, ships and ports have been targeted, and a range of plausible threat scenarios exist for future maritime attacks. This, together with the effects of conflict spill over from land and the link between extremism and blue crime, show the need for ongoing attention to

---

[32] Paul A. Povlock, "A Guerilla War At Sea: The Sri Lankan Civil War," *Small Wars Journal*, September 2011, https://smallwarsjournal.com/jrnl/art/a-guerilla-war-at-sea-the-sri-lankan-civil-war.

[33] Nagapushpa Nagarajan Devendra, "Brewing Yemen Civil War and Its Implication on International Maritime Security," *Journal of Maritime Research* 15, no. 1 (April 2018): 15–19.

this dimension of maritime security. However, it is also important to note that the distinction between state and nonstate actors, and between legitimate and illegitimate violence, is often blurred. In practice, the lines between terrorism, extremist violence, resistance movements, revolution, civil war, and interstate conflicts can be difficult to draw. For this reason, it is important to pay attention to the intersections and boundary spaces between the three dimensions of the maritime security triangle. In the next section, we turn to an example of this ambiguity in practice by investigating how so-called grey-zone activities at sea blur the boundaries.

4.4 Grey Zones

Grey-zone activities are coercive actions by states or their proxies which avoid the overt or attributable use of military force and so fall below the threshold of outright war.[34] The aim is to achieve tactical or strategic gains while avoiding the costs and risks of military confrontation.[35] In the maritime domain, examples include cyberattacks on civilian infrastructures such as ports, or actions by civilian coast guards and commercial fishing vessels to contest (sometimes aggressively) territorial claims sea. Since they are neither actions of war nor rule following activities, they are often difficult to classify under established legal categories. Grey-zone activities risk undermining international institutions and eroding their purpose and meaning. Hence, they are an increasingly prominent matter of concern on the maritime security agenda.

Grey-zone activities are characterized by their ambiguity, deniability, and incrementality. They may be provocative, belligerent, or norm-breaking, but in ways that muddy the waters of responsibility or fall below generally accepted thresholds for an armed response.[36] It is often hard to establish whether a state authorized an action, and how to link it to the organization or individual who carried it out. As a result, holding the culprits responsible is challenging as they can conveniently deny their involvement or place the blame on someone else.

---

[34] Several analysts prefer the term "hybrid warfare," and the relation between the two terms is debated. For a discussion of both terms, see Tahir Mahmood Azad, Muhammad Waqas Haider, and Muhammad Sadiq, "Understanding Gray Zone Warfare from Multiple Perspectives," *World Affairs* 186, no. 1 (March 2023): 81–104; Andrew Dowse and Sascha-Dominik Bachmann, "Explainer: What Is 'Hybrid Warfare' and What Is Meant by the 'Grey Zone'?," *The Conversation*, June 2019, http://theconversation.com/explainer-what-is-hybrid-warfare-and-what-is-meant-by-the-grey-zone-118841.

[35] Geraint Hughes, "War in the Grey Zone: Historical Reflections and Contemporary Implications," *Survival* 62, no. 3 (May 2020): 131–158.

[36] Michael J. Mazarr, "Mastering the Gray Zone: Understanding a Changing Era of Conflict," *Monographs, Books, and Publications.* 428 (2015): 55.

These activities are incremental in nature because they can look differently when seen over time. Indeed, they are often described as "salami-slicing" tactics: Individually, each action may seem relatively insignificant, but in combination and over time, they can result in a significant political or strategic outcome. The burden is therefore placed on the adversary to either accept the new situation or to respond in ways that may be costly, appear disproportionate in terms of the specific action at stake, or have a high escalatory potential.[37] For this reason, the management of the narrative around grey-zone activities is key to fostering uncertainty of intention, justification, and blame.

The blurring of legal categories together with uncertainty over intent, accountability, and response make grey-zone activities difficult to deal with. In the following section, we discuss these problems by investigating a range of examples that have been interpreted as grey-zone activities in the maritime domain. We then discuss how far these actions represent a new problem for international security.

Contemporary Examples

Grey-zone tactics have become increasingly prominent in the maritime domain, with China, Iran, and Russia being notably linked with their adoption.[38] This does not imply that it is only these countries that make use of the grey zone, or that others have not done so too. However, the activities of China, Iran, Russia, particularly since 2010, have attracted particular attention and intensified international concerns about the use of such tactics at sea.

China

China has developed and adopted a range of maritime grey-zone tactics, especially in the East and South China Seas, as well as in its dispute over the sovereignty and status of Taiwan. While other countries involved in these disputes have deployed grey-zone tactics of their own, Chinese activities stand out by their scope, innovativeness, and scale.

---

[37] James Goldrick, "Grey Zone Operations and the Maritime Domain" (The Australian Strategic Policy Institute, 2018), 24, https://www.aspi.org.au/report/grey-zone-operations-and-maritime-domain.

[38] Michael J. Green, John Schaus, Jake Douglas, Zack Cooper, and Kathleen H. Hicks, *Countering Coercion in Maritime Asia* (Washington, DC: Center for Strategic and International Studies, 2017), https://www.csis.org/analysis/countering-coercion-maritime-asia; Geoffrey Till, "Maritime Security and the Gulf 1," in *Security Dynamics in The Gulf and The Arabian Peninsula: Contemporary Challenges and Opportunities*, ed. Howard M. Hensel (London: Routledge, 2022), 135–152.

Perhaps most remarkably, since 2014 China has engaged in an extensive process of island-building in the Spratly and Paracels region of the South China Sea. This has comprised major land reclamation projects to convert seven reefs into large man-made islands, capable of supporting military bases, including deepwater harbors and airstrips.[39] Island building in this context functions as a highly visible assertion of Chinese control over contested territories. It has also enabled the construction of new military facilities from which to exert influence in the region and served the government to justify its excessive claims in the region.

China has also made extensive use of its civil maritime security agencies to assert and enforce its claims in contested territories, to harass and intimidate rival parties and test the limits of their response, and to do so while remaining below the threshold of outright military confrontation. These actions have been facilitated by the expansion and militarization of the China Coast Guard and Maritime Safety Administration since 2012.[40] Both agencies frequently engage in provocative and coercive activities at sea, including patrolling in disputed waters, conducting dangerous maneuverers in the vicinity of other states' vessels, preventing the arrest of Chinese fishers accused of illegal fishing, and, in one case, forcibly liberating a Chinese fishing vessel from the custody of Indonesian maritime authorities.[41] The China Coast Guard and Maritime Safety Administration have pursued similar tactics in the East China Sea, especially in the vicinity of Senkaku/Diaoyu islands, whose ownership China contests with Japan. They have also been used to disrupt foreign military operations, such as by the US Navy.

These activities have been accompanied by the deployment of China's state-owned fishing fleet. Many of these vessels are believed to be part of the People's Armed Forces Maritime Militia, a paramilitary formation that operates under the command of the Chinese military. As with the China Coast Guard, China has used its fishing fleet to conduct harassment or presence operations in disputed areas, while maintaining the plausible deniability of state involvement.[42] For example, in March 2021, around 200 Chinese fishing vessels concentrated and loitered at Whitson Reef in the Philippines' EEZ. While the actions themselves

---

[39] Robert Beckman, "China's 'Island-Building' in the South China Sea: Implications for Regional Security," in *Regional Security Outlook 2017*, ed. Ron Huisken (Council for Security Cooperation in the Asia Pacific, 2017), 40–42.

[40] The CCG's largest ships are the size of naval cruisers, weighing in at 12,000 metric tons and carrying naval guns, helicopters, and anti-aircraft defences. See Alessio Patalano, "When Strategy Is 'Hybrid' and Not 'Grey': Reviewing Chinese Military and Constabulary Coercion at Sea," *The Pacific Review* 31, no. 6 (November 2018): 811–839.

[41] Guilfoyle and Chan, "Lawships or Warships?," 5–6.

[42] Rob McLaughlin, "The Law of the Sea and PRC Gray-Zone Operations in the South China Sea," *American Journal of International Law* 116, no. 4 (October 2022): 834.

were not unlawful, in that the vessels did not actually engage in any fishing activity, they were interpreted as a deliberate provocation by the Philippine government, which lodged a diplomatic protest. At other times, the fleet has been deployed alongside the China Coast Guard. In 2014, for example, around 100 fishing vessels accompanied an oil exploration mission into waters claimed by Vietnam. The mission was escorted by the China Coast Guard and resulted in direct clashes with Vietnamese coast guard forces. Chinese fishing vessels also regularly operate in the waters of the Senkaku/Diaoyo islands.

Taken together, China's grey-zone activities have enabled an expansion and consolidation of its regional maritime presence through island building and the construction of new military facilities. It has also deployed its maritime security agencies and fishing fleet to press home its territorial claims, while obstructing and frustrating those of others. Through these tactics, China has tested the limits of international law and the UNCLOS consensus, established new realities of occupation and possession in contested areas, and worked to delegitimize and constrain the actions of neighboring states.

Iran

Iran's grey-zone activities take place in the context of ongoing sanctions on the Iranian regime over its nuclear policy, as well as its regional rivalry with Israel sometimes described as a "shadow war."[43] Iran has used grey-zone tactics to assert its regional influence, and to demonstrate its ability to restrict shipping movements in the Persian Gulf and Strait of Hormuz—one of the major transit routes for oil and gas from the Middle East.

When in 2017 the United States withdrew from the Joint Comprehensive Plan of Action—commonly known as the "Iran nuclear deal"—that had been established to regulate Iran's nuclear activities in exchange for the withdrawal of international sanctions, the Iranian regime threatened to close the Strait of Hormuz to international shipping.

From May to June 2019, a series of attacks on vessels took place in the Persian Gulf. In May, four ships anchored in United Arab Emirates territorial waters were damaged by limpet mines. The following month, two oil tankers were attacked using similar methods while transiting the Strait of Hormuz. Subsequent investigations by the United Arab Emirates, the United States, and a Norwegian insurance company pointed to Iran's Islamic Revolutionary Guard Corps as the perpetrator. Iran denied any involvement in the affair, raised the possibility of a

---

[43] Alexander Lott and Shin Kawagishi, "The Legal Regime of the Strait of Hormuz and Attacks Against Oil Tankers: Law of the Sea and Law on the Use of Force Perspectives," *Ocean Development & International Law* (July 2022): 1–24.

potential "false flag" operation by the United States or Israel, and called for an international investigation.

Another series of incidents occurred the following month. In July 2019, the *Grace 1*—a tanker transporting oil from Iran to Syria—was detained by British Royal Marines in Gibraltar over sanctions violations. Iran reacted with fury to what it called the "illegal seizure" of the vessel and summoned the British ambassador to complain. Ten days later, the *Stena Impero*, a Swedish owned chemical tanker flagged in the United Kingdom, was seized by Iranian forces. After a period of intense diplomatic activity, the *Grace 1* was released in August, and the *Stena Impero* a month later. Iran claimed that its legal process over the incident had been completed, but without ever specifying what charges had been brought against the ship. In response to these incidents, two naval operations, led respectively by the United States and a coalition of European states, were launched to deter further attacks in the region (see Chapter 7).

Even so, grey-zone incidents attributed to Iran continued. In July 2021, the tanker *MT Mercer Street* was targeted in a drone attack, which led to the deaths of a Romanian and a British crew member. The vessel was Japanese owned and flagged in Libera but managed by an Israeli company. Iran denied any involvement and the issue was discussed in a closed session of the UN Security Council. Further incidents followed. In August 2021, four ships were boarded in the Gulf of Oman under unclear circumstances. In April 2022, Greece seized an Iranian flagged tanker, the *Lana*, on suspicion of violating EU sanctions on Russia. In response, Iran seized two Greek owned vessels on unclear charges. In November 2022, another drone attack occurred on a tanker with close ties to Israel.

These incidents document how Iran has been able to use the vulnerability of maritime transport and its geographical location to disrupt a key global shipping lane, to contest international sanctions, and to pursue its conflict with Israel below the threshold of war. The Iranian goals seems to have been to test the boundaries of any international response, as well as to demonstrate its capability and intent in ways that are easily deniable or retain a high degree of legal ambiguity.

Russia

Russia has long been considered an innovator of grey-zone tactics.[44] It has been accused of engaging in activities such as extra-territorial killings, cyber security

---

[44] Christopher Chivvis, *Understanding Russian "Hybrid Warfare": And What Can Be Done About It* (Santa Monica, CA: RAND Corporation, 2017).

operations, and disinformation and influencing campaigns aimed at regime destabilization in foreign states, and the extensive use of semiautonomous mercenary forces in African states. The use of proxy forces and other grey-zone tactics were key to its invasion of the Crimean Peninsula in 2014, and the ongoing war in Ukraine since.

The frequency and scope of these activities has led to concerns that Russia might exploit the maritime domain in a similar way.[45] To date, little hard evidence of such activities exists. However, since 2014 observers have pointed to increased Russian naval activities within or bordering European EEZs. These include military exercises and surveillance operations, often in the vicinity of critical underwater infrastructures such as pipelines and data cables. These actions have spurred fears that Russia might engage in acts of sabotage on these installations with the aim of disrupting critical energy supplies or global communications.

As we discuss in more depth in Chapter 8 when reviewing the critical maritime infrastructure protection agenda, a major re-evaluation of Russian naval activities occurred in 2022 following a series of underwater explosions that destroyed the Nord Stream pipelines supplying gas from Russia to Germany. The explosions took place in the EEZs of Denmark and Sweden and were later confirmed by investigators to have been the result of deliberate sabotage. The situation was swiftly interpreted in the context of Russo-European tensions over the war in Ukraine. In response, Norway and other European states increased the protection of their underwater infrastructures through naval patrols and other activities. Because there was no evidence of an overt military attack, nor of criminal or extremist involvement in the incident, it has been widely interpreted as a grey-zone attack, likely conducted by a civilian vessel and not easily attributable to any state actor. Russian officials blamed the United States and later the United Kingdom for carrying out the attack, while their western counterparts pointed to Russia.

The Nord Stream incident had many of the classic attributes of a grey-zone attack. It was politically impactful and created uncertainty and a sense of vulnerability among affected states. The nonattributable nature of the sabotage also meant that no one actor could be held responsible or made subject to retaliatory action. The incident also showed how competing narratives of blame allocation are used for political purposes.

---

[45] Gary Schaub, Martin Murphy, and Frank G Hoffman, "Hybrid Maritime Warfare," *The RUSI Journal* 162, no. 1 (January 2017): 32–40.

Contextualizing Maritime Grey Zones

The examples of China, Iran, and Russia are in many ways paradigmatic in terms of how grey-zone activities challenge the boundaries between war in peace. However, to some degree, there is nothing new about the use of grey-zone tactics at sea. States have long exploited the maritime domain to intimidate, pressure, or otherwise influence their adversaries in ways that fall short of direct military action.[46] Increasing naval presence in contested areas, firing warning shots, or placing flags on contested territories have been long standing practices, as we have observed in our discussion of interstate disputes above. What is often described as either deterrence, or power projection, for example through US freedom of navigation operations, arguably falls into the grey zone too.

Maritime forces offer plentiful advantages in this regard. The interconnected nature of the ocean space and its lack of borders or territorial obstacles means that ships can move freely to or withdraw from pressure points or areas of crisis. They can also be used for a range of different missions, including the projection of military power, but also the deterrence of adversaries, the assertion of sovereign rights in contested territories, or the signaling of support for allies.[47] These characteristics mean that maritime deployments can have a flexibility and ambiguity of purpose which is at home in the grey zone.

Nevertheless, there is reason to think that the recent growth in grey-zone activities at sea has features which distinguish it from traditional notions of naval or "gunboat" diplomacy, in character if not always in concept. In particular, and as discussed in Chapter 3, the UNCLOS settlement of 1982 created a new patchwork of institutional disputes between states over their maritime territorial rights. It also opened new spaces of contestation and ambiguity to which grey-zone tactics could be applied.

In addition, UNCLOS and other maritime conventions increased the importance of non-naval maritime actors such as coast guards. Many states have strengthened these agencies in ways that blur the boundaries between traditional law enforcement and military roles, sometimes deliberately so (see Chapter 6). As the case of the South China Sea shows, this blurring of roles has meant that nonmilitary agencies can sometimes be deployed for coercive purposes, in ways that fall below the traditional threshold for a military response and minimize the risk of escalation.

---

[46] Ken Booth, *Navies and Foreign Policy* (London: Routledge, 2014 [1977]), 34–36; Goldrick, "Grey Zone Operations and the Maritime Domain," 69.

[47] J. J. Widen, "Naval Diplomacy—A Theoretical Approach," *Diplomacy & Statecraft* 22, no. 4 (December 2011): 718.

Finally, and as we have seen with the case of Iran, technological developments have provided new capabilities through which to pursue grey-zone tactics. These include the use of drones or cyberattacks to damage adversaries' interests or disrupt their activities, and in ways that obscure responsibility and maintain deniability.

Summary

Grey-zone activities take place at the boundary between war and peace. The aim is to achieve tactical or strategic goals, while avoiding the risks of outright military conflict. Grey-zone tactics are characterized by their ambiguity, deniability, and incrementality. They consist of actions that fall below accepted thresholds for an armed response and present a significant challenge to existing maritime security norms and institutions. Grey-zone activities in the maritime domain have included the use of maritime law enforcement agencies to dispute and contest maritime boundaries, as well as nonattributable attacks on shipping and shipping infrastructures by drones or other methods, including cyber warfare.

Insofar as these activities challenge interpretations of legal obligations and treaties, they raise the question of whether such disputes can be managed by existing international institutions. While Iranian actions have, for example, been discussed in the UN Security Council, the veto powers of permanent members Russia and China have blocked any effective action on this issue. These developments raise questions about the limits of international institutions on the one hand, while others argue that they show the need for institutional redesign and the development of alternative forms of dispute settlement and norm enforcement.

4.5 Understanding Conflict and Terrorism at Sea

In this chapter we have investigated two of the core dimensions of maritime security: interstate conflicts and violent extremism. As we have shown, different forms of interstate conflict persist in the maritime domain. While some of these are minor, they have a potential to be intractable or escalate if the symbolic value attached to these disputes increases. Diplomatic negotiations and international courts provide a solid legal infrastructure for resolution, but as the Chagos or South China Sea dispute reveal, also have limitations. Interstate conflicts will thus continue to occupy a central place on the maritime security agenda. Maritime terrorism incidents and activities, if compared to land, are less severe. Yet the activities of militant organizations have significant potential to disrupt international trade or cause mass casualties and severe environmental damage. Restricting terrorist activities, is hence an important objective of maritime security actions.

Interstate conflict and terrorism are two categories that provide useful intellectual starting points for thinking about issues on the maritime security agenda. However, the distinction between them is sometimes unclear in practice. This is especially so in the case of grey-zone tactics, where the nature of the threat and the question of who is responsible for it can be unclear. Grey-zone activities are on the rise, and not only question current understandings of rules and institutions but call for new strategies and tools to address the challenges they present.

What unites all the issues we have discussed in this chapter is that they are challenges that arise from political motivations and contestations. This distinguishes them from blue crimes, where profit is at stake. At an international level, the problems linked to crime are also less contentious and the relevant legal regime is better defined. For this reason, we discuss blue crimes in a separate chapter. However, it is important for the analyst and professional to recognize the interconnections between issues. Conflicts between states create uncertainties and might lead to weak law enforcement in contested areas—conditions which in turn may allow blue crimes to thrive. Equally, civil wars and the activities of extremist groups create conditions of insecurity that can be beneficial to maritime criminals.

5

Blue Crime: Pirates, Smugglers, and Ecocriminals

5.1 The Variety of Crime at Sea

The maritime space has always been conducive to illicit activities. The ocean covers more than 70% of the earth's surface. It is easy to hide in, and difficult to monitor and police. It allows movement across and between different legal regimes, often in spaces of loose or ambiguous regulation and variable jurisdictional responsibility. The seas offer many opportunities for criminality.[1] Pirates hijack and rob vessels at sea; smugglers use the sea to transport illicit cargos. Others pollute the oceans, evade environmental regulations and international labor conventions, or fish illegally.

Transnational organized crime at sea, or blue crime, has, over the years, become increasingly recognized as a major security issue that requires political attention. States and regional organizations across the world have made the fight against blue crime a core component of their maritime security strategies. Blue crimes have also been addressed at the highest levels of international security, with the UN Security Council issuing several resolutions on piracy and holding an open debate on transnational organized crime at sea in February 2019.[2]

We begin this chapter by exploring the concept of blue crime and demonstrate how it enables the categorization of crimes and the identification of links

---

[1] For an insightful popular account of the variety of crime, see Ian Urbina, *The Outlaw Ocean: Journeys Across the Last Untamed Frontier* (New York: Knopf, 2019).

[2] United Nations Security Council, "High Seas Crime Becoming More Sophisticated, Endangering Lives, International Security, Speakers Tell Security Council," accessed June 23, 2023, https://press.un.org/en/2019/sc13691.doc.htm; See also Brian Wilson, "The Turtle Bay Pivot: How the United Nations Security Council Is Reshaping Naval Pursuit of Nuclear Proliferators, Rogue States, and Pirates," *Emory International Law Review* 33, no. 1 (2019 2018): 1–90.

between them. We then move on to the most important manifestations of blue crime. First, we discuss crimes against shipping and maritime movement, focusing on piracy off the coast of Somalia, in Southeast Asia, and in the Gulf of Guinea. Next, we turn to maritime smuggling. After a general overview, we focus on narcotics and people smuggling as emblematic examples. Finally, we examine environmental crimes, looking particularly at illicit fishing as a crime that causes harm to the marine environment, but also to people and their sustainable futures.

5.2 What Is Blue Crime?

The term "blue crime" refers to serious organized crimes or offences that take place in, on, or across the maritime domain and which have the potential to inflict significant harms.[3] This definition understands crime through the harms it causes rather than the extent to which activities are criminalized in national or international law. This avoids the problem that specific illicit activities may be subject to different levels or degrees of criminalization between states and over time. A focus on harm also facilitates the integration of evidence and frameworks from criminology—that is, the scientific study of crime—to maritime security.[4] By referring to crimes that are "serious" and "organized," we exclude low-level or petty crimes such as those which take place for ad hoc or even banal reasons, such as ignorance (of environmental regulations for example) or opportunism.[5]

Three Categories of Blue Crime

A focus on harms leads the discussion to three broad categories of blue crime. Each of these categories differs in terms of where and to whom or what harms are caused and how they relate to the sea.

---

[3] For an expanded discussion of this definition in the context of international law, see Christian Bueger and Timothy Edmunds, "Blue Crime: Conceptualising Transnational Organised Crime at Sea," *Marine Policy* 119 (September 2020): 104067.

[4] See for example: Paddy Hillyard and Steve Tombs, "From 'Crime' to Social Harm?," *Crime, Law and Social Change* 48, no. 1 (September 2007): 9–25. Our understanding of harms draws particularly on the work of green criminologists around notions of environmental harm. For a survey see Avi Brisman and Nigel South, "Green Criminology and Environmental Crimes and Harms," *Sociology Compass* 13, no. 1 (2019): e12650.

[5] As we have argued in our discussion of the root causes of maritime insecurity (see Chapter 3, Section 3.5), this does not imply that such lower-level crimes should not equally deserve attention, since they can contribute to an environment in which more serious crimes thrive.

The first category is *crimes against mobility*. These are crimes that cause harm to global maritime transport, shipping, and its supporting infrastructures such as ports. They disrupt supply chains and logistical routes and can cause direct harms to people such as seafarers and dock workers. The most important crime in this category is piracy. However, other activities belong here too. Stowaways, for example, can be highly organized and cause significant disruption to shipping, while cyber criminals can damage or extort port operations by installing ransomware (see Chapter 8, Section 8.2).

The second category comprises *illicit flows* across the maritime space. These are sometimes called "transit crimes."[6] They are crimes in which the oceans function primarily as a conduit for criminal enterprise between two points on land. In consequence, the harms caused by these crimes also tend to be felt on land rather than at sea. Smuggling and trafficking activities of various sorts fall into this category. A wide range of illicit goods and cargos are illicitly smuggled by sea, including narcotics, arms, and controlled substances such as wildlife products or pharmaceuticals. People are also smuggled for the purposes of irregular migration, and sometimes trafficked against their will.

Our third category incorporates *environmental crimes*, including illicit fishing and marine pollution. These are crimes that cause significant harms in and to the marine environment, with nature, marine biodiversity, ecosystems, oceanic life, and marine heritage being the main victims. These crimes often have second order effects on people too. For example, pollution can damage human health, while biodiversity loss can impact food production or the income generated by fisheries or tourism. These crimes take place in the sea. They exploit or degrade the resources, fauna and flora of the oceans, or damage infrastructures or cultural heritage, such as shipwrecks and war graves.

Figure 5.1 provides a systematic overview of blue crime using these categories. It illustrates the activities they include and the harms they cause, as well as a series of cross-cutting or facilitating practices that are common across categories.

The Intersections Between Blue Crimes

Each of these categories of blue crime clusters a set of problems together. These problems often manifest differently in specific places and situations. However, they also share common features and interconnections. While it can be worthwhile to analyze individual expressions of blue crime in isolation, it is equally important to connect the dots and consider how they relate to one another.

---

[6] Edward R. Kleemans, "Organized Crime, Transit Crime, and Racketeering," *Crime and Justice* 35 (January 2007): 163–215.

	Crimes against mobility	Illicit flows	Environmental crimes
Relation to the sea	On the sea	Across the sea	In the sea
Main harm	Global trade	Economy & society	Ecosystems
Expressions	Kidnap and ransom; ship & cargo seizure; robbery and theft; crimes in and against ports; stowaways; cyber crimes	Arms; narcotics; illicit goods; counterfeits; wildlife; waste; people smuggling; human trafficking; sanction violations	Illicit fishing; pollution; illicit resource extraction; crimes against critical infrastructures and cultural heritage
Associated harms and problems	Supply chain disruptions; economic losses; seafarers; passengers; coastal economies; port facilities	Formal economy; public health; public safety; environmental destruction; human suffering;	Environmental destruction; biodiversity loss; legitimate coastal economy; coastal livelihoods; food security
Cross-cutting & facilitating	Bribery, blackmail, and corruption; slavery, forced and child labor; insurance, cargo and document fraud, money laundering; obstruction of justice; other forms of support for criminal groups		

Figure 5.1 Three blue crimes

The ocean is a legally complex and variegated space. As we discussed in our exploration of legal perspectives (Chapter 3, Section 3.2), it incorporates a patchwork of different jurisdictional zones and legal regimes, including territorial waters, exclusive economic zones (EEZs), the high seas, and international straits. Vessels sailing under multiple, indefinite, or weakly regulated flag state authority add further intricacy to the picture.[7] What counts as serious crime also depends on legal statutes and processes of criminalization, which can differ widely across societies and over time. Some states, for example, do not have laws in place to deal with many common forms of crime at sea.[8] These legal complexities, absences, and ambiguities create opportunities for blue crime to flourish, since law enforcement actors often struggle to navigate across and between different legal jurisdictions. The fact that blue crimes have land-based aspects—including their organization, financing, and the need to launder illicit profits and goods—also complicates law enforcement.

---

[7] Jessica H. Ford and Chris Wilcox, "Shedding Light on the Dark Side of Maritime Trade—A New Approach for Identifying Countries as Flags of Convenience," *Marine Policy* 99 (January 2019): 298–303.

[8] Patrick Vrancken, "State Jurisdiction to Investigate and Try Fisheries Crime at Sea," *Marine Policy* 105 (July 2019): 129–139.

As our discussion of the root causes of maritime insecurity has shown (Chapter 3, Section 3.5), blue crimes intersect in important ways. In many cases, the organization, material, and skills required to engage in one crime are transferable to others. All that is often required is access to a boat and a crew with the necessary seamanship skills, and sometimes an ability or willingness to threaten or use violence. These capacities are generally widely available in coastal regions and the wider maritime economy.

Different types of blue crimes can also share common forms of criminal enterprise or business practices. Blue crimes often rely on access to finance and money laundering channels, as well as practices such as fraud or forgery, the use of forced labor, or corrupt payments to officials or other gatekeepers. Crimes tend to cluster in specific geographical locations, sometimes called "hot spots."[9] Busy trade routes provide ample opportunities for robbery or for concealment among legitimate traffic. Regional or local political instability or historically grown cultures of crime can lead to weak law enforcement, widespread corruption, or economic conditions that facilitate criminal recruitment and organization. Under some circumstances these factors can lead to a spiral of insecurity, whereby criminal activities become gradually more severe and serious over time.[10]

These interconnections mean that blue criminals can be highly adaptable, able to switch between different types of crime or different geographic spaces as circumstance dictates. For example, if the risks of one form of crime become too high due to law enforcement countermeasures, or if new opportunities emerge in other areas, criminals can change the nature of their enterprise or the location of their activities. Criminologists refer to this problem as "displacement."[11] Intersections between criminal activity and the legitimate maritime economy can also make it difficult to distinguish illicit actors at sea from their licit counterparts. A fishing vessel, for example, can be equally used in legitimate fishing activities on some days, but also for smuggling or even piracy.

We explore these issues in more depth in the following sections. We focus on key examples from each of three categories of blue crime: piracy as a crime

---

[9] Jessica Di Salvatore, "Does Criminal Violence Spread? Contagion and Counter-Contagion Mechanisms of Piracy," *Political Geography* 66 (September 2018): 14–33.

[10] A problem studied in debates on broken windows theory, see for example: Joshua Tallis, *The War for Muddy Waters: Pirates, Terrorists, Traffickers and Maritime Insecurity* (Annapolis, MD: Naval Institute Press, 2019).

[11] Shane D. Johnson, Rob T. Guerette, and Kate Bowers, "Crime Displacement: What We Know, What We Don't Know, and What It Means for Crime Reduction," *Journal of Experimental Criminology* 10, no. 4 (December 2014): 549–571.

against mobility, narcotics and people smuggling as illicit flows, and illicit fishing as an illustration of environmental crimes.

5.3 The Perils of Piracy

Piracy is the blue crime that has had the biggest impact on the maritime security agenda and shaped what we described as the second wave of thinking in Chapter 2. Thanks to novels and Hollywood movies, it is also the issue that most people are familiar with in one way or the other. Obviously, piracy today differs in important ways from the swashbuckling adventure stories of Treasure Island or the Pirates of the Caribbean, but there are also commonalities. Piracy is about theft, armed robbery, and kidnap and ransom for profit at sea. It can stretch from smaller scale crimes, such as climbing on board a ship to steal cash, to hijacking and kidnapping incidents that involve millions of US dollars of ransoms paid to release crews, cargos, and vessels.

The contemporary history of piracy starts in the 1980s when the shipping industry became concerned about the problem. These concerns initiated a systematic collection of incident data, which demonstrated growing regional piracy trends. Today the industry-run International Maritime Bureau as well as the International Maritime Organization (IMO) record piracy incidents globally, while dedicated information sharing centers conduct similar work for regional hot spots. In consequence, and contrary to many other blue crimes, there are numerous data sources available on the number and type of piracy incidents worldwide.[12]

In the 2000s the focus of counterpiracy activities was Southeast Asia, where new regional maritime security operations and institutions were developed in response to pirate activities in the Strait of Malacca. The rise of piracy off the coast of Somalia from 2008 led to the issue becoming a significant international security concern. The problem of piracy was discussed in the UN Security Council and a broad international coalition was formed to combat it. While Somali piracy was brought under control in 2012, the situation in Southeast Asia continues to be difficult. From 2010, pirate activities in the Gulf of Guinea also increased in scale and intensity and triggered a major international response.

---

[12] Lydelle Joubert, "What We Know about Piracy" (Stable Seas/SafeSeas, May 2020), https://www.stableseas.org/post/manage-your-blog-from-your-live-site. Even then, it should be noted that piracy activity still often goes unreported, especially in cases where the victims are local fishers or nonindustrial users of the sea.

Defining Piracy

Contrary to many other blue crimes, piracy is clearly specified in international law. Under article 101 of the United Nations Convention on the Law of the Sea (UNCLOS), it is defined as:

a. any illegal acts of violence or detention, or any act of depredation, committed for private ends by the crew or the passengers of a private ship or a private aircraft, and directed:
   i. on the high seas, against another ship or aircraft, or against persons or property on board such ship or aircraft;
   ii. against a ship, aircraft, persons or property in a place outside the jurisdiction of any State;
b. any act of voluntary participation in the operation of a ship or of an aircraft with knowledge of facts making it a pirate ship or aircraft;
c. any act of inciting or of intentionally facilitating an act described in subparagraph (a) or (b).

This definition is highly specific and stipulates that piracy is about "private ends." It hence excludes acts of politically motivated violence and terrorism. It also specifies that only acts on the high seas or outside the jurisdiction of any state count as piracy. For this reason, attacks in territorial waters are commonly referred to as "armed robbery against ships" rather than piracy per se and are subject to national laws and jurisdiction rather than UNCLOS provisions. Some institutions address this issue by creating novel categorizations. For example, the Information Fusion Centre in Singapore employs the category and acronym of TRAPS—theft, robbery, and piracy at sea—to collate data on any kind of piratical act, wherever it occurs.[13]

Piracy incidents are well recorded and studied. However, definitional difficulties can lead to conflicting statistics and trend analyses because piracy monitoring organizations will often use their own verification standards and classify similar incidents differently from one another (see Chapter 7, Section 7.5). In addition, some types of pirate attacks—such as those on yachts or artisanal fishing vessels—are less frequently or consistently reported and attract far less political attention. This is a notable oversight given that these kinds of attacks form the bulk of piracy incidents in some regions of the world, such as the Caribbean or Bay of Bengal. It is also important because it suggests that a

---

[13] IFC, "Maritime Security Situation IFC AOI 2022" (Singapore: Information Fusion Centre, 2022), 2–3, https://www.ifc.org.sg/ifc2web/Publications/Half-Yearly%20Report/2022/Mid-year%20Report%202022.pdf.

significant proportion of pirate attacks go unrecorded or even unnoticed beyond the immediate environs in which they take place.[14]

Piracy Hotspots

Three major regional hot spots of piracy have emerged in Southeast Asia, off the coast of Somalia, and in the Gulf of Guinea. Other parts of the world are also affected by piracy, but at a lower level. For example, smaller scale piracy incidents are frequently reported in Latin America and the Caribbean, where it is often sailing yachts or local fishing vessels rather than commercial ships which are attacked. The modalities of piracy operations can differ substantially across geographical regions.

Somalia

Somalia has experienced two substantial waves of piracy. The first occurred in 2005 but was limited in nature.[15] The second took place between 2008 and 2012 on a much greater scale. Statistics show that 548 attacks, with 122 vessels pirated, took place in the period 2009–2012.[16] In 2012 alone more than 580 seafarers were taken hostage, and 851 attacked with firearms.[17] Piracy off the coast of Somalia primarily followed a kidnap for ransom model.[18] Operating from small, fast skiffs, pirates would climb on board a vessel in open waters, hold the crew at gunpoint, and then take control of the ship. The vessel was then steered to the Somali coastline. Anchored close to coastal villages, the pirates would initiate negotiations with the ship owner over the ransom to be paid to release it and its crew. These negotiations, depending on tactics, could last for weeks and months and cause severe stress for hijacked crews, many of whom were mistreated. Once a ransom amount was agreed, the money would be flown to the location and waterproof packets of cash dropped on the hijacked vessels. Pirates would then divide up the profits and release the ship.

---

[14] Bryan C. Peters and Letizia Paoli, "Neglected Facets of Maritime Piracy: A Global Overview," forthcoming paper, n.d.

[15] Martin N. Murphy, *Small Boats, Weak States, Dirty Money: Piracy and Maritime Terrorism in the Modern World* (New York: Columbia University Press, 2009).

[16] Michele Vespe, Harm Greidanus, and Marlene Alvarez Alvarez, "The Declining Impact of Piracy on Maritime Transport in the Indian Ocean: Statistical Analysis of 5-Year Vessel Tracking Data," *Marine Policy* 59 (September 2015): 9–15.

[17] Kaija Hurlburt, Conor Seyles et al., *The Human Cost of Piracy 2012* (One Earth Future Foundation, 2013).

[18] Sarah Percy and Anja Shortland, "The Business of Piracy in Somalia," *Journal of Strategic Studies* 36, no. 4 (August 2013): 541–578.

This business model was very profitable. Pirate negotiators were able to gradually increase the size of the ransoms paid up to figures of million US dollars. It is estimated that between USD 339 and USD 413 million was taken in ransom from ships hijacked off the coast of Somalia between 2005 and 2012.[19] These costs were usually covered by insurance companies. However, in several cases, these hijacking incidents ended in tragedy, with crew members dying or being abandoned if ransoms went unpaid.[20]

The business model was continuously adjusted. When international navies introduced a transit system to protect shipping in vicinity to the Somali coast, pirates branched out into the wider Indian Ocean to attack shipping many hundreds or even thousands of miles from the Somali coast. To enable these long-distance operations, pirates used so-called motherships. These were vessels, such as dhows or fishing boats, which could be used to launch an attack with smaller skiffs.

The shipping industry and international navies responded with a range of countermeasures, which were summarized in dedicated best-practice manuals. These manuals recommended self-defense practices designed to make it more difficult for pirates to climb on board a ship or take it over. Navies improved their response time to distress calls, sometimes arriving on site within hours of an incident being reported. They also organized protected convoys. Increasing numbers of pirates were arrested and prosecuted, with the number of pirates in jail reaching more than a thousand in 2013.[21] As a measure of last resort, shipping companies started to employ private armed guards on their vessels to deter pirates and fend off any potential attacks (see Chapter 6, Section 6.4). By 2012, protection by navies, the arrest and prosecution program, self-defense measures, and armed guards on vessels had together proved effective at containing piracy in the region.

One notable feature of the Somali case was that pirate gangs justified their work by claiming they were acting as informal coast guards protecting Somali waters from illicit intrusion and resource exploitation by foreign actors.[22] This narrative was effective for gaining the local support needed from coastal villages and to recruit gang members. A further reason for the decline of piracy was that

---

[19] World Bank, "Pirate Trails: Tracking the Illicit Financial Flows from Pirate Activities Off the Horn of Africa," 2013, 40–42, https://www.imolin.org/pdf/imolin/piracy/Pirate_Trials.pdf.

[20] Colin Freeman, *Between the Devil and the Deep Blue Sea: The Mission to Rescue the Hostages the World Forgot* (London: Icon Books, 2021).

[21] "Sentencing of Somali Pirates Involved in the Attack on the S/V QUEST," US Department of State, accessed July 2, 2023, https://2009-2017.state.gov/r/pa/prs/ps/2013/08/212809.htm.

[22] Christian Bueger, "Practice, Pirates and Coast Guards: The Grand Narrative of Somali Piracy," *Third World Quarterly* 34, no. 10 (November 2013): 1811–1827.

this justification became less convincing as the naked criminality of many pirate gangs intensified, leading coastal communities to withdraw their support.

The international community also established a series of maritime security capacity-building programs aimed at assisting local states to deal with the piracy problem in their own waters (see Chapter 7, Section 7.6). At first, these initiatives focused on criminal justice reforms onshore to enable the prosecution and imprisonment of piracy suspects according to international human rights standards. However, they gradually expanded to include activities targeted at strengthening maritime law enforcement, regional cooperation, and information sharing between agencies and states.

The story of Somali piracy is important for maritime security. It was the first blue crime that was dealt with at the highest levels of international security. It also brought about remarkable international cooperation in various formats and was highly influential in shaping the repertoire of maritime security solutions that we discuss in Chapter 7.

Southeast Asia

Two areas of Southeast Asia are especially prone to pirate attacks.[23] The first and most enduring piracy hotspot is the Strait of Malacca. This is a narrow chokepoint in the waters between Indonesia, Malaysia, and Singapore. It is also one of the busiest shipping routes in the world, with most transits between Asia and Europe running through it. Due to the importance of Singapore as a hub for global transshipment, many ships also anchor in the area, providing ample targets for piracy operations. Piracy in this region tends to comprise small-scale thefts from ships and crew, or armed robberies of ship cargos. Kidnap for ransom piracy also occasionally takes place, but with much less frequency than was the case off the coast of Somalia between 2008 and 2012. Many of these incidents take place in territorial waters, and so are not formally classed as piracy under the UNCLOS framework.

In 2006, a dedicated regional organization was created to manage piracy and armed robbery at sea in this area—the Regional Cooperation Agreement on Combating Piracy and Armed Robbery against Ships in Asia (ReCAAP).[24]

---

[23] In-depth analyses of Southeast Asian piracy are provided in Caroline Liss, *Oceans of Crime: Maritime Piracy and Transnational Security in Southeast Asia and Bangladesh* (Singapore: ISEAS Publishing, 2011); John F. Bradford, "Shifting the Tides against Piracy in Southeast Asian Waters," *Asian Survey* 48, no. 3 (June 2008): 473–491; Caroline Liss and Ted Biggs, eds., *Piracy in Southeast Asia: Trends, Hot Spots and Responses* (Abingdon: Routledge, 2017).

[24] Kornwika Poonnawatt, "Multilateral Cooperation against Maritime Piracy in the Straits of Malacca: From the RMSI to ReCAAP," *Marine Policy* 152 (June 2023): 105628.

ReCAAP is a pioneering counterpiracy organization. Working with 16 members, including regional states but also external actors such as Australia, China, the United Kingdom, and the United States, its primary purpose is to collect data on piracy attacks and act as a reference point for coordinating incident responses. Two key regional states, Malaysia and Indonesia, decided not to join the agreement due to suspicions over external involvement and concerns over intrusions into their sovereignty. These countries instead favored a smaller regional response, and in 2004 launched a coordinated air and maritime patrol program and intelligence sharing initiative with Singapore and Thailand.

A second piracy hotspot in Southeast Asia is in the Sulu and Celebes Seas.[25] This is a weakly governed maritime border region between Malaysia, Indonesia, and the Philippines. The region is known for various illicit activities, including smuggling and irregular migration. Here piracy attacks on ships took mainly place between 2014 and 2019 and were largely attributed to the Abu Sayaf extremist group (see Chapter 4, Section 4.3). Contrary to the incidents in the Strait of Malacca, piracy in the Sulu and Celebes Seas consisted primarily of kidnap for ransom, often with high levels of violence including the killing of crews. Pirates targeted both cargo and fishing vessels. Attacks in the region were eventually contained through military action on land, with Philippine armed forces targeting the operational headquarters of the militant group. Malaysia, Indonesia, and the Philippines also increased their maritime security patrols in the area and strengthened their collaboration and information exchange activities through the Trilateral Maritime Patrols initiative.

The Gulf of Guinea

In 2020 the Gulf of Guinea had become the major global hotspot for maritime piracy. For example, of 195 piracy incidents reported to the International Maritime Bureau in 2020, 81 took place in the Gulf of Guinea.[26] The region also accounted for 130 of the 135 globally reported cases of kidnap for ransom piracy that same year. While these numbers declined between 2021 and 2023, piracy in the region continues to be an issue of significant international concern. The

---

[25] Alexandra Amling et al., "Stable Seas: Sulu and Celebes Seas" (Stable Seas, February 2019), https://www.stableseas.org/post/stable-seas-sulu-and-celebes-seas; Ian Storey, "Trilateral Security Cooperation in the Sulu-Celebes Seas: A Work in Progress," *Perspective, Review of Maritime Transport*, no. 48 (August 2018), https://www.iseas.edu.sg/images/pdf/ISEAS_Perspective_2018_48@50.pdf.

[26] IMB, "Piracy and Armed Robbery Against Ships, Report for the Period 1 January 2020—31 December 2020" (ICC International Maritime Bureau, 2021), https://www.icc-ccs.org/reports/2020_Annual_Piracy_Report.pdf.

piracy problem in the Gulf of Guinea has existed since the 1990s, but gathered pace in the early 2010s, with the UN Security Council issuing its first resolution on the matter in 2012. The character of piracy in the Gulf of Guinea differs from that in Somalia or Southeast Asia. This is due both to the local geographic, political, and socioeconomic context, but also the of business models and modus operandi of the pirates themselves.

Most pirate groups in the Gulf of Guinea operate in and around the environment of the Niger Delta, including the territorial waters of Nigeria, Benin, Togo, and Cameroon. Attacks became more ambitious and wide ranging, extending as far as Côte d'Ivoire in the West and the Democratic Republic of Congo to the south and at distances of up to 170 nautical miles from the coast.[27] However, and for the most part, one of the distinguishing features of piracy in this part of the world is that many attacks take place relatively close to land or when ships are at anchor. Because so many incidents occur within the territorial waters of states, pirate incidents in the region often fall into the category of armed robbery against ships rather than piracy per se.

The inshore nature of some pirate attacks in the Gulf of Guinea is in large part a consequence of the political economy of shipping in the region, which is dominated by the oil industry. In contrast to the Somali case, where pirates preyed on the high volume of vessels transiting shipping lanes in the high seas, in the Gulf of Guinea they frequently target the tanker traffic that clusters around the Niger Delta. Pirate attacks tend to be more diverse and violent than was the case off the coast of Somalia, comprising theft of ship cargoes, oil bunkering, and theft from crews, as well as the hijacking of ships and the kidnap of crews for ransom. This business model requires a developed land-based infrastructure to offload stolen cargos and launder them into the legitimate economy. These operations are also facilitated by corruption on land, as well as close ties between pirate groups and militant organizations operating in the region.[28]

Piracy in the Gulf of Guinea has been met with a vigorous regional and international response. At a national level, regional states including Nigeria have strengthened their maritime security law enforcement capacities and introduced new laws for the suppression of piracy, though actual prosecutions have been rare. Regional cooperation and coordination mechanisms have also been established, many of which were modeled on arrangements first developed in the Western Indian Ocean (see Chapter 7, Section 7.2). The Yaoundé Code of

---

[27] Ifesinachi Okafor-Yarwood et al., "Stable Seas: Gulf of Guinea" (One Earth Future Foundation, April 2020), 39.

[28] Justin V. Hastings and Sarah G. Phillips, "Maritime Piracy Business Networks and Institutions in Africa," *African Affairs* 114, no. 457 (October 2015): 569–576.

Conduct was established in 2013 to support regional maritime security cooperation and information sharing. The G7++ Friends of the Gulf of Guinea group was created the same year to coordinate activities between coastal states, international actors, and the private sector. A Shared Awareness and Deconfliction group was established in 2021 to assist operational coordination in the region. International states have also deployed warships to counterpiracy operations in the region, including under the EU's Coordinated Maritime Presence initiative (see Chapter 7, Section 7.3).

Despite these efforts, piracy in the Gulf of Guinea continues to present a difficult problem, with roots in the socioeconomic and political inequities and conflicts that are widespread across the region. While strengthened operations at sea and continued regional cooperation might go some way toward containing the problem, it is likely to present a pressing challenge to maritime security in coming years.

Summary

Piracy is one of the defining blue crimes on the maritime security agenda. The measures adopted to respond to it have been extensive and wide ranging, in large part because it is the blue crime that impacts trade routes and the commercial sector most directly. It is important to recognize that there is no single model of piracy, with significant regional variation in pirate activities and business models. The goal of controlling piracy at reasonable levels may be more realistic than striving for its complete eradication, especially given the challenges of addressing its socioeconomic and political root causes.

5.4 Smuggling by Sea

Like piracy, maritime smuggling has a long history. The seas are advantageous to the movement of illicit goods and cargos because they connect different parts of the world without hard borders or checkpoints, and exchanges of goods can take place outside the jurisdictional territories of states. Of course, smuggling by sea requires departure and arrival points on land, which means that many goods must also pass through ports and customs posts. However, because larger ports today process such huge volumes of cargo, much of it containerized, they offer numerous opportunities for the onward movement of illicit goods without detection. Smugglers can also avoid these facilities altogether, making use of remote or unpoliced landing points on coastlines, close to shore drop-off locations, or smaller harbors with weaker or nonexistent security measures in place.

We now explore some general characteristics of maritime smuggling and then zoom in on key smuggling routes for narcotics and for people to provide a better understanding how such operations work and the kinds of consequences the crime has.

Varieties of Smuggling

A wide variety of goods and cargos are smuggled by sea. Many, such as narcotics, illicit arms, wildlife, or counterfeits, are explicitly illegal at their point of destination. Others, such as fuel, cigarettes, or waste products, may be legal but are smuggled through illicit routes to avoid taxation, customs duties, or regulatory measures. People smuggling along maritime routes is a common practice to avoid immigration restrictions or other border controls. Humans can also be trafficked against their will for the purposes of forced labor in agriculture, domestic service, or the sex industry.

Other types of smuggling are carried out to evade UN Security Council sanctions against countries or extremist groups. Sanctions often target small arms, weapon systems, and ammunition. They are also used to restrict exports and imports of key goods such as oil and gas by sanctioned countries, or to target the sources of income of states or extremist groups, such as the sanctions imposed by the Council on charcoal trading by the Somali group Al Shabab.

Maritime smuggling exhibits a diversity of scale, organization, and harms that reflects the range of goods being smuggled. While the illicit nature of these activities means that exact figures on their global nature and extent are difficult to come by, what is clear is that smuggling by sea is ubiquitous in all regions of the world and can be a highly profitable activity. For example, the global market for illicit narcotics was estimated at between USD 426 and USD 652 billion in 2014 alone, perhaps as much as 1% of all global trade.[29] Not all narcotics smuggling takes place by sea, with smuggling routes varying by drug type and region. However, maritime flows make up a significant proportion of this figure.

Maritime smugglers use different methods to transport illicit cargos according to the type of goods being smuggled, including their physical characteristics, value, and the laws they seek to evade. Illicit items are often concealed among other cargos or in shipping containers and moved under false documentation or cloned customs seals to disguise evidence of tampering. Containers can also be shipped from port to port to obscure their origin in what are known to

---

[29] Channing May, "Transnational Crime and the Developing World," *Global Financial Integrity* 3, August 2021, https://gfintegrity.org/report/transnational-crime-and-the-developing-world/.

high-risk countries. The large volume of global container traffic makes detection difficult without specific prior intelligence to target interceptions. It has been estimated that port authorities in Africa and Europe, for example, have an average capacity to physically screen fewer than 2% of containers moving through their ports.[30] The detection of some illegal items—such as counterfeits, illicit waste, or weapon precursors—requires specialized expertise if they are to be distinguished from their legitimate counterparts.

Illicit goods and irregular migrants can also be shipped in smaller vessels, including yachts, fishing boats, and dhows. These often land their cargos at smaller harbors, where customs and surveillance procedures may be less rigorous, or at isolated coastal spots such as beaches and coves. In the case of people smuggling into Europe, unsuitable or unsafe craft have sometimes been used, either in disregard of migrants' safety or in the expectation that people will be rescued by coast guard agencies and disembarked at a destination from which they can later apply for asylum or refugee status.

Maritime smugglers show considerable innovation in the methods they use to transport goods and people. This is especially so in the case of the trade in illicit narcotics. Examples include the use of canisters containing drugs that are towed behind ships, transshipment of drug cargos from one vessel to another on the high seas, discarding packages with GPS transmitters overboard to be later collected by smaller vessels, and, in the case of cocaine trade, the use of submersibles and submarines.

Maritime smuggling operations have varying degrees of criminal organization, depending on the goods being moved. Narcotics trafficking of all types tends to be highly organized. This is in part because the lucrative nature of the trade attracts more organized criminal groups. However, it is also because the logistical demands of moving such widely prohibited items are considerable and they tend to be a high priority for law enforcement countermeasures. Other forms of smuggling take place in a more loosely distributed network. People smuggling, for example, often takes place through what the Organization for Economic Co-Operation and Development has called a "pay as you go" model, in which migrants use different people smugglers at different points in a journey, ranging from criminal gangs to opportunistic individuals.[31]

---

[30] Lucia Bird, "West Africa's Cocaine Corridor: Building a Sub-Regional Response" (Global Initiative Against Organized Crime, April 2021), 5, https://globalinitiative.net/wp-content/uploads/2022/07/GB-W-Africa-Corridor.July22.REV-web.pdf.

[31] OECD, "Can We Put an End to Human Smuggling?," Migration Policy Debates, December 2015, https://www.oecd.org/migration/mig/Can%20we%20put%20an%20end%20to%20human%20smuggling.pdf.

Some forms of smuggling can come to be seen as legitimate for some groups and under certain circumstances. This is the most obvious for cases of sanctions against armed groups or states. Yet it is also often a humanitarian question. People smuggling, for example, offers a mechanism through which vulnerable individuals can access asylum routes that might otherwise be closed to them. The illicit trade in otherwise licit goods can also support informal and barter economies in poverty-stricken countries and provide access to necessities for poor and marginalized communities.[32]

Narcotics Smuggling

Information on narcotics smuggling is mainly based on seizures. Seizure data allows law enforcement officials to reconstruct smuggling routes and understand their develop over time.[33] In this section we discuss three key maritime smuggling routes for narcotics: the cocaine trade between South America and West Africa, heroin smuggling from Afghanistan across the Indian Ocean, and the methamphetamine trade in Southeast Asia.

The Western African Cocaine Route

The global trade in cocaine boomed in the 1970s and 1980s, primarily in response to the growing popularity of the drug in the United States. Cocaine was trafficked from producer countries in South America, particularly Columbia, to United States markets by air and sea routes. Export patterns began to change in the 1990s, due to a major law enforcement response by United States authorities and others, and the emergence of a lucrative new European market. In consequence, transatlantic smuggling routes saw significant growth. By 2009 it was estimated that Europe was the source of more than half the smuggling profits, while the United States share had fallen to a third.[34] Much of this trade takes place directly between South American and European ports. However, since the mid-2000s West Africa has also emerged as an important transit point for cocaine trafficking into Europe.

---

[32] Asia Foundation, *Trade in the Sulu Archipelago: Informal Economies amidst Maritime Security Challenges* (The Asia Foundation, 2019), https://asiafoundation.org/publication/trade-in-the-sulu-archipelago-informal-economies-amidst-maritime-security-challenges/.

[33] Kendra McSweeney, "Reliable Drug War Data: The Consolidated Counterdrug Database and Cocaine Interdiction in the 'Transit Zone,'" *International Journal of Drug Policy* 80 (June 2020): 102719.

[34] Jeremy McDermott, James Bargent, Douwe den Held, and Maria Fernanda Ramírez, "The Cocaine Pipeline to Europe" (Global Initiative Against Organized Crime, February 2021), 8, https://insightcrime.org/investigations/cocaine-pipeline-europe/.

Smugglers use the western African route because it helps to conceal the origin of shipments and facilitates the disaggregation of wholesale cargos into smaller packages for onward transit. These methods make it more difficult for law enforcement agencies in Europe to intercept incoming cargos. The route is believed to work as follows.[35] Cocaine is moved by land from producer countries such as Columbia, Bolivia, and Peru to ports on the eastern seaboard of South America, particularly in Brazil and Venezuela. There it is concealed within shipping containers to be shipped onward to West African destinations, which function as storage sites and transit hubs for the onward movement of cocaine to Europe. Methods used include the re-containerization of illicit cargos for shipment along legitimate maritime trade routes, the movement of cocaine by land routes through Mali and Niger into Libya and beyond, and a coastal route whereby cocaine is moved from its entry ports to Mauritania, from where fishing boats transfer cargoes to European destinations.

The development of a western African cocaine route has caused significant harms to African states, particularly those most impacted such as Guinea Bissau. It has fueled corruption and political instability and led to a rise in cocaine use among local populations. It also illustrates how criminals are able exploit the international connectivity of maritime routes to adapt to changing circumstances and undermine law enforcement responses.

Heroin and the Western Indian Ocean's Narcotics Problem

Afghanistan is the world's largest producer of opium and heroin.[36] There is a long history of opium poppy cultivation in the country, which intensified over decades of instability and war to the point where opiate products became Afghanistan's most profitable export.[37]

Traditionally, most Afghan heroin was smuggled to Europe and beyond via land routes, including a so-called Balkan route which runs through Iran, Türkiye, and Syria, then on through Southeastern Europe to markets in Western and Central Europe, and a northern route through Central Asia and Russia into

---

[35] Bird, "West Africa's Cocaine Corridor: Building a Sub-Regional Response," 4–6.

[36] For an analysis of the political and socioeconomic dynamics of opium production in Afghanistan see David Mansfield, *A State Built on Sand: How Opium Undermined Afghanistan* (London: C. Hurst & Co., 2016).

[37] UNODC, "Afghanistan Opium Survey 2021: Cultivation and Production" (UN Office on Drugs and Crime, March 2022), https://www.unodc.org/documents/crop-monitoring/Afghanistan/Afghanistan_Opium_Survey_2021.pdf; UNODC, "Opium Cultivation in Afghanistan: Latest Findings and Emerging Threats" (UN Office on Drugs and Crime, November 2022), https://www.unodc.org/documents/crop-monitoring/Afghanistan/Opium_cultivation_Afghanistan_2022.pdf.

Eastern Europe.[38] However, since the early 2010s, strengthened law enforcement along both routes, as well as the wars in Syria and Ukraine, have made them less attractive. In a telling example of how security developments on land can become entangled with maritime security, traffickers have increasingly shifted to maritime methods, with the expansion of a southern route through the Western Indian Ocean.

The southern route begins in Afghanistan, from where heroin is moved to the Makran coast in Iran-Pakistan borderlands. This is an isolated region where law enforcement is weak. From there it is moved onward by sea. One branch goes southeast toward markets in Asia and Australia. A second branch goes southwest toward countries in eastern Africa, which function as transshipment points for onward movement to destinations in Europe and elsewhere. Heroin is trafficked using smaller vessels such as dhows and fishing vessels, as well as by concealment in shipping containers. Using dhows and fishing boats enables traffickers to hide their activities among the busy maritime traffic in the Arabian sea and off the coast of East Africa. Because these vessels frequently do not have an Automatic Identification System (AIS), conduct few port visits, and are often unflagged, they are especially difficult targets for inspection and interception. On reaching their destinations, they reportedly anchor in international waters, where they are met by smaller boats who then ferry their cargos to isolated landing points or small commercial harbors. Trafficking via containers is reportedly facilitated by political corruption and criminal influence in ports and customs.[39] On arrival cargos are moved onward by land for later transshipment to Europe and elsewhere, primarily in shipping containers.

Seizure data confirms the scale of the problem. In 2021 alone, maritime security operations have reported the seizure of over six metric tons of heroin, with one bust alone netting more than one metric ton on board a single dhow.[40]

The emergence of the southern route has turned countries such as Kenya, Tanzania, and Mozambique into key transit destinations for the heroin trade, with small island states such as Seychelles functioning as important staging posts. While most of the narcotics trafficked in this way are in transit to Europe, there has also been a flood of cheap heroin into local drug markets.

---

[38] UNODC, "World Drug Report 2015" (UN Office on Drugs and Crime, 2015), 43, https://www.unodc.org/wdr2015/.

[39] Simone Haysom, Peter Gastrow, and Mark Shaw, "Tackling Heroin Trafficking on the East African Coast" (ENACT, July 2018), 2, https://enactafrica.org/research/policy-briefs/tackling-heroin-trafficking-on-the-east-african-coast.

[40] UNODC, "Analysis of Opiate Stamps Seized in the Indian Ocean, 2017–2021," Afghan Opiate Trade Project (UN Office on Drugs and Crime, 2022), 16, https://www.unodc.org/documents/data-and-analysis/AOTP/Drug_Stamp_Report_Online_1.pdf.

Although the revenues generated are lower than those in western Europe, profits are still substantial, and African countries have seen the sharpest increase in heroin usage worldwide. This influx has had a significant impact on countries in the region, leading to public health problems, political corruption, and gang violence. In Seychelles, for example, it is estimated that up to 10% of the population are heroin users.[41] The rise in the number of addicts has led to a spike in local crime rates. It has also placed pressure on the available workforce given the overall size of the Seychelles population is only 100,000 people. In consequence, heroin smuggling has become the leading maritime security priority for the Seychelles government.

The Methamphetamine Trade in Southeast Asia

Southeast Asia's Golden Triangle region, which straddles the borders between Myanmar, Thailand, and Laos, has long been notorious as a hotspot for opium and heroin production. The Golden Triangle was the source of most of the world's heroin until the early 2000s, when Afghanistan took over as the world's largest producer. Since 2015, however, heroin production in the region has been eclipsed by the manufacture of synthetic drugs, particularly methamphetamine and its potent derivative, crystal meth. Methamphetamine is a cheap, highly stimulating, and addictive narcotic that is increasingly popular in Asia and Oceania. Contrary to heroin and cocaine, which both derive from plants and require farmland to produce, the production of crystal meth only requires access to its chemical precursors. This means that industrial scale quantities of the drug can be manufactured in relative secrecy, particularly if production facilities can be concealed in remote areas. The operations are highly profitable, with estimates indicating a market value in East and Southeast Asia was worth 61.4 billion USD in 2019.[42] By comparison, the regional heroin trade was valued at around 10 billion USD in 2022.[43]

Methamphetamine production in Southeast Asia is concentrated in Myanmar.[44] The narcotics are then smuggled across the Thai and Laotian borders,

---

[41] Louise Adamou and Chris Alcock, "Seychelles: The Island Paradise Held Prisoner by Heroin," *BBC News*, March 2023, https://www.bbc.com/news/world-africa-64785171.

[42] UNODC, "Synthetic Drugs in East and Southeast Asia: Latest Developments and Challenges" (UN Office on Drugs and Crime, May 2020), 8, //www.unodc.org/unodc/en/scientists/2020-regional-synthetic-drugs-in-east-and-southeast-asia.html.

[43] Jonathan Head and Kelly Ng, "Opium Production in Myanmar Surges to Nine-Year High," *BBC News*, January 2023, https://www.bbc.com/news/world-asia-64409019.

[44] UNODC, "Synthetic Drugs in East and Southeast Asia: Latest Developments and Challenges" (UN Office on Drugs and Crime, May 2022), 8–10, https://www.unodc.org/documents/scientific/Synthetic_Drugs_in_East_and_Southeast_Asia_2022_web.pdf

for onward movement throughout the region. Traffickers use Southeast Asia's extensive network of maritime routes and ports to access markets in Indonesia, Malaysia, and the Philippines, as well as further afield reaching markets in Japan and South Korea, but even Australia, New Zealand, South Asia, and the South Pacific Island states.

The growth in the Southeast Asian methamphetamine trade continues to expand and for instance 172 metric tons of the drug, including over a billion tablets were seized in 2021.[45] Maritime routes are at the heart of the trade. They provide drug traffickers with the means to cascade their product through the entire region, in ways in ways that are highly resistant to interdiction by law enforcement agencies. Indeed, despite increased awareness and a year-on-year growth in seizures, the drug has become cheaper and purer, suggesting an abundance of supply.

The proliferation of cheap methamphetamine has caused significant harms across the region, with growing numbers of users and drug related social problems. It has also kindled new drug markets in transit countries along the supply chain. This is perhaps most evident in the South Pacific, where small island states have functioned as transshipment points for methamphetamine shipped from Southeast Asia to Australia, New Zealand, and the United States. Methamphetamine use in small island states has accelerated significantly; in Fiji, for example, drug-related offences have increased 560% between 2013 and 2018.[46]

The three narcotics smuggling routes discussed above indicate the scale of the issue and how detrimental the effects of maritime trafficking in illicit substances can be, especially in vulnerable countries such as small island states. We now turn to the problem of people smuggling as a second paradigmatic example of illicit maritime flows.

The Illicit Movement of People

The illicit movement of people by sea routes has attracted significant political and popular attention. This is in large part due to the scale and visibility of the so-called migration crisis in the Mediterranean starting in 2015, but also the humanitarian tragedy of the Rohingya refugees in Southeast Asia from 2017. Maritime migration is a complex issue in its own right and causes different forms of harms.[47]

---

[45] UNODC, "Synthetic Drugs in East and Southeast Asia," 7.
[46] UNODC, "Synthetic Drugs in East and Southeast Asia," 12.
[47] See for example: Itamar Mann, *Humanity at Sea: Maritime Migration and the Foundations of International Law* (Cambridge: Cambridge University Press, 2016).

For an informed debate and analysis, it is important to be aware of the different terms used and their implications. The term "irregular migration" describes the movement of people across borders without following the regulations of origin, transit, and destination countries. Examples include avoiding passport controls or border checks, travel without the required documentation, and overstaying visas without permission. "Migrant," "people," or "human smuggling," by contrast, refers to "the facilitation, for financial or other material gain, of irregular entry into a country where the migrant is not a national or resident."[48] "Human trafficking" designates situations where people are smuggled against their will or through deception, generally for the purposes of forced labor. Irregular migration is not necessarily organized, and hence not a blue crime, unless it involves people smuggling or human trafficking for profit.

Irregular migration is driven by a complex combination of pressures and incentives.[49] While it is difficult to generalize given the great diversity of irregular migrant circumstances and motivations, common pressures include issues of poverty, unemployment, conflict, or repression at home. Incentives include the prospect of better economic opportunities or life chances abroad, as well as safety from war or persecution. A right to asylum is enshrined in UN Universal Declaration of Human Rights and in international refugee law.[50] This gives people fleeing their homes from persecution or civil war the right to claim protection and refugee rights in the first safe country they come to, even if they enter that country by irregular means. Few migrants use such methods by choice. They do so because they are unable to access legal routes.[51]

Irregular migration takes place by air, land, and sea. Of these, maritime routes tend to be the most dangerous due to the hazards of traveling in a volatile and weather dependent environment. Because of these dangers, sea routes are mainly used when no other options are available. Maritime migration is commonly facilitated by people smuggling groups of varying scale, organization, and sophistication. At the lowest levels, this may only comprise a handful of individuals with access to boats. In other cases, smuggling takes place through

---

[48] UNODC, "Migrant Smuggling," United Nations: Office on Drugs and Crime, n.d., //www.unodc.org/unodc/en/human-trafficking/migrant-smuggling/migrant-smuggling.html.

[49] See for example Nozomi Matsui and James Raymer, "The Push and Pull Factors Contributing Towards Asylum Migration from Developing Countries to Developed Countries Since 2000," *International Migration* 58, no. 6 (2020): 210–231.

[50] See the contributions in Cathryn Costello, Michelle Foster, Jan McAdam, eds. *The Oxford Handbook of International Refugee Law* (Oxford: Oxford University Press, 2021).

[51] Nina Perkowski and Vicki Squire, "The Anti-Policy of European Anti-Smuggling as a Site of Contestation in the Mediterranean Migration 'Crisis,'" *Journal of Ethnic and Migration Studies* 45, no. 12 (September 2019): 2178–2180.

more organized networks with the involvement of internationally operating criminal organizations or corrupt law enforcement officials.[52]

In the following sections, we explore two examples of the irregular movement of people by sea. Our first case, the so-called European migration crisis starting in 2015, led to a major response and a series of international naval and coast guard operations. Our second example is the Western Indian Ocean region, which hosts some of the busiest and most dangerous maritime migration routes in the world, but only receives limited coverage in the international news media, resulting in a correspondingly diminished response.

The European Migration Crisis of 2015

What became known as the European migration crisis in 2015 comprises of the mass movement of people to EU states, including by maritime routes originating in North Africa and Türkiye.[53] The rise in maritime migration in 2015 was in large part a consequence of the escalating impact of instability and conflicts in North Africa and the Middle East, especially the conflicts in Libya, Mali, and Syria. For this reason, the very term "migration" (or "migrant crisis") is highly contested because it implies that people were seeking to migrate to Europe voluntarily, when in fact most were fleeing conflict or persecution and so properly fall into the category of refugees, asylum-seekers, and displaced people.

Over a million illegal border crossings into the EU were recorded over the course of the year, most of them taking place across the Mediterranean.[54] In 2015, the majority of these movements took place along the so-called southeastern route between Türkiye and Greece across the Aegean Sea, but also along the longer and more dangerous Central Route between Libya and Italy. Smaller though significant maritime routes for migrants included a Western Route from Morocco to Spain, and a Western African route to the Canary Islands. Over 3,700 deaths were recorded among people attempting these crossings in 2015, with many more deaths likely going unrecorded.

In the absence of easily accessible legal routes for migration into the EU, an estimated 90% of these movements were facilitated by people smuggling

---

[52] Tuesday Reitano and Lucia Bird Ryuiz-Benitez de Lugo, "Understanding Contemporary Human Smuggling as a Vector in Migration" (Global Initiative Against Organized Crime, May 2018), 5–12, https://globalinitiative.net/wp-content/uploads/2018/05/TGIATOC-Understanding-Contemporary-Human-Smuggling-1936-hi-res.pdf.

[53] Helen Crawley et al., *Unravelling Europe's "Migration Crisis": Journeys over Land and Sea* (Bristol: Policy Press, 2018).

[54] Europol and INTERPOL, "Migrant Smuggling Networks: Joint Europol-INTERPOL Report," May 2016, https://www.europol.europa.eu/cms/sites/default/files/documents/ep-ip_report_executive_summary.pdf, 8.

groups.[55] These comprise networks of smugglers and facilitators, cooperating with each other at local level, rather than hierarchical criminal organizations. The methods of these smuggling networks differ across routes. On the southeastern route crossings are relatively short and passage takes hours rather than days. On this route, migrants are crowded into small boats such as rubber dinghies and given basic instruction on how to maneuver them on their own. On the longer and more dangerous Central Route, larger vessels, often unseaworthy and overloaded, are used to move people into Italian waters to be intercepted by coast guard vessels.

The growth of irregular migration in the Mediterranean led to a range of maritime security operations, including Operation Triton (2014–2018), conducted by the European Border and Coast Guard Agency, commonly known as Frontex and Operation Sophia (2015–2020), an EU naval mission aimed at countering people smuggling networks. These operations have also been followed by various successor missions. In 2013, the EU also launched a program aimed at capacity-building with the Libyan Coast Guard to prevent people smuggling. In 2015 and since, a significant number of nongovernmental organizations (NGOs) have been active in saving lives at sea, including SOS Mediterranee, Médecins Sans Frontières, and Sea-Watch (see Chapter 6, Section 6.5).

Throughout the crisis and beyond, the EU response struggled to balance the competing demands of border protection, saving lives at sea, and addressing its root causes.[56] Some European states were accused of using dangerous and illegal pushback methods to turn migrants back at sea at a risk to their lives. Search and rescue missions were also criticized for their potential to create an incentive for migrant boats to risk a dangerous crossing in the expectation of rescue should they get into trouble.[57] These tensions were also visible in the political controversy over the work of NGOs, who later found their vessels impounded by Italian authorities and were prevented from disembarking rescued migrants in harbor.[58] The EUs capacity-building work with the Libyan Coast Guard was also controversial, with the latter accused of multiple human rights abuses, torture, and corruption, including toward the migrants themselves.

---

[55] Europol and INTERPOL, "Migrant Smuggling Networks," 2.

[56] Eugenio Cusumano, "Humanitarians at Sea: Selective Emulation across Migrant Rescue NGOs in the Mediterranean Sea," *Contemporary Security Policy* 40, no. 2 (April 2019): 239–262.

[57] It should be noted that this claim is highly contested and controversial. See for example: Eugenio Cusumano and Matteo Villa, *Sea Rescue NGOs: A Pull Factor of Irregular Migration?* (Fiesole: European University Institute, 2019); Glenda Garelli and Martina Tazzioli, "Migration and 'Pull Factor' Traps," *Migration Studies* 9, no. 3 (September 2021): 383–399.

[58] Eugenio Cusumano and Matteo Villa, *Sea Rescue NGOs: A Pull Factor of Irregular Migration?* (Fiesole: European University Institute, 2019).

Irregular Migration in the Western Indian Ocean

People smuggling by sea is a worldwide phenomenon. Often irregular migration patterns are complex and intersect in particular regions. One example is the Western Indian Ocean. Here, maritime routes for irregular migration interlink with a series of wider migrant routes, including land-based ones, that traverse the Horn of Africa and lead into the Arabian Peninsula and Europe. A major maritime migration route runs across the Gulf of Aden, from Somalia and Djibouti to Yemen and vice versa. This is one of the busiest maritime migration routes in the world, with an estimated 160,000 people making the crossing to Yemen in 2018.[59] A second route comprises displaced people fleeing fighting in the Cabo Delgado region of northern Mozambique by sea to other, safer regions of the country, and sometimes on to other countries in Southern Africa by land routes. A third route is between the island state of Comoros and the nearby French overseas department of Mayotte,[60] and a fourth leads from Sri Lanka, northward to the Red Sea, where people migrate to escape the instability and poverty at home.

In all cases, migrants are motivated by a complex mixture of pressures, incentives, and motivations. Conflict at home is a key factor for many, including the wars and insurgencies in Yemen, Somalia, Sudan, Mozambique, and the Tigray region of Ethiopia. Environmental stressors and natural disasters, such as Eastern Africa's ongoing drought crisis and governmental oppression, as in Eritrea, are also key drivers. Incentives such as the prospect of employment in the richer countries of the Gulf region or South Africa also play a key role. The International Organization for Migration suggests that most migrants making the crossing to Yemen, for example, do so with the aim of finding employment in Saudi Arabia.[61] At the same time, there is also a smaller flow of people the other way from Yemen into Djibouti and Somalia. These movements include people returning home from the Gulf, but also Yemenis seeking safety and new economic opportunities in the Horn of Africa. Often, of course, pressures and incentives combine, with people who have been displaced from conflict seeking to relocate in countries where they expect a more secure environment and better economic prospects.

---

[59] IOM, "A Region on the Move: 2018 Mobility Overview in the Horn of Africa and the Arab Peninsula" (IOM Regional Office for the East and Horn of Africa, May 2019), 28, https://returnandreintegration.iom.int/en/resources/report/region-move-2018-mobility-overview-horn-africa-and-arab-peninsula.

[60] Kelly Moss and Masie Pigeon, "Stable Seas: Western Indian Ocean" (Stable Seas, March 2022), https://www.stableseas.org/post/stable-seas-western-indian-ocean, 18–21.

[61] IOM, "A Region on the Move."

The absence of easily accessible safe and legal routes for migration means that migrants are often forced to rely on people smugglers to make their journeys. Human trafficking gangs are also active in the region, with people being trafficked by sea either against their will or under false pretenses for the purposes of forced labor or sex work in the Gulf countries and elsewhere. In the case of the Gulf of Aden, these movements are facilitated by the already busy maritime traffic between Somalia and Yemen, including fishing and trading vessels of various sorts. However, the crossings are often also very dangerous, with migrants crowded onto unsafe vessels and moving across busy shipping lanes or dangerous waters. Reports cite officials as estimating that as many as 50,000 people may have died attempting the crossing from Comoros to Mayotte, for example.[62]

Summary

Illicit flows are one of the key categories of blue crime. Smuggling features differently in national and regional priorities by what is being moved. Narcotics trafficking, for example, is generally a high priority for maritime security agencies in richer countries, while sanctions violations tend to be dealt with by states with highly capable navies. People smuggling is a major priority across countries, yet as shown attention and responses have been concentrated on some regions and routes and not others. Other illicit goods, such as waste or counterfeits, attract far less attention. This can be particularly so in countries where customs authorities lack enforcement capacity or where legal regulations are undeveloped or sporadically enforced. It is also noteworthy that while smuggling has long been recognized as a transnational organized crime, it was only in the late 2000s that it came to be recognized as a distinct maritime issue and a key priority of the maritime security agenda.

5.5 Illicit Fishing and Other Environmental Crimes

While smuggling and piracy are crimes with long histories, the same is not true for our third category of environmental crimes. The detrimental effects of industrial activities on nature have been well understood and recognized since the mid-nineteenth century at least.[63] However, it was only in the 1960s that

---

[62] Moss and Pigeon, "Stable Seas," 21.
[63] George Perkins Marsh, *Man and Nature: Or, Physical Geography as Modified by Human Action* (Seattle: University of Washington Press, 2003 [1864]).

deliberate environmental damage began to be understood as a form of crime to be controlled by regulations and bans on harmful activities, or made subject to criminal law.[64] In the maritime domain, understandings of environmental crime have been most closely linked to the harmful consequences of the fishing and shipping industries. A complex regulatory response, which at least in part criminalizes such activities, has been under development since the 1960s.

A decline in fish stocks due to overfishing has been apparent since mid-twentieth century, when the first restrictions on species were introduced. One prominent case was the collapse of the Monterrey sardine fishery off the Pacific coast of the United States in the 1950s and 1960s. This led to a moratorium on commercial fishing in the area in 1967. Internationally, fishing became regulated by newly created Regional Fisheries Management Organizations (RFMOs), which focused on specific migratory species such as tuna. RFMOs such as the Inter-American Tropical Tuna Commission or the Pacific Islands Forum Fisheries Agency developed programs to manage fish stocks and allocate catch levels and quotas. However, compliance and enforcement were left in the hands of member states, and the RFMOs were unable to regulate the activities of nonmembers.

It was not until the 1980s that more robust international measures were agreed. An important example is the 1982 moratorium of the International Whaling Commission banning commercial whaling to prevent the extinction of species. The UN Food and Agriculture Organization (FAO), which provides the secretariats for most RFMOs, also enabled a major shift in thinking when it introduced the concept of Illegal, Unregulated and Underreported (IUU) fishing in the 1990s, discussed below.[65] This development was significant because it consolidated the view that illicit fishing activities should be classed as crimes.

Responses to marine pollution developed over a similar timeline.[66] Here, the role of the IMO was key. In 1973, it oversaw the adoption of the International Convention for the Prevention of Pollution from Ships (known as MARPOL). The Convention was amended in 1978, after a series of pollution incidents involving oil tankers. The focus at this time was on the prevention of accidents, with less attention paid to deliberate acts of marine pollution. These only entered

---

[64] Brisman and South, "Green Criminology and Environmental Crimes and Harms."

[65] See Tore Henriksen, "The FAO and Ocean Governance," in *The IMLI Treatise on Global Ocean Governance: Volume II: UN Specialized Agencies and Global Ocean Governance*, ed. Malgosia Fitzmaurice and Alexandros Ntovas (Oxford: Oxford University Press, 2018).

[66] For a historical overview see James Parsons and Chad Allen, "The History of Safety Management," in *Managing Maritime Safety*, ed. Helle Oltedal and Margareta Lützhöft (London: Routledge, 2018), 16–32.

the discussion later as regulations were tightened and broader understandings of what was considered pollution (such as the discharge of noxious substances from ships) came to the fore. Several annexes have since been added to MARPOL, and other treaties, such as the Convention on the Control of Transboundary Movements of Hazardous Waste and their Disposal (Basel Convention) of 1989, have come into force. Taken together, these regulations have de facto criminalized various forms of pollution at sea.

Today environmental crime is a well-established category, on land as well as at sea.[67] Seen from the perspective of harm, marine environmental crimes include illicit fishing, pollution, and waste dumping at sea or into the sea from land; the discharge of ballast and wastewater from ships; unregulated breakage activities; the abandonment of ships; and the illicit extraction of natural resources other than fish. Insofar as undersea installations and maritime heritage such as shipwrecks and war graves form an integrated part of the marine environment, the deliberate destruction or tampering with such objects can also be considered a maritime environmental crime.

The fight against environmental crime at sea is especially challenging because many activities which cause significant harm to the marine environment are only lightly criminalized, or may not be criminalized at all, depending on where they take place. Environmental crimes that are carried out on the High Seas are subject to much looser forms of criminalization and regulation because they depend almost wholly on flag state legislation and enforcement.

In the following sections we investigate the case of illicit fishing as an emblematic example of maritime environmental crime. While certainly not the only important crime in this category, the issue has played a significant role in driving the global debate on environmental crime at sea.

Illicit Fishing

A prominent understanding of illicit fishing is the FAO concept of "illegal, unreported, and unregulated fishing," commonly abbreviated to IUU fishing. The IUU concept specifically clusters together three different practices. Illegal fishing takes place in direct contravention of national and regional fisheries management laws, for example on access, species quotas or acceptable fishing methods. It also includes fishing conducted by vessels without nationality. "Unreported fishing" refers to catches that are not reported or misreported to relevant

---

[67] For a useful overview of current instruments see Nicola Giovannini, Luigi Melica, Marco Giannotta, and Malena Zingoni, *Addressing Environmental Crimes and Marine Pollution in the EU: Legal Guidelines and Cases* (Brussels: Droit au Droit, 2013).

national authorities or RFMOs. Unregulated fishing refers to activities that take place outside of conservation or management measures, and that are "inconsistent with State responsibilities for the conservation of marine living resources under international law."[68] It also might refer to vessels flagged in countries who are not members of the relevant RFMOs or parties to the main environmental treaties and conventions. Not all these activities are blue crimes, insofar that unregulated activities might be neither clearly harmful, nor illegal. For this reason, we here prefer the term "illicit fishing," which in line with our general definition of blue crime, centers on harms.

Illicit fishing is also associated with a series of wider crimes connected with the fisheries sector, such as document forgery or tax avoidance, bribery and corruption of politicians and officials, and the exploitation of crew members on board ship, including forced labor and slavery. Some analysts use the term "fisheries crimes" to capture this wider set of criminal practices.[69]

Illicit fishing is recognized as a key priority by most coastal states and a growing range of maritime security related international organizations, as well as by NGOs, activists, and civil society groups. The extent to which illicit fishing is formally criminalized varies across jurisdictions and activity types.

Organization and Scale

Illicit fishing is a global problem. It takes place at varying levels of organization and scale. At its least egregious, it is conducted by groups of artisanal fishers who flout regulations, use banned fishing methods such as explosives, or fish in restricted areas on an opportunistic basis. However, illicit fishing is often a highly sophisticated, organized, and industrialized practice conducted by transnational networks of criminals, working through shell companies and operating vessels under flags of convenience.[70] Some illicit fishing activities take place under license from an appropriate authority, but in circumstances where this has been facilitated through bribery, corruption, or other forms of abuse.[71]

Many of the vessels implicated in illicit fishing originate in (though are not necessarily flagged to) a small number of states. China, Iran, Spain, and Vietnam

---

[68] FAO, "What Is IUU Fishing?," n.d., https://www.fao.org/iuu-fishing/background/what-is-iuu-fishing/en/.

[69] Eve de Coning and Emma Witbooi, "Towards a New 'Fisheries Crime' Paradigm: South Africa as an Illustrative Example," *Marine Policy* 60 (October 2015): 208–215.

[70] NCM, "Chasing Red Herrings" (Copenhagen: Nordic Council of Ministers, October 2018).

[71] Maurice Beseng, "Cameroon's Choppy Waters: The Anatomy of Fisheries Crime in the Maritime Fisheries Sector," *Marine Policy* 108 (October 2019): 103669.

are most often referred to in this regard.[72] This has led to speculation over whether some of these activities may be state-sponsored or condoned, such as through the deliberate neglect of compliance measures or the use of such fishing activities to pursue geopolitical objectives (see Chapter 4, Section 4.4). These practices or allegations have the potential to fuel interstate conflicts at sea. For example, a core driver of the 1994 Turbot war between Canada and Spain that we discuss in detail in Chapter 4 was the Canadian accusation that Spanish vessels were engaged in unregulated fishing that did not respect the quotas established by the Northwest Atlantic Fishery Organization RFMO.

Illicit fishing is also often implicated in wider networks of blue crime.[73] Because fishing vessels are so numerous and well-suited to the concealment of illicit cargos, they have frequently been linked to smuggling activities of various types, including narcotics and arms.

Harms Caused By Illicit Fishing

Illicit fishing causes significant harms. It undermines the legitimate maritime economy with estimates suggesting that activities account for between 15% and 30% of the total global catch,[74] at a potential cost to global economy of USD 23.5 billion.[75] As much as 90% of the world's fish stocks are already either depleted or overexploited,[76] and illicit fishing intensifies these pressures.

Illicit fishing also damages marine ecosystems, local fisheries, and coastal economies. Many protected species are often actively targeted by illicit fishing vessels due to their high market value. Illicit fishers also sometimes employ destructive or indiscriminate fishing methods which can produce high levels of "bycatch"—unwanted species that are later discarded; a practice which can cause large-scale damage to ecosystems. Illicit fishing can also lead to a depletion of fish stocks in areas used by subsistence or artisanal fishers, with significant negative impacts on coastal livelihoods, especially in vulnerable areas of the Global South. Local fishers may also be subject to violence and intimidation by

---

[72] Dyhia Belhabib and Philippe Le Billon, "Fish Crimes in the Global Oceans," *Science Advances* 8, no. 12 (2022): 1–15.

[73] UNODC, "Transnational Organized Crime in the Fishing Industry" (UN Office on Drugs and Crime, 2011), www.unodc.org/unodc/en/human-trafficking/2011/issue-paper-transnational-organized-crime-in-the-fishing-industry.html; and Belhabib and Le Billon, "Fish Crimes in the Global Oceans."

[74] NIC, "Global Implications of Illegal, Unreported and Unregulated (IUU) Fishing)" (National Intelligence Council of the United States, September 2016), 3, https://irp.fas.org/nic/fishing.pdf.

[75] NCM, "Chasing Red Herrings," 11.

[76] UNCTAD, "90% of Fish Stocks Are Used up—Fisheries Subsidies Must Stop," UNCTAD, July 2018, https://unctad.org/news/90-fish-stocks-are-used-fisheries-subsidies-must-stop.

foreign-flagged illegal fishing vessels. Industrial fishing practices such as illicit bottom trawling can also cause long-term damage to entire ecosystems, such as coral reefs.

Finally, illicit fishing can spur and legitimate other blue crimes. Environmental degradation caused by overfishing, damage to coastal livelihoods, violence and intimidation at sea, and the perception that fish is being "stolen" by outsiders can provide motivations to engage in or support other crimes. This link is well illustrated by the case of piracy off the coast of Somalia, where piracy gangs legitimized their activities and recruited members with the claim that they were protecting local waters from foreign illicit fishing vessels (see Chapter 5, Section 5.3).

Responses

The international response to illicit fishing is led by the FAO.[77] The FAO International Plan of Action to Prevent, Deter, and Eliminate IUU Fishing of 2001 provides a common framework of action for states.[78] The subsequent FAO Agreement on Port State Measures to Prevent, Deter and Eliminate IUU Fishing of 2009 focuses on measures to be taken in the ports where fish are landed. Interpol, the International Criminal Police Organization, is another international organization active in the fight against illicit fishing. It provides Investigative Support Teams to assist member countries with criminal investigations into fisheries crimes. It also issues regular notices, which are formal requests for cooperation or alerts between states, for illicit fishing activities.[79] In addition, RFMOs maintain blacklists of vessels known to engage in illicit fishing or suspected of doing so to inform regional maritime law enforcement actors. Various other regional information-sharing and surveillance initiatives enable the cross-national exchange of data and evidence on suspicious vessels and facilitate interceptions by enforcement agencies (see Chapter 7, Section 7.5). A growing number of non-governmental organizations also support fisheries protection. Examples include the provision of satellite surveillance and algorithms that can detect suspicious

---

[77] See for example NCM, "Chasing Red Herrings"; Andrew M. Song, Joeri Scholtens, Kate Barclay, Simon R. Bush, Michael Fabinyi, Dedi S. Adhuri, and Milton Haughton, "Collateral Damage? Small-Scale Fisheries in the Global Fight against IUU Fishing," *Fish and Fisheries* 21, no. 4 (2020): 831–843.

[78] FAO, "International Plan of Action to Prevent, Deter and Eliminate Illegal, Unreported and Unregulated Fishing" (Food and Agriculture Organization, 2001), https://www.wto.org/english/tratop_e/rulesneg_e/fish_e/2001_ipoa_iuu.pdf.

[79] "Fighting Illegal, Unreported and Unregulated Fishing," accessed June 26, 2023, https://www.interpol.int/en/News-and-Events/News/2019/Fighting-illegal-unreported-and-unregulated-fishing.

fishing activities, and sometimes even direct interdiction of vessels at sea (see Chapter 6, Section 6.5).

The Chase of the Thunder

A noteworthy episode that shines a light on the challenge posed by illicit fishing but also potential responses to it is the chase of the vessel *Thunder*. The case received significant news coverage and was the subject of a video documentary released in 2018.[80] This incident stands out due to the extensive duration and geographic range of the pursuit, spanning 110 days and encompassing a distance of 10,000 nautical miles. Furthermore, it serves as an illustration of how various maritime security actors, from across the globe and including an NGO, can cooperate to tackle illegal fishing activities.

By 2013, the *Thunder* was one of the most notorious illicit fishing vessels in the world. At nearly 62 meters in length and with a crew of 40, the *Thunder* conducted illicit fishing on an industrial scale, netting an estimated USD 76 million from sales of the sought-after (though tightly regulated) Patagonian toothfish. In 2013 the vessel was placed on an Interpol Purple Notice, indicating a "most wanted" status alongside only a handful of other vessels in the world. The *Thunder* had in fact earlier been apprehended in Malaysia in May 2014, though was later released after the payment of a USD 90,000 fine.

In December 2014, the *Thunder* was spotted in Antarctic waters by the *Bob Baker*, a vessel owned and operated by the Sea Shepherd NGO. The *Bob Baker* gave chase, and was later joined by another Sea Shepherd ship, the *Sam Simon*. Their aim was to keep track of the *Thunder*'s position and to disrupt any attempted fishing activities. The chase unfolded over the course of four months. It involved multiple confrontations at sea, including net cutting. It finally came to an end in early April in the Gulf of Guinea, not far from the islands of São Tomé and Príncipe. Running low on fuel, the *Thunder* reported a collision and began to sink. Its crew were picked up by the pursuing Sea Shepherd vessels and later handed over to local police authorities and Interpol representatives. Three of the ship's officers were later charged with illegal fishing offences, sentenced to up three years in prison, and fined a total of USD 17 million.

The role of maritime domain awareness in the pursuit of the *Thunder* was crucial. The surveillance centers that we review in Chapter 7, provided critical information and intelligence regarding the vessel's location, movements, and activities. This helped track the *Thunder* throughout the chase, enabling effective

---

[80] "A Renegade Trawler, Hunted for 10,000 Miles by Vigilantes," accessed May 19, 2023, https://www.nytimes.com/2015/07/28/world/a-renegade-trawler-hunted-for-10000-miles-by-vigilantes.html.

coordination with regional maritime security forces, and provided evidence for prosecution.

The case of the *Thunder* is illustrative of the global challenge posed by industrial scale illicit fishing. The *Thunder* was able to operate with impunity for many years by fishing in areas beyond national jurisdiction, with its AIS transponder turned off. While in principle any state could have hunted and pursued it under the Interpol Purple notice, the difficulty and cost of doing so was prohibitive to action. It took the intervention of Sea Shepherd to put an end to its activities, demonstrating the key role that NGO actors can play in fisheries enforcement activities at sea (see Chapter 6, Section 6.5).

The case is also indicative of the difficulties of prosecuting illicit fishing activities. Over its lifetime, the *Thunder* operated under seven different names and seven different flags, while its ownership was shrouded in multiple shell companies based in Seychelles, Nigeria, and Panama. It is notable in this respect that even when prosecutions did occur, these were limited to the ship's officers rather than its beneficial owners, whose identity remains uncertain. Even the final denouement of the episode posed an obstacle to prosecution, with many suspecting that the ship was deliberately scuttled in bid to destroy evidence.

Summary

The different forms of environmental crime at sea are a growing challenge in the light of pollution of the sea and biodiversity loss. While we have focused on illicit fishing as the problem that is the most clearly tackled on the maritime security agenda, environmental crime is a field with a broad scope. Pollution caused by the shipping and cruise line industry, which includes greenhouse gas emissions,[81] ballast water, noise pollution, disposal of chemicals, oil and waste, and container losses, but also potentially accidents that involve negligence can be included here.[82] Other forms of illicitly harvesting ocean resources, such as the illicit mining of seabed minerals, are likely to become more important in the future. As we discuss in Chapter 8, a key reason for the development of this debate is the growing awareness that the oceans are in a crisis state. Declining ocean health requires better protection from marine activities, including through more studies that document harm, but also stronger criminal laws.

---

[81] Judith van Leeuwen and Jason Monios, "Decarbonisation of the Shipping Sector—Time to Ban Fossil Fuels?," *Marine Policy* 146 (December 2022): 105310.

[82] Tony R. Walker et al., "Environmental Effects of Marine Transportation," in *World Seas: An Environmental Evaluation (Second Edition)*, ed. Charles Sheppard (Cambridge, MA: Academic Press, 2019), 505–530.

While regulations and laws at national and international levels are expanding as a better understanding of the harms caused by environmental crimes spreads, the effectiveness of these regulations can be undermined by weak maritime law enforcement. At the same time, maritime environmental crimes are often considered to be of lower legal or political priority than other forms of blue crime.

5.6 Interlinkages

In this chapter we have explored the problem of crime at sea as a core component of the maritime security agenda. We defined blue crime as comprising serious organized crimes or offences that take place in, on, or across the maritime domain, and that have the potential to inflict significant harms. Our focus on harms redirects our attention from the question of what has been criminalized in national and international legislation—something that can vary widely by jurisdiction and over time—to the negative impacts of these activities.

The three dimensions of blue crime we outline are an encouragement to consider the linkages between different types of crime. This is an important exercise given that most international treaties and responses are fragmented across issues and between regions. Recognizing these interlinkages is key if the root causes of blue crime are to be understood and addressed (see Chapter 3, Section 3.5), but also to ensure that maritime security solutions are formulated in a joined-up manner. This is important to prevent spirals of crime and the rise of new hot spots, and also to avoid potential displacement effects, in that success in addressing one particular crime can sometimes lead to the rise of another.

In the next two chapters, we explore the actors and solutions of maritime security in more detail. In Chapter 6, we discuss the "who's who" of maritime security. Our aim is to introduce the complex range of different actors and agencies who have a role to play in maritime security, including who they are, what they do, and how they relate to each other. In Chapter 7 we turn to the toolbox of maritime security solutions. Here we examine the approaches that maritime security actors have developed to combat insecurity at sea. We highlight the strengths and challenges of these responses and show how a common repertoire of maritime security solutions has emerged.

6

The Who's Who of Maritime Security

6.1 Actors in Maritime Security

A characteristic of maritime security is the high number of different actors involved and the complexity of their relations. In this chapter we unpack this complexity through an analysis of different types of actors: states, international organizations, private companies, and civil society organizations. For the maritime security analyst and professional, it is important to understand the plurality of actors, and that these follow different rationales and logics and have specific roles and capabilities.

We start by addressing the state. States are key players in maritime security. However, individual states have different positions and capabilities, and face different challenges in the maritime domain. They tend to organize their solutions to maritime security in different ways, shaped by their histories, political cultures, and governance regimes. We examine the internal dimensions of states by focusing on how they organize enforcement at sea. A key issue here is in how far maritime security is approached as a military (naval) responsibility, or as a civil law enforcement (coast guard) one. Most states face the challenge of how to organize relations between these agencies.

We go on to investigate the role of international and regional organizations. These organizations are important because they set and enforce rules and norms, but also provide discussion forums, dispute settlement mechanisms, and deliver capacity-building and technical assistance. Our next section addresses the role of commercial actors. A wide range of commercial sectors are present in the maritime domain and there is a growing role for private security providers. Our final section discusses the role of nongovernmental organizations (NGOs) and activists. As we show, these actors are often challenge state policies, but can also assume important support functions.

6.2 What's In a State? Navies, Coast Guards, and Other Agencies

Legal obligations under the UN Convention on the Law of the Sea (UNCLOS), conventions by the International Maritime Organization (IMO), and other international treaties, and the rise of the maritime security agenda, imply a significant spectrum of obligations and responsibilities for states in the maritime domain. International rules require that states be able to ensure safety in their ports, police their territorial waters, manage and protect their exclusive economic zones (EEZs), and regulate and inspect their flagged vessels and those coming into their ports. States also have responsibilities outside their immediate areas of national jurisdiction, including the protection of maritime trade routes, counterterrorism, and the fight against blue crimes abroad.

As detailed in figure 6.1, states have four different roles to play in maritime security. As a *coastal state* they safeguard territorial waters and EEZs. As a *port state* they ensure safety in ports, control what goods and ships enter and exit the country by sea, and ensure that ships coming into and leaving port comply with international regulations. As a *flag state* they regulate shipping and fishing and enforce laws on board vessels under their authority. Finally, as an *international state* they secure international waters and assist other states in fulfilling their obligations.

While all states are equal and have the same obligations under international law, in practice their capabilities differ quite substantially. Some states can draw on significant naval capabilities and economic resources for maritime security, while others lack those means. The United States, for example, operates the largest navy and second largest coast guard in the world, with naval bases

Role	Tasks	Examples
Coastal State	Safeguard coastline, fisheries control	Marine protection, fishery control, border control
Port State	Security and safety in ports, ship compliance, cargo inspections	Countersmuggling, ISPS Code
Flag State	Legislation on board ships, compliance with international law, protection of ships	ISPS Code, MARPOL
International State	Sanctions enforcement, tsunami relief operations	Counterpiracy operations, tsunamis

Figure 6.1 State roles in ocean governance

and stations across the globe. Australia, Brazil, China, Japan, Russia, the United Kingdom, and European Union (EU) member states have sizable navies and coast guard agencies and have global maritime security ambitions. All are also major coastal, flag, port, and international states according to the roles above.

Yet maritime security is also a widely distributed and indeed global task, in which many smaller states are important too. Small island states, such as those in the Caribbean, South Pacific, or Indian Ocean, for example, often have large territorial seas and EEZs. For this reason, they are often referred to as "large ocean states."[1] However, many lack the human, material, and financial resources to secure their waters. Other states have unique positions as port and flag states. Malta, Singapore, and the United Arab Emirates are important port states. The Bahamas, Liberia, the Marshall Islands, and Panama are major flag states with responsibility for many thousands of vessels around the world.

In other cases, employment and income from the shipping industry makes a sizable contribution to the national gross domestic product, as is the case in Denmark, Greece, Norway, and Switzerland. Other countries are leading fishing nations, such as Chile, Indonesia, Peru, or Vietnam. Still others, such as Belgium, Denmark, or the Netherlands, are leading offshore wind power providers. Even landlocked states are important in maritime security because they are economically dependent on trade. Landlocked countries such as Austria, Switzerland, or Mongolia operate flag state authorities, while some, such as Ethiopia, even operate a navy.

States Are Not Unitary Actors

States are not unitary actors. They have different constitutional arrangements, governance forms, and political systems, and accordingly organize their maritime security responses in various ways. To deal with the broad spectrum of maritime security tasks, states delegate responsibilities to different ministries, departments, and dedicated agencies. While working under a common jurisdictional umbrella and under the same government, most states maintain an array of different maritime agencies for historical, constitutional, or political reasons and in relation to their position as a coastal, flag, port, and international state.

The number of state agencies involved in maritime security can be substantial. To take an example, the United Kingdom's 2022 National Strategy for Maritime Security lists fully 35 distinct government entities with a role in maritime

---

[1] Nicholas Chan, "'Large Ocean States': Sovereignty, Small Islands, and Marine Protected Areas in Global Oceans Governance," *Global Governance: A Review of Multilateralism and International Organizations* 24, no. 4 (December 2018): 537–555.

security, including ministerial portfolios as diverse as transport, defense, home and foreign affairs, and the environment. At the agency level alone, the strategy identifies the Royal Navy, the Royal Air Force, the Border Force, the Maritime and Coastguard Agency, the Police Service, and four nationally devolved marine environmental management agencies as dealing with aspects of UK maritime security in home waters and beyond.[2] Taken together, these actors make up the governmental maritime security sector in the United Kingdom.

Not all countries exhibit such diversity. States such as Denmark, for example, have subsumed many of these individual agency functions into a single navy organization. Even so, it is commonly the case that maritime security tasks are distributed between at least three, and often many more, distinct national agencies.

Broadly speaking, three main types of maritime security agencies can be distinguished. The first of these are military actors. In the maritime domain, it is generally navies that are dominant in this respect, though other military services may also conduct maritime security tasks, as when air forces provide surveillance or search and rescue functions. Military forces most often have a mandate outside the areas of national jurisdiction and work under ministries of defense.

A second category of agencies are civil in character and primarily engaged in maritime law enforcement. Most commonly, this includes coast guard organizations and maritime police. These agencies are mandated to operate in territorial waters as well as EEZs and are generally responsible to ministries of the interior or equivalent. In some cases, as with China, Japan, or the United States, coast guards may also be deployed to regional or global tasks too.

Finally, there are those agencies engaged in marine safety, port security, and environmental protection and management tasks such as fisheries control, which can also have enforcement responsibilities. These agencies tend to focus their operations on areas under national jurisdiction, as well as vessels under their flag. They generally operate under a more diverse set of ministerial portfolios, such as transport, agriculture, the economy, or the environment, depending on national political systems.

While it is difficult to generalize across diverse national approaches, agencies are distinguished by their expected roles and functions, the legal frameworks they operate under, their technical skills and specializations, their resourcing and equipment, and the degree to which they are organized along military command and control structures. Navies, for example, are explicitly military actors, generally equipped with ocean-going warships, and specialized in coercion and

---

[2] Her Majesties Government of the United Kingdom, "National Strategy for Maritime Security, CP 724" (HMG, August 2022), 96–105, https://www.gov.uk/government/publications/national-maritime-security-strategy.

combat at sea.[3] Many democratic countries, including Germany, Japan, the United States, and United Kingdom, restrict the role of naval actors in domestic law enforcement due to their norms of civil–military relations and expectations of civilian control over the military.

Coast guards specialize in maritime law enforcement and search and rescue.[4] They are mostly equipped and resourced at a lower level than their naval counterparts, with fleets of inshore and offshore patrol vessels rather than warships (though in some cases, as with the Chinese, Japanese, or United States coast guards, these may include large ocean-going vessels with naval armaments). Alongside maritime police formations, they generally have the power of arrest, as well as specialist law enforcement skills such as evidence collection and crime scene investigation.

Other types of agencies, such as port customs, fisheries control, maritime search and rescue, or marine environmental management organizations, have equipment and skill requirements relevant to their expected functions. Normally these agencies will maintain a fleet of vessels of varying size and capability, and often have enforcement powers in their areas of specific responsibility.

Role-Based Accounts

Studies of national maritime security sectors reveal a significant diversity of organizational and governance structures.[5] Depending on the case, any one individual agency may fulfil various tasks according to political decisions, context, and circumstance. In this respect, there is a risk that focusing too much on the formal institutional mandates and names of organizations and the way that they are configured obscures the political and strategic logics that underpin their deployment and operations. This obscurity may even be deliberate in some cases, such as when coast guards are used as part of grey-zone activities (see Chapter 4, Section 4.4).

Attempts to streamline the debate to provide orientation for professionals, enable international cooperation, or inform restructuring efforts, address this problem by focusing on the functions and tasks that a national maritime security sector performs. While it may be the case that certain roles are most frequently

---

[3] Ian Speller, *Understanding Naval Warfare*, 2nd ed. (London: Routledge, 2018); Geoffrey Till, *Seapower: A Guide for the Twenty-First Century*, 4th ed. (London: Routledge, 2018), 114–144.

[4] Ian Bowers and Swee Lean Collin Koh, eds., *Grey and White Hulls: An International Analysis of the Navy-Coastguard Nexus* (Singapore: Springer Singapore, 2019).

[5] See for example the case studies in Bowers and Koh, *Grey and White Hulls*; Christian Bueger, Timothy Edmunds, and Robert McCabe, eds., *Capacity Building for Maritime Security: The Western Indian Ocean Experience* (Basingstoke: Palgrave, 2021).

conducted by specific agencies—such as navies fulfilling military tasks and coast guards law enforcement ones—a focus on functions does not assume that they do so exclusively. Moreover, these role distributions are not static. They are subject to change according to political priorities and decisions. For example, a new government or a new maritime security strategy might very well restructure and redistribute roles.

There are several outlines of the functions and roles that are helpful to organize the discussion. The EU, for example, has published a "coast guard functions" handbook that lays out 11 tasks,[6] while the United States produced a Maritime Security Sector Reform Guide that specifies the functions of agencies.[7] Summarized, the spectrum of coast guard functions includes eight crucial tasks, each complex and potentially wide ranging in its own right.

1. Maritime safety, such as ensuring the compliance of vessels with national and international laws, and operating vessel traffic management, e.g., the traffic separation schemes and lighthouses.
2. Assistance to mariners in distress and ship casualties, search and rescue, accident, and disaster response.
3. Border control, including the prevention of irregular migration.
4. Customs activities, such as the enforcement of import and export tax regulations.
5. Prevention and suppression of trafficking and smuggling, such as through interceptions and inspections.
6. Fisheries inspection and control to ensure compliance with regulations and prevent and address illicit fishing.
7. Environmental protection and response, including in marine protected areas, to prevent environmental crimes, such as illicit waste disposal.
8. General monitoring and surveillance and contributing to maritime domain awareness, for instance, to identify suspicious behavior.

Other outlines of functions can be found in naval strategies and doctrines. These usually identify three main categories of operational activity for navies: combat operations at sea, constabulary operations, and naval diplomacy. Since the focus is on military operations, these outlines tend to concentrate on the combat functions of navies. Key concepts include that of "sea control"—that is, securing

---

[6] European Commission, "Annex to the Commission Recommendation Establishing a 'Practical Handbook' on European Cooperation on Coastguard Functions" (European Union, June 2021), https://oceans-and-fisheries.ec.europa.eu/system/files/2021-07/c-2021-5310-annex_en.pdf.

[7] United States Government, "Maritime Security Sector Reform Guide" (Washington, DC, n.d.), https://2009-2017.state.gov/documents/organization/154082.pdf.

the sea or parts of the sea so that friendly fleets and shipping can move unhindered by enemy action;[8] "sea denial"—in the sense of denying an enemy's freedom of movement at sea or in parts of the sea without necessarily attempting to control it for one's own use;[9] and "power projection"—meaning the use of naval forces for the purposes of blockade or to deploy military force from sea onto land, often in areas distant from national territory.[10]

Constabulary operations refers to those tasks most directly associated with maritime security, and crosses over significantly with the spectrum of coast guard functions, including carrying them out in international or foreign waters.[11] They include actions such as measures to ensure freedom of navigation; the protection of sea lanes and chokepoints from pirates and other malign actors; the enforcement of laws and regulations in the maritime domain and in ports, including in the fight against blue crime and marine environmental degradation; and the policing of maritime territories and claims.

Navies, coast guards, and maritime security agencies can also be used for diplomatic and political tasks of various types, including for purposes of deterrence or reassurance, through maintaining presence at sea, port visits, or capacity-building activities.[12] Another spectrum of activities are in international humanitarian and disaster relief operations, where maritime security forces are often well equipped to provide rapid emergency support from the sea, and interventions at the invitation of countries in distress.[13]

A role-based account encourages us to consider the range of different functions that maritime security agencies may be deployed to carry out, whatever their notional organizational ideal-type mandate might be. Coast guards and other non-naval maritime security actors can be used for coercive purposes, if, for example, they are deployed to dispute maritime claims in contested areas. By the same token, navies regularly engage in constabulary tasks of various sorts, such as in counterpiracy operations in the Western Indian Ocean and Gulf of Guinea.

---

[8] Till, *Seapower*, 157.

[9] Jonathan D. Caverley and Peter Dombrowski, "Cruising for a Bruising: Maritime Competition in an Anti-Access Age," *Security Studies* 29, no. 4 (August 2020): 671–700.

[10] Speller, *Understanding Naval Warfare*, 129–149.

[11] Till, *Seapower*, 150–169.

[12] J. J. Widen, "Naval Diplomacy—A Theoretical Approach," *Diplomacy & Statecraft* 22, no. 4 (December 2011): 715–733; Bama Andika Putra, "The Rise of Paragunboat Diplomacy as a Maritime Diplomatic Instrument: Indonesia's Constabulary Forces and Tensions in the North Natuna Seas," *Asian Journal of Political Science* (June 2023): 1–19.

[13] David Capie, "The United States and Humanitarian Assistance and Disaster Relief (HADR) in East Asia: Connecting Coercive and Non-Coercive Uses of Military Power," *Journal of Strategic Studies* 38, no. 3 (April 2015): 309–331.

Not all the roles discussed here are necessarily of direct relevance to maritime security. Warfighting concepts, for example, tend to be less relevant to the maritime security agenda, while search and rescue tasks are often understood primarily as a function of marine safety rather than maritime security per se. Even so, in practice these functions can easily become folded into wider maritime security operations. Interstate disputes and grey-zone confrontations can escalate to include activities on the warfighting spectrum, while maritime border policing operations (such as controlling irregular migration by sea) often have a search and rescue component too.

The Interagency Coordination Challenge

The complexity of the maritime security sector creates challenges of how to achieve coherence, adjust and integrate sector policies and management, optimize resource utilization, ensure information sharing, and minimize interagency competition and bureaucratic partisanship.[14]

At a political level, agencies can find themselves competing for resources, status, or attention. This can especially be the case if agency roles and responsibilities overlap or conflict. However, at the operational level, they must work together closely to achieve their goals within existing resource limits. Maritime security thus requires ongoing coordination between departments and agencies. The greater the number of organizations involved, the more challenging this task becomes. Governments address these issues through initiatives framed as "whole of government," "joined-up government," or "interagency coordination" approaches.

There are several, sometimes concurrent, ways that states commonly approach this issue.[15] The first is a division of labor model. Here, a clear division of responsibilities, specializations, and hierarchy of relations between agencies is established. Often this entails assigning a dedicated lead agency to a particular issue area, to which other agencies are subordinated for operational command and control purposes. This has the advantage of demarcating clear lines of authority and accountability and centralizing operational command and control. Specialization also ensures the build-up of expertise and dedicated training programs in technical areas, such as fisheries control or narcotics detection. However, the model can run into difficulties if there are significant status or

---

[14] Brian Wilson, "The Complex Nature of Today's Maritime Security Issues: Why Whole-of-Government Frameworks Matter," in *Routledge Handbook of Naval Strategy and Security*, ed. Joachim Krause and Sebastian Bruns (Abingdon: Routledge, 2016), 153–165.

[15] Evan Laksmana, "Remodelling Indonesia's Maritime Law Enforcement Architecture: Theoretical and Policy Considerations," *Contemporary Southeast Asia* 44, no. 1 (2022): 122–149.

resource differences between the agencies concerned, or if they have different organizational cultures, priorities, or ways of working. Civil and military organizations, for instance, have quite different management styles and organizational cultures. This can be especially problematic if a more powerful agency is subordinated to what it considers to be a junior partner or institutional rival.

A second model is to establish joint command and coordination structures to manage relations between agencies. Coordinating committees and dedicated multiagency maritime security centers provide a mechanism whereby policy priorities can be identified and negotiated between departments, information sharing is enabled, and through which joint operations at sea can be orchestrated. They are often multipurpose and serve policy, strategic and operational coordination as well as maritime domain awareness goals. This is the currently preferred model of many countries. The primary drawback of this model lies in a potential lack of accountability as any failure or underperformance can be attributed to a collective committee rather than a specific agency.

Examples of this model include the Global Maritime Operational Threat Response Coordination Center of the United States, which was created to support interagency responses to maritime threats in 2010.[16] The United States also published a Maritime Security Cooperation Policy in 2013 and a National Fleet Plan in 2015 to help align planning, resources, and operations across the Navy, Marine Corps and Coastguard.

Similarly, since 2010, the United Kingdom established a series of cross-departmental maritime security coordination and information sharing mechanisms.[17] These include an information sharing center (National Maritime Information Centre), which provides a common picture across agencies, and a Joint Maritime Operations Coordination Centre to coordinate the government's at-sea assets and capabilities to provide a "whole system" response to incidents. In 2020, both of these centres were incorporated into a new Joint Maritime Security Centre, whose role is to fuse intelligence, data, and capabilities as well as to coordinate operations. The center is supported by a high-level Maritime Threat Group to coordinate at the level of strategy and policy.[18]

The Australian government created a civil-military multiagency Joint Offshore Protection Command in 2005, which then became the Border Protection Command in 2006. It also established the Australian Maritime Security Operations Centre which coordinates maritime response and

[16] Wilson, "The Complex Nature."

[17] Christian Bueger, Timothy Edmunds, and Scott Edwards, "Innovation and New Strategic Choices: Refreshing the UK's National Strategy for Maritime Security," *The RUSI Journal* 166, no. 4 (June 2021): 66–75.

[18] Bueger, Edmunds, and Edwards, "Innovation and New Strategic Choices."

surveillance activities.[19] Related examples from Southeast Asia are Thailand's Maritime Enforcement Command Centre and Indonesia's maritime security agency (known as BAKAMLA). Many states also run joint maritime security exercises to enable agencies to get used to working with each other and to build trust between them.

Finally, coordination between agencies can also be based on ad hoc and informal channels (see Chapter 7, Section 7.2). These might include personal relations between individual officials or nonofficial communication channels such as WhatsApp groups. These informal channels can provide an important addition to more formal administrative structures, and in practice often play a critical role in coordinating between agencies on a day-to-day basis.

Dealing with effective coordination is not just a technical and operational challenge. It requires institutional buy-in and commitment to succeed and may struggle in contexts where organizational tensions or rivalries are pronounced. Under these circumstances, processes of confidence and trust building are critical.

Summary

States are the most important actors in maritime security. They are obliged to police and protect their own waters and EEZs, meet various obligations under UNCLOS and other international law, and participate in global and regional maritime security operations. There is no single model of how states organize their maritime security sectors, though most states maintain some mix of military and civil agencies who fulfil a variety of maritime security roles depending on context and circumstances. Coordinating between agencies is a common challenge in maritime security even at the intrastate level. Solutions include the assignment of a lead agency on specific issues, the creation of coordinating committees and structures, and the holding of joint exercises and strategic planning processes to build familiarity and trust.

6.3 A Global Field: International and Regional Organizations

While states and their agencies are important actors in maritime security, governments have delegated many issues to regional and international

---

[19] James Wraith and Clive Schofield, "Australia's Endeavours in Maritime Enforcement. Securing Vast and Vital Oceans," *Korean Journal of International and Comparative Law* 6 (2018): 219–44.

organizations (IOs). Within IOs states agree on norms, rules, and technical standards. The secretariats of IOs prepare and facilitate such negotiations, but also run programs for implementation and often monitor compliance. While to some degree IOs act on behalf of states, they have grown and developed expertise to a degree that often they act independently from direct state mandates.[20] Indeed, there is a notable trend of IOs expanding their mandates to ensure their continued relevance and maintain their status.

The global field of IOs that matter in maritime security is quite complex. There is no clear hierarchy between IOs. Instead, there are numerous practical relations between organizations. IOs also sometimes compete over resources or authority, especially in areas of maritime security where numerous different organizations are involved and prospects for donor funding are higher.

IOs in maritime security can broadly be distinguished along two lines. The first is geographical scope, that is, whether organizations are international and operate globally or whether they are regional. International organizations have a global spectrum of work and are often part of the UN system. They tend to focus on specific issues, such as development or environmental protection and are based on (a set of) specific international treaties. Regional organizations are formed to address a particular geographical space, such as Europe or Southeast Asia. They are often more integrated, tend to form "security communities,"[21] focus on multiple issues, and have restrictive membership criteria. Regional organizations sometimes act outside the territories of their members. For example, the EU is not only very active in its own regional waters—the Atlantic, the Baltic, the Mediterranean, and the North Sea—but also engaged in the Indian Ocean, Gulf of Guinea, and elsewhere.

The second important distinction is between those organizations which are formal and those that are informal.[22] Formal organizations, such as those in the UN family are based on multilateral treaties and have standing secretariats, while informal organizations are looser formations, with some of them relying only on vague terms of references and memoranda of understanding. Informal organizations are also often issue-specific and can be more short-lived, as they can lose purpose and relevance once they have delivered their main task.

We start our overview with the formal level and first look at global and then regional organizations. We then discuss the role of informal organizations.

---

[20] As discussed in Michael N. Barnett and Martha Finnemore, *Rules of the World: International Organizations in Global Politics* (Ithaca, NY: Cornell University Press, 2004).

[21] See Chapter 3, Section 3.3 for a discussion of the concept of security community.

[22] The notion of informality is well explained in Thomas Kwasi Tieku, "Ruling from the Shadows: The Nature and Functions of Informal International Rules in World Politics," *International Studies Review* 21, no. 2 (June 2019): 225–243. See also Chapter 7, Section 7.2.

Global IOs

There is no IO that is exclusively dedicated to maritime security, nor is there an IO in charge for all matters dealing with the oceans. Instead, ocean governance takes place through a complex web of IOs.[23] This complexity is well illustrated by UN Oceans—the UN body that aims to coordinate agencies. Its website lists no less than 23 distinct participating UN entities.[24] Figure 6.2 provides an overview of the key IOs drawing on the maritime security matrix (see Chapter 3, Section 3.4).

Three IOs of the UN family are particularly important for maritime security. The International Maritime Organization (IMO) and the Food and Agricultural Organization (FAO) were the first to address ocean governance concerns and have assumed a significant profile in maritime security. The United Nations Office on Drugs and Crime (UNODC) has also emerged as an innovator in maritime security, especially following the outbreak of Somali piracy in the 2000s.

The IMO is the main authority that governs shipping and port facilities. It is a UN specialized agency that was created by a convention adopted in 1948 and opened its headquarters in London in 1958. The main tasks of the IMO focus on health and safety in shipping, ship building, the prevention of accidents, and environmental issues such as pollution from shipping. The name of the

MARINE ENVIRONMENT			ECONOMIC DEVELOPMENT	
MARINE SAFETY		BLUE ECONOMY		
	IMO	UNEP	UNDP	UNCTAD
	UNODC			
UNSC		**MARITIME SECURITY**	ILO	FAO
INTERPOL				IOM
	ITLOS			UNHCR
	SEA POWER		RESILIENCE	
NATIONAL SECURITY				**HUMAN SECURITY**

Figure 6.2 Priority areas of global IOs

---

[23] See the discussions in Seline Trevisanut, Nikolaos Giannopoulos, and Rozemarijn Roland Holst, eds., "Regime Interaction in Ocean Governance: Problems, Theories and Methods," in *Regime Interaction in Ocean Governance* (Leiden: Brill Nijhoff, 2020).

[24] See UN Oceans, accessed January 11, 2024, www.unoceans.org.

organization is somewhat misleading, and perhaps the "international ship and port organization" might be more accurate, given the remit of its mandate.

Initially, maritime security concerns held a low position on the IMO's list of priorities and were discussed in one of its three committees—the Maritime Safety Committee. Following concerns from the industry, the IMO began monitoring piracy incidents in the 1980s, and continues to offer guidance to shipping in this area. The IMO explicitly engaged in security matters for the first time after the adoption of the Convention for the Suppression of Unlawful Acts against the Safety of Maritime Navigation in 1988 (known as SUA Convention), following the hijacking of the cruise liner *Achille Lauro* in 1985 (see Chapter 4, Section 4.3).[25]

The IMO's role changed significantly in the aftermath of the 9/11 terrorist attacks on the United States, when the international community sought ways to address the vulnerabilities of maritime trade to terrorism. The outcome was the adoption of the International Ship and Port Facility Security (ISPS) Code, which introduced obligatory security measures for governments, ports, and ships.[26] As the guardian of the code, the IMO expanded its technical assistance to ensure ISPS standards worldwide. The role of the IMO increased with the rise of piracy in the mid-2000s. The Maritime Safety Committee became one of the core sites where the role of the shipping industry in counterpiracy was discussed. The IMO also expanded its capacity-building work in response to piracy and began to address other maritime security issues, such as supporting maritime domain awareness and information sharing initiatives (see Chapter 7, Section 7.6).

The FAO is a UN specialized agency that was created in 1945 to eliminate hunger and improve nutrition and standards of living by increasing agricultural productivity. Based in Rome, it was mandated by states to oversee all aspects of food production and agriculture, including fisheries management and aquaculture. The FAO assists with the regulation of national fisheries, and also operates the secretariats of Regional Fishery Monitoring Organizations (RFMOs) that manage migratory fish stocks and aquaculture in regional settings. With fish stocks in decline, the FAO and the regional organizations it supports have focused on illicit fishing activities. The FAO coined the concept of Illegal Unregulated and Underreported (IUU) fishing, which has widely structured the

---

[25] "Convention for the Suppression of Unlawful Acts against the Safety of Maritime Navigation" (United Nations, 1988), accessed January 11, 2024, https://treaties.un.org/doc/db/terrorism/conv8-english.pdf.

[26] "International Ship and Port Security Code" (IMO, 2003), https://portalcip.org/wp-content/uploads/2017/05/ISPS-Code-2003-English.pdf.

debate on this problem (see Chapter 5, Section 5.5). The FAO's fisheries department is one of the key actors in the fight against illicit fishing.

The UNODC was established in 1997 out of the merger of the UN Centre for International Crime Prevention and the UN International Drug Control Programme. Based in Vienna, it is tasked with supporting states in the fight against transnational organized crime. It is the guardian of two international treaties on organized crime. The 2000 UN Convention against Transnational Organized Crime[27] and the 2003 Convention against Corruption.[28]

The smuggling of illicit goods has been a key focus of the UNODC since its inception. An early focus on narcotics was expanded to goods such as wildlife, counterfeits, arms, and ammunition. The UNODC did not originally address these issues as a dedicated problem of the maritime domain. This changed substantially with the creation of its Global Maritime Crime Programme (GMCP) in 2010. Initiated as a project that aimed to ensure human rights standards in the prisons where Somali pirates were incarcerated, the program has significantly expanded as the main provider of maritime security capacity-building in the criminal justice sector (see Chapter 7, Section 7.6).

A second set of global IOs was established through UNCLOS (see Chapter 3, Section 3.2). The International Tribunal for the Law of the Sea (ITLOS) is a court in Hamburg established to settle maritime boundary disputes and competing territorial claims. Since its inception in 1996 it has resolved more than 25 cases through arbitration and judgments. UNCLOS also established the International Seabed Authority (ISA) based in Kingston, Jamaica. The ISA has responsibility for the governance of deep-sea ocean resource exploitation in areas outside national jurisdiction. Its task is to provide rules for deep seabed mining and ensure the equitable distribution of risks, technologies, and revenues from such activities. While not directly relevant to the maritime security agenda of the present, it could become important if deep-sea mining and disputes become common in the future. Finally, the Division for Ocean Affairs and the Law of the Sea was installed in the UN General Secretariat as the secretariat of UNCLOS. Its mandate is to oversee ratification, to store submissions of countries concerning territorial claims, to provide capacity-building on the law of the sea, and to organize a regular assessment of the state of the oceans, which includes maritime security concerns.

With the expansion of the maritime security agenda, other IOs have also become active in the maritime domain. The International Criminal Police

---

[27] "United Nations Convention against Transnational Organized Crime" (UNDOC, 2023), www.unodc.org/unodc/en/organized-crime/intro/UNTOC.html.

[28] "Convention against Corruption" (UNDOC, 2003), www.unodc.org/unodc/en/treaties/CAC/index.html.

Organization (Interpol) coordinates information sharing and international law enforcement operations and provides capacity-building to help combat issues such as piracy, illicit fishing, or pollution crimes. The UN Environment Programme (UNEP) runs the Regional Seas Programme. This focuses on sustainable development and environmental protection, including issues such as pollution crimes. Likewise, the UN Development Programme (UNDP) is active in ocean governance and capacity-building, including the fight against environmental crimes at sea. The International Organization for Migration (IOM) and the UN High Commissioner for Refugees (UNHCR) addresses irregular migration at sea. The UN Conference on Trade and Development (UNCTAD) monitors maritime shipping trends, while the International Labour Organization (ILO) is in charge of regulating employment conditions at sea. The World Tourism Organization (UNWTO) regulates the maritime tourism industry, and IOs such as the International Hydrographic Organization (IHO), the UN Educational, Scientific, and Cultural Organization (UNESCO), and the World Meteorological Organization (WMO) provide standards, maps, navigational aids, and data for maritime domain awareness.

Our short review of relevant global organizations would not be complete without also flagging the importance of the UN Security Council in maritime security. As the most important global international security forum with substantial legal powers, the Security Council has assumed an important role in maritime security. Starting out from resolutions on piracy in the 2000s (see Chapter 5, Section 5.3), it has since become an important venue for the discussion of issues such as illicit migration by sea and grey-zone incidents such as those in the Strait of Hormuz and Baltic Sea. The number of Security Council statements and resolutions on maritime security has expanded significantly since the 2000s, making it one of the key global forums for maritime security matters.[29] This role was reinforced in 2021 when the Council held its first general debate on maritime security, including a discussion on whether a new permanent institutional structure for the issue should be established.[30]

This review documents how complex and multifaceted the landscape of global IOs is, which raises questions of their relations, how complexity can be managed, and how duplication of effort and competition between IOs can be avoided. This complexity increases significantly when regional IOs are also considered.

---

[29] Brian Wilson, "The Turtle Bay Pivot: How the United Nations Security Council Is Reshaping Naval Pursuit of Nuclear Proliferators, Rogue States, and Pirates," *Emory International Law Review* 33, no. 1 (2018): 1–90.

[30] UN Security Council, S/2021/722, August 12, 2021.

Regional IOs

Major regional organizations have also incorporated maritime security into their agendas in one way or another. In Europe, both the North Atlantic Treaty Organization (NATO) and the EU have significant ambitions to develop maritime security solutions. Both organizations have been proactive in running counterterrorism and countersmuggling operations in the Mediterranean. They have also been involved in counterpiracy off the coast of Somalia, sending multinational naval missions to the region. NATO's primary focus is on counterterrorism operations and grey-zone activities with a focus on European waters and the North Atlantic. The EU has a dedicated maritime security strategy that lays out its ambition to become a global maritime security provider.[31] It runs a wide range of naval operations and capacity-building initiatives with a focus on the Mediterranean, the Gulf of Guinea, and the Western Indian Ocean.[32]

The Association of Southeast Asian Nations (ASEAN), the Pacific Islands Forum, and the Indian Ocean Rim Association are examples of other regional IOs that have developed key maritime security roles. On the African continent, all major regional organizations discuss maritime security and some have produced dedicated strategies and policies, including the African Union , the Southern African Development Community, the Economic Community of Central African States, the Economic Community of West African States , the Indian Ocean Commission , and the Gulf of Guinea Commission. On the American continent likewise a range of organizations have developed a profile in maritime security. These include the Organization of American States , the Caribbean Community , the Organisation of Eastern Caribbean States , and the Southern Common Market. These IOs are important for regional coordination, but also play a significant role in regional capacity-building (see Chapter 7, Section 7.6) and facilitate informal partnerships with regional nonmembers.

Informal Organizations

As we discuss in greater detail in Chapter 7, many maritime security issues are dealt with through informal international and regional arrangements. These organizational formats provide greater flexibility and are often used to develop standards and guidelines, which later inform formal decisions in global and regional IOs.

---

[31] European Commission, "The EU Maritime Security Strategy and Its Action Plan," 2023, https://eur-lex.europa.eu/legal-content/EN/TXT/?uri=CELEX:52023JC0008.

[32] Christian Bueger and Timothy Edmunds, "The European Union's Quest to Become a Global Maritime Security Provider," *US Naval War College Review* 76, no. 2 (Spring 2023): xx–xx.

Maritime security has been discussed at a high level of political representation in the Group of 7 (G7) and the Group of 20 (G20) where joint declarations have been issued. For example, the G7's 2015 Lübeck Declaration on Maritime Security was an important milestone advancing holistic maritime security thinking among senior political decision-makers.[33] Other important examples at a strategic governmental level relevant for maritime security include so-called mini-lateral arrangements. The trilateral agreement for security cooperation between Australia, the United Kingdom, and the United States, known as AUKUS, was formed in 2021 out of an earlier intelligence partnership and aims at strengthening the relation between these countries in information sharing, naval capability development, and interoperability.[34] The Quadrilateral Cooperation mechanism, known as the Quad, between Australia, India, Japan, and the United States, started as a loose coordinating body and dialogue forum on security in the Indo-Pacific and has increasingly become more institutionalized.[35] As part of this process it has developed significant ambitions in maritime security too.[36] The cooperation between Brazil, Russia, India, China, and South Africa, known as BRICS, is another example for such a format. While initially less focused on maritime or security questions, it has started to address issues of ocean governance and blue crimes.[37]

A wide range of informal formats address maritime security at a more technical and operational level. These include regional coast guard forums, such as the Arctic Coast Guard Forum, North Atlantic Coast Guard Forum, or European Coast Guard Functions Forum; navy-to-navy forums, such as the Indian Ocean Naval Symposium; and coordination mechanisms, such as the Shared Awareness and Deconfliction mechanisms in the Western Indian Ocean and Mediterranean or the Yaoundé Code of Conduct, the Djibouti Code of Conduct, or the Co-ordination for the South Atlantic Maritime Area. Many of

---

[33] "G7 Foreign Ministers' Declaration on Maritime Security" (Lübeck, April 2015), https://www.mofa.go.jp/files/000076378.pdf.

[34] Niklas Swanström and Jagannath Panda, eds., *AUKUS: Resetting European Thinking on the Indo-Pacific?* (Stockholm: Institute for Security and Development Policy, 2021), https://isdp.eu/content/uploads/2021/10/AUKUS-Resetting-European-Thinking-on-the-Indo-Pacific-9.11.21.pdf.

[35] Siling Yang and Jilei Ren, "The Quad: From Loose Coordination Toward an Alliance," *East Asian Affairs* 02, no. 01 (June 2022): 2250004.

[36] Tom Corben, Blake Herzinger, Tomohiko Satake, Ashley Townshend, and Darshana M. Baruah, *Bolstering the Quad: The Case for a Collective Approach to Maritime Security* (Sydney: United States Studies Centre, 2023), https://www.ussc.edu.au/analysis/bolstering-the-quad-the-case-for-a-collective-approach-to-maritime-security.

[37] Adriana Erthal Abdenur, Maiara Folly, Kayo Moura, Sergio A. S. Jordão, and Pedro dos Santos Maia, "The BRICS and the South Atlantic: Emerging Arena for South–South Cooperation," *South African Journal of International Affairs* 21, no. 3 (September 2014): 303–319.

these technical informal formats also promote information sharing and maritime domain awareness.

There are also numerous issue specific informal IOs. The Contact Group on Piracy off the Coast of Somalia (see Chapter 7, Section 7.2), for example, was a core vehicle to organize the fight against piracy in the region, while the Southern Route Partnership is an informal alignment to coordinate counternarcotics operations and capacity-building across the Indian Ocean. Several important agreements also are run under the auspices of the UNEP Regional Seas program and focus on marine pollution specifically with various degrees of formality. Often these informal arrangements are the outcome of international capacity-building activities by formal IOs, such as the IMO, UNODC, or the EU.

A telling example of how such informal, technical organizations evolve over time and increasingly institutionalize is the Djibouti Code of Conduct (DcoC).[38] Starting out from a series of meetings facilitated by the IMO, states from the Arab Peninsula and Eastern and Southern Africa agreed in 2009 on an officially signed code to collaborate closely and share information. This collaboration was a response to the problem of piracy off the coast of Somalia, and the agreement initially limited to it. The states agreed to work through three information sharing centers and to develop a joint regional training center. While the centers were formally established their activity was limited, and the DcoC instead became an important vehicle to coordinate and deliver capacity-building with support of the IMO secretariat. Meetings of member states led to the conclusion that the remit of the agreement should be widened to include the full spectrum of maritime security issues (known as the Jeddah amendments of 2017). With the widened mandate in place and with a steer by the IMO secretariat and a donor trust fund, the frequency of meetings increased, and governance structures were developed. The focus turned toward national capacity-building and formulating regional standards. The quest to turn the agreement into a legally binding regional treaty, or to install a permanent secretariat, however, was ongoing in 2023.

Summary

IOs are important in maritime security because they allow for the negotiation of shared standards and norms, provide mechanisms for ensuring compliance

---

[38] Formally the Djibouti Code of Conduct concerning the repression of piracy, armed robbery against ships in the Western Indian Ocean and the Gulf of Aden. The history of the arrangement is well documented at IMO. Djibouti Code of Conduct, available at www.dcoc.org; see also Robert McCabe, "Western Indian Ocean: Multilateral Capacity Building Initiatives," in *Capacity Building for Maritime Security: The Western Indian Ocean Experience*, edited by Christian Bueger, Timothy Edmunds and Robert McCabe (Basingstoke: Palgrave MacMillan, 2021), 131–162.

with these, and offer means for conflict resolution. They enable the pooling of resources and expertise to enhance the effectiveness of operations or capacity-building. They are also important watchdogs for alerting the international community to new risks and threats. However, the complexity of different mandates and sheer number of organizations involved in the global field of maritime security also implies that there is the risk of competition between IOs, as well as the potential for duplication and even contradiction in their activities.

One key governance challenge is the question of whether maritime security is better approached at a global level or on a regional one. While the argument can be made that maritime security issues differ radically across regions, the regional approach faces the challenge of establishing the right scope, such as whether piracy off the coast of Somalia is an African or an Indian Ocean problem, but also how to transfer lessons and coordinate across regions. Given the global character of transport and fisheries, the connectivity of maritime ecosystems, and the lack of funding and resources for maritime security, a regional approach to maritime security is also dependent on the global level.

6.4 Profit: The Industry and Private Security Providers

Throughout history commercial interests have played a defining role in the exploration, use, and exploitation of the global ocean. Today, the commercial maritime economy has grown to an unprecedented extent. Over 80% of the volume of global trade is carried by sea, and some predictions indicate that the value of the international maritime economy will rise to USD 3 trillion by 2030.[39] The maritime industry is also recognized to be a significant factor in economic growth. This is captured by terms such as "blue growth" or "blue economy," which refer to attempts to increase maritime economic activities in a sustainable and environmentally friendly way.[40]

Private companies are important actors in maritime security. They assume two roles. First, they can become the target of maritime threats, such as piracy

---

[39] UNCTAD, "Review of Maritime Transport 2022: Navigating Stormy Waters" (New York: United Nations Publications, 2022), https://unctad.org/system/files/official-document/rmt2022_en.pdf, xv; OECD, "The Ocean Economy in 2030" (Paris: OECD Publishing, 2016), https://www.oecd.org/ocean/topics/ocean-economy/, 13.

[40] See the discussion of the blue economy in Christian Bueger and Felix Mallin, "Blue Paradigms: Understanding the Intellectual Revolution in Global Ocean Politics," *International Affairs* 99, no. 4 (June 2023), 1719–1739.

or terrorist attacks. This raises the question of who has the responsibility of protecting them. However, private companies are also sometimes directly or indirectly involved in blue crimes, for example if they engage in (or are used to facilitate) environmental crimes such as illicit fishing or pollution. They might also indirectly spur extremist violence or blue crimes if they carry out their business in a way that exacerbates the root causes of maritime insecurity (see Chapter 3, Section 3.5).

The main interest of maritime commercial actors is the pursuit of profit. While in principle they share a common interest with other actors in creating a secure maritime environment, their primary rationale for doing so is to reduce costs and potential liabilities. High levels of maritime insecurity can interfere with legitimate economic activities, while countermeasures such as diverting ships or installing new security systems can also be expensive. For this reason, the industry has tended to try to place the burdens and costs for maritime security solutions and protection on states. Insecurity at sea has also created new business opportunities for some commercial actors such as the insurance and private security sectors.

In this section, we first provide an overview of the different types of maritime commercial sectors. We then zoom in on the specific role of the shipping industry and private security providers, focusing on the case of piracy off the coast of Somalia. We end with a discussion of the wider relationship between maritime security issues and the blue economy.

An Overview of Commercial Actors in the Maritime Sector

The private commercial actors relevant for maritime security span a range of different sectors. These include the transport industry, such as shipping, ports, and logistics, together with associated service industries such as insurance or salvage companies. Extractive industries are also active in the maritime domain, including those sourcing energy from the sea through oil and gas platforms or offshore wind and solar farms, and those in the food sector who derive revenue from aquaculture and fisheries. Seabed mining is a prospectively emerging sector too. Cable industries in telecommunication and electricity own and operate cables on the ocean floor. Tourism companies offer services ranging from beach holidays, diving tours, and ocean cruises, to running luxury superyachts. Manufacturing companies build and repair ships, and supply vessels and equipment to maritime security agencies. Finally, the private security industry provides a range of protective services to various actors working in or moving through the maritime domain.

Maritime industries are highly concentrated, and a large share of the maritime economy is in the hands of a few transnational companies. A 2021 study found that the 100 largest corporations, across sectors, accounted for 60% of total revenues, or USD 1.1 trillion.[41] About half of these companies are in the oil and gas sector. Five of the 10 largest companies are in container shipping, which together control 85% of the market. There is also a concentration of profit, with around half the revenue from the global maritime economy ending up in only seven countries: the United States, Saudi Arabia, China, Norway, France, and the United Kingdom.[42] This means that some maritime companies have significant international power and influence. In some countries, such as Denmark or Norway, a large part of the gross domestic product is created by maritime industries, while some small island states, such as Seychelles, are fully dependent on them.

The maritime economy is well organized in associations that represent the industry's interests. In the shipping world, the International Chamber of Shipping, the World Shipping Council, the Baltic and International Maritime Organization, and the International Association of Independent Tanker Owners are key actors; the port industry is organized in associations such as International Association of Ports and Harbors; extractive industries in bodies such as the International Association of Oil & Gas Producers and the International Coalition of Fisheries Associations; and cable operators are organized in the International Cable Protection Committee, while the offshore wind industry coordinates through bodies such as the Global Wind Energy Council or the Global Wind Organisation. These associations are important because companies tend to delegate negotiations with states or lobbying work to them. They also often have an important standard-setting role for their members, for instance by providing maritime security guidance or standard contracts. Figure 6.3 provides examples of key maritime industries and associations.

Maritime industries have a long history of self-governance and regulation based on private contracts and industry standards. The major international shipping associations, for example, convene a regular roundtable in London to coordinate and discuss maritime security and how to represent their interests at the IMO. The Baltic and International Maritime Organization is one of the most important developers of standard contracts for shipping and produces guidance documents on issues such as maritime cyber security. The Lloyds War Committee is the main international body that determines shipping insurance premiums and maritime security risk. Classification societies not only implement international conventions for the safety of shipping, but also introduce and

---

[41] J. Virdin, T. Vegh, J.-B. Jouffray, R. Blasiak, S. Mason, H. Österblom, D. Vermeer, H. Wachtmeister, and N. Werner, "The Ocean 100: Transnational Corporations in the Ocean Economy," *Science Advances* 7, no. 3 (January 2021): 1–2.

[42] Virdin et al., "The Ocean 100," 3.

Sector	Examples of Key Associations	Major Companies
Shipping	International Chamber of Shipping (ICS), the World Shipping Council (WSC), the Baltic and International Maritime Organization (BIMCO), the International Association of Independent Tanker Owners (INTERTANKO), classification societies	A.P. Moeller-Maersk, Mediterranean Shipping Company, Cosco Shipping
Ports	International Association of Ports and Harbors (IAPH)	DP World, Shanghai International Port Group, CK Hutchinson Holdings
Energy	International Association of Oil & Gas Producers (IOGP), Global Wind Energy Council, the Global Wind Organisation, the Oil Companies Marine Forum (OCIMF)	Saudi Aramco, Petrobas, ExxonMobil, Royal Dutch Shell, Oested
Seafood	International Coalition of Fisheries Associations (ICFA)	Maruha Nichiro, Nippon Suisan Kaisha, Dongwon Enterprise
Communication	International Cable Protection Committee (ICPC)	Meta, Google
Tourism	Cruise Lines International Association (CLIA)	Carnival Corporation, Royal Caribbean Cruises, Norwegian Cruise Lines
Insurance	International Union of Marine Insurance (IUMI), The International Group of P&I Clubs (IGP&I)	Lloyds of London, Gard P&I, Assuranceforeningen SKULD, UK Mutual Steam Ship

Figure 6.3 Key maritime industries and associations

monitor their own technical standards, which in turn has consequences for insurance costs.

This culture of self-governance has deep historical roots linked to the need to manage the risks of colonial trade and exploration. It also derives from the fact that so much maritime industry activity takes place in lightly regulated spaces such as EEZs, or in areas beyond national jurisdiction on the high seas. In addition, the principles of flag state regulation under UNCLOS give the industry significant autonomy (see Chapter 3, Section 3.2). These factors can make the industry resistant to cooperation with maritime security initiatives, for instance if they introduce new regulations or reporting requirements or increase costs of operation in other ways.

Industry autonomy under the open registry regime also has important implications (see Chapter 3, Section 3.2). Many shipping companies flag their vessels to open registry states to save costs. However most open registry states only have limited regulatory capacity and minimal naval forces. This means that they have few, if any, means to provide protection for the vessels they are responsible for, prosecute criminal activities on board, or in some cases enforce regulations.

Maritime Security Responses and the Commercial Sector

Shipping has long been regulated to avoid accidents, improve working conditions, and save lives at sea.[43] The most important treaty in this respect is the International Convention for the Safety of Life at Sea (SOLAS).[44] SOLAS traces its origins to the Titanic disaster of 1912, after which the first version of the Convention was adopted. SOLAS, which now operates under the auspices of the IMO, specifies minimum standards for shipping. These are formally enforced by flag states and informally by classification societies and insurance. The convention has been frequently amended with new provisions.

One of the most important amendments to SOLAS for maritime security purposes was the ISPS Code.[45] Adopted in 2002 in reaction to the 9/11 attacks, it was the first time that the shipping industry was specifically asked to pay attention to maritime security concerns. The Code sets out technical standards for the industry, including the need for a dedicated company security officer, ship security assessments and internal audits. It thus placed a significant burden on the shipping industry to contribute to counterterrorism efforts. The ISPS Code was important because it clarified that the shipping industry is a significant and direct actor in maritime security and confirmed the expectation that it should take over certain responsibilities in this area.

The role and responsibilities of the shipping industry in maritime security were the subject of intense debate during the rise of piracy off the coast of Somalia (see Chapter 5, Section 5.3). Piracy had been on the industry's radar since the 1980s, and associations recurrently called on states to take the issue seriously. Piracy off the coast of Somalia, however, made the problem more serious and costly. When the number of attacks increased, shipowners faced higher insurance premiums, higher fuel costs due to the rerouting of vessels, delays, and

---

[43] For a historical overview see James Parsons and Chad Allen, "The history of safety management," in *Managing Maritime Safety*, edited By Helle Oltedal and Margareta Lützhöft (London: Routledge, 2018), 16–32.

[44] "International Convention for the Safety of Life at Sea (SOLAS)" (IMO, 1974), accessed January 11, 2024, https://www.imo.org/en/About/Conventions/Pages/International-Convention-for-the-Safety-of-Life-at-Sea-(SOLAS),-1974.aspx.

[45] "International Ship and Port Security Code."

onerous new liabilities and insurance costs. There was also a significant human cost to shipping company employees subject to threat, kidnap, and violence.

In consequence, the shipping industry advocated for a strong state-led counterpiracy response, initially favoring solutions such as naval patrols. This position derived from a common view in the industry that security at sea was the business of states who were obliged to ensure freedom of navigation. It was also due to concerns about the potential cost of an integrated response with industry, especially given experiences with the ISPS Code and counterterrorism. The gathering pace and severity of the piracy problem in the Western Indian Ocean forced shipowners to revisit this position.

At the heart of this change was a collective decision, by key international organizations, states, and the shipping industry itself, to accommodate the use of armed private security guards on ships.[46] Historically, this practice had been strongly resisted by the industry due to concerns about cost and liability. However, the rising cost of piracy and the initial limited success of state-led counterpiracy responses to eliminate the problem encouraged the sector to reconsider. These changes were facilitated by the IMO in partnership with shipping industry representatives and other actors, which, in 2011, offered tentative support for the employment of military or private armed guards on vessels transiting areas at risk from piracy attack. This position was adopted by a range of other public and private maritime stakeholders, including, significantly, the maritime insurance industry, which began to offer lower premiums to shipping companies employing such measures.

This shift in the IMO and industry's position was accompanied by a series of other measures. These included the industry-led delineation of a high-risk area for shipping, where vessel self-protection measures were recommended, and the publication of best management practices to support this. At the heart of these recommendations, was close collaboration between the shipping industry and the navies operating in the region (see Chapter 7, Section 7.1). Commercial shipping was also integrated into various maritime domain awareness and information sharing systems, the aim of which was to coordinate across the various actors involved in counterpiracy and other maritime security responses (see Chapter 7, Section 7.5).

Taken together, these developments have had significant consequences for maritime security. They have led to a partial shift in responsibility from the state to the private sector in the fight against piracy and other areas of maritime security, such as the protection of offshore installations. While states have continued to engage in counterpiracy efforts of various sorts, greater emphasis has been placed

---

[46] Åsne Kalland Aarstad, "Maritime Security and Transformations in Global Governance," *Crime, Law and Social Change* 67, no. 3 (April 2017): 313–331.

on shipowners to ensure (and pay for) their own protection, whether through vessel hardening measures or the employment of armed guards. It is notable that at least in the case of counterpiracy, for example, it is the shipping industry that set the agenda for the wider global response to the problem, albeit in ways that were facilitated and enabled by international organizations such as the IMO.

The practice of using armed guards on commercial vessels when transiting areas where there is a significant risk of pirate attack became normalized. In 2010, for example, only 5% of vessels attacked by Somali pirates were armed, while by 2012 as many as 33,000 merchant ships—over half of all those passing off the coast of Somalia—carried armed guards.[47]

In consequence of these developments, the maritime private security sector has grown significantly since 2010, to an estimated global value of nearly USD 25 billion in 2019.[48] Maritime private security companies provide a range of services to shipping and other commercial actors in the maritime sector. These include intelligence services to inform route planning and company risk assessments; protective services such as advice on vessel hardening measures and the supply of guards to ports and installations and on board vessels; and crisis response services, such as ransom negotiations and the repatriation of kidnapped seafarers. In some cases, private security providers have been used to supply or augment coast guard functions too, including migrant rescue in the Mediterranean, the provision of helicopter and drone surveillance services to national agencies, and undertaking patrolling tasks in the Gulf of Guinea. In Nigeria, for example, private security providers operate in a complex hybrid system with state security actors, including the assignment of naval personnel to privately owned and operated patrol vessels. This approach has been controversial due to accusations that it has fueled corruption and criminalization in the Nigerian security sector.[49]

The Blue Economy and Maritime Security

Another way of framing the discussion of the role of commercial actors is through the link between blue economy and maritime security.[50] Both are

---

[47] Jan Stockbruegger, "US Strategy and the Rise of Private Maritime Security," *Security Studies* 30, no. 4 (August 2021): 597.

[48] Stockbruegger, "US Strategy and the Rise of Private Maritime Security," 583.

[49] Okechukwu Iheduru, "Hybrid Maritime Security Governance and Limited Statehood in the Gulf of Guinea: A Nigerian Case Study," *Journal of Military and Strategic Studies* 22, no. 3 (2023): 133–138.

[50] See the discussion in Michelle Voyer, Clive H. Schofield, Kamal Azmi, Robin M. Warner, and Alistair McIlgorm, "Maritime Security and the Blue Economy: Intersections and Interdependencies in the Indian Ocean," *Journal of the Indian Ocean Region* 14, no. 1 (January 2018): 28–48.

mutually interdependent. Seizing new economic opportunities at sea requires a certain level of maritime security to be viable. Yet as we have emphasized in our discussion of root causes (see Chapter 3, Section 3.5), economic dislocation can also facilitate the growth of blue crimes. This relationship makes the commercial sector an important potential factor in addressing some of the core drivers of maritime insecurity. Since industry can create job opportunities for coastal communities in sustainable sectors such as tourism or green energy, it can also play an indirect role in enhancing maritime security.

The reverse can also be true. Extractive industries have been linked to the rise of extremist violence and blue crimes.[51] If extraction causes environmental destruction through pollution or overfishing, and if revenues from exploitation are not equitably distributed, then this can provide justifications for supporting or engaging in terrorism or criminal activities at sea. The outbreak of piracy in the Gulf of Guinea, for instance, has been at least partially linked to resistance against the extractive industries in Nigeria.[52] Another example is the rise of extremist violence in Northern Mozambique that was linked to the start of gas extraction activities off the coast.[53] There is also a risk that companies feed corruption in their businesses and hence weaken national and local maritime security sectors.

Summary

The role of the private sector in maritime security has been concentrated around those threats and issues most directly linked to the interests of global capital such as piracy. International shipping and the protection of global trade is the emblematic example in this respect. Other maritime security issues, such as those relating to environmental crime or trafficking activities, have attracted considerably less attention. In part this is because such issues do not impact directly on company profits. It is also because the countermeasures they imply, such as greater scrutiny or regulation of company activities, may impose additional costs to industry and undermine commercial autonomy. For this reason, it should be recognized that while the private sector remains a critical actor in maritime security, it is also one whose engagement can be highly problematic as

---

[51] For a review, see Michael L. Ross, "The Political Economy of the Resource Curse," *World Politics* 51, no. 2 (January 1999): 297–322.

[52] Martin N. Murphy, "Petro-Piracy: Oil and Troubled Waters," *Orbis* 57, no. 3 (June 2013): 424–437.

[53] Fernando Jorge Cardoso, "Cabo Delgado: Insurgents, Jihadists or Terrorists?," IMVF Policy Paper, 2021, https://www.imvf.org/wp-content/uploads/2021/08/imvf-policy-paper-9-2021-cabo-delgado-insurgents-jihadists-or-terrorists.pdf.

it is driven primarily by the logic of the market rather than notions of security as a public good.

6.5 More Than Protest? Nongovernmental Organizations and Activists

Nongovernmental, civil society and activist organizations are of growing importance in maritime security.[54] They perform many different roles. Often they act as watchdogs and critical voices evaluating state or company activities, but they can also provide important support functions, such as expertise, data, or even directly take over maritime security tasks at sea.

What constitutes an NGO can be difficult to determine.[55] While NGOs are nonstate and nonprofit actors that work for political, humanitarian, environmental, or community goals, the boundaries with those pursuing commercial interests or even with violent actors are sometimes difficult to draw. Some NGOs use direct action and violence in their protests, for example, and have been labeled by some as "ecoterrorists" as a result. The work of others is directly funded by companies who have an underlying business interest in the issue at hand.[56] Still others rely on philanthropies, which might have specific partisan priorities.[57] Other NGOs, such as the International Union for Conservation and Nature, have governments as members or funders, further complicating the picture. Often NGOs form transnational coalitions and alliances, collapsing these distinctions further. Examples include the Ocean Risk and Resilience Action Alliance, which aims at developing innovative funding solutions, or the Universal Ranger Support Alliance, which develops professional standards for coast guards and other staff working in protected areas.

Keeping these classification challenges and substantial number of NGOs working in various networks, coalitions, and alliances in mind, it is useful to categorize organizations according to the scale in which they work (local, national, or international) and the issue area they focus on. Grassroots organizations in

---

[54] Antje Scharenberg, "Sea Changes: How Ocean Activism Reshapes the Way We See Borders, Sovereignty and Power," *The Sociological Review Magazine*, August 2022.

[55] See for example: Anna C. Vakil, "Confronting the Classification Problem: Toward a Taxonomy of NGOs," *World Development* 25, no. 12 (December 1997): 2057–2070.

[56] This includes, for instance, industry funded NGOs such as the International Maritime Bureau or the Maritime Anti-Corruption Network.

[57] Marc-Andrej Felix Mallin, Dennis C. Stolz, Benjamin S. Thompson, and Mads Barbesgaard, "In Oceans We Trust: Conservation, Philanthropy, and the Political Economy of the Phoenix Islands Protected Area," *Marine Policy* 107 (September 2019): 103421.

coastal communities, such as associations of fishermen often play a key role at a local level, support those in need, and do not necessarily specialize in issues. Other NGOS engaged in advocacy and activism in the environmental or human rights field commonly work at a regional, transnational, or even global level.

In the following section we discuss these types of NGOs before focusing on two issues where the sector is particularly active: illicit fishing and irregular migration. We then sum up the major functions that NGOs perform in maritime security.

Local NGOs

Local NGOs are primarily interested in a specific local region or country, where they represent the interests of coastal communities, subsistence fishermen, and leisure activities (e.g., sailing or surfing clubs), or address local environmental concerns.

The recognition that maritime security is often driven by local logics has done much to increase the influence of such organizations (see Chapter 3, Section 3.5). Security actors have come to realize that listening to these actors can facilitate their understandings of when and how marine security threats emerge. Counterpiracy in Somalia, for example, benefitted from direct engagements with village elders and women's rights organizations. This helped to decrease the legitimacy of and public support for pirate organizations, making recruitment and logistics more difficult.[58]

Local NGOs can also be important partners in raising awareness, drawing attention to suspicious activities, or in combating blue crimes more directly. In this way, they can play an important role in wider maritime domain awareness activities (see Chapter 7, Section 7.5). The United Kingdom, for example, established an initiative called Project Kraken in 2007 to encourage members of the public and community organizations to report suspicious incidents that might indicate preparations for criminal or terrorist activities on the coastline.[59] The Joint Maritime Information Coordination Center of Pakistan's navy has staff that regularly tour through regional communities and meet representatives to gather knowledge and ensure collaboration and reporting.

In some cases, local or national NGOs can also contribute to maritime safety and security directly. The United Kingdom's Royal National Lifeboat Institution,

---

[58] Christian Bueger, "Drops in the Bucket? A Review of Onshore Responses to Somali Piracy," *WMU Journal of Maritime Affairs* 11, no. 1 (April 2012): 15–31.

[59] Duncan Weaver, "Project Kraken: Surveillance and Liminality "On the Edge" of Land and Water," *Geopolitics* 27, no. 1 (January 2022): 334–335.

for example, is the country's largest charity and plays a critical role in national search and rescue operations at sea.[60] Others, such as the NGO Eco-Sud in Mauritius, take up direct environmental management responsibilities in marine protected areas.

International NGOs

At an international level, a wide range of NGOs address maritime security related issues. These can be broadly clustered around the scope of their work, with the majority of NGOs addressing environmental policy and protection issues, followed by those working in the humanitarian field, and to a lesser extent NGOs that target crime, or maritime security specifically. Figure 6.4 provides a range of paradigmatic examples of such NGOs.

Focus Area	Examples	Issues
Environment	Environmental Justice Foundation (EJF), Greenpeace, International Union for the Conservation of Nature (IUCN), World Wide Fund for Nature (WWF), SkyTruth	Environmental crimes, marine protection
Oceans	Global Fishing Watch, Oceana, Ocean Conservancy, Pew Charitable Trusts, Sea Shepherd Conservation Society, Spyglass, Too Big To Ignore	Illicit fishing, marine protection
Humanitarian	International Red Cross and Red Crescent Movement (ICRC), Médecins Sans Frontières (MSF), Sea-Watch, SOS Méditerranée	Irregular migration, trafficking, people smuggling
Human Rights	Human Rights at Sea	Slavery and human rights violations
Crime	Transnational Initiative against Organized Crime, Wildlife Justice Commission	Narcotic and people smuggling, illicit fishing
Maritime Security	International Maritime Bureau (IMB), Maritime Anti-Corruption Network (MACN), SafeSeas, Stable Seas, Stop Illegal Fishing	Blue crimes, maritime terrorism, corruption

Figure 6.4 Examples of global NGOs in the maritime security field

---

[60] Royal National Lifeboat Institution, accessed June 7, 2023, https://rnli.org/.

In the environmental field, NGOs have emerged as an important challenger to state policies. Greenpeace, the Sea Shepherd Conservation Society, and Ocean Rebellion are the most well-known NGOs in this regard.

An early influential case of the role of NGOs in marine environmental security was the Rainbow Warrior incident of 1985.[61] Greenpeace had been actively protesting at sea against whaling and seal hunting since the 1970s, but also against nuclear testing and nuclear waste dumping in the South Pacific. Greenpeace acquired a range of vessels to stage protests at sea, one of which was the Rainbow Warrior. Planning to protest against French nuclear testing, the vessel was sunk while anchored in New Zealand's territorial waters with involvement of the French government, leading to the death of one activist. The incident led to a public outcry and substantial support for Greenpeace.

The role of NGOs in maritime security has changed substantially since then. While some activists, such as Ocean Rebellion, continue to act primarily as protest platforms raising awareness of climate change and blue justice concerns, other NGOs have turned toward supporting states with weak maritime security and maritime domain awareness capacities.

This shift is perhaps most visible in the case of the Sea Shepherd Conservation Society.[62] Formed in the late 1970s by former Greenpeace members that were ousted because they supported direct action rather than peaceful protest, the NGO primarily focused on disrupting whaling and seal hunting operations. From the 1990s it turned its attention to the fight against illicit fishing, and increasingly understands itself as an anti-poaching organization. In this role, Sea Shepherd has worked to assist states in their efforts to combat IUU fishing (see Chapter 5, Section 5.5). This includes direct support at sea, working with navies and coast guards in states such as Costa Rica, Gabon, and São Tomé and Príncipe.

NGOs often take over important functions that governments do not want or are not able to perform. An example is the role of NGOs in providing maritime security expertise such as data collection and statistical analyses to provide orientation and guidance for policymakers and practitioners. The Global Initiative against Transnational Organized Crime, for instance, operates an IUU Fishing Index, laying out how well countries are equipped to deal with the problem of illicit fishing.[63] The United States-based NGO Stable Seas runs a Maritime

---

[61] Ramesh Thakur, "A Dispute of Many Colours: France, New Zealand and the 'Rainbow Warrior' Affair," *The World Today* 42, no. 12 (1986): 209–214.

[62] Claude Berube, *Sea Shepherd: The Evolution of an Eco-Vigilante to Legitimized Maritime Capacity Builder* (Newport, RI: US Naval War College, 2021).

[63] "IUU Fishing Index 2021," Global Initiative Against Organized Crime, accessed June 7, 2023, https://globalinitiative.net/analysis/iuu-fishing-index-2021/.

Security Index detailing how countries are affected by maritime insecurities and how well they govern their maritime sector.[64]

Stable Seas itself evolved from the Oceans Beyond Piracy initiative, a dedicated NGO established by the One Earth Future Foundation in 2010, to support international actors in counterpiracy efforts off the coast of Somalia. The program initially acted as a facilitator between different actors engaged in counterpiracy work in the region, including hosting meetings between stakeholders. Over time, it became an important knowledge provider analyzing the human and economic costs of piracy and advocating for international action on the issue. It also supported information sharing between actors and assisted in the coordination of capacity-building work.

Key Issues Areas for NGOs

The area of maritime security where NGOs are perhaps most active is the campaign against illicit fishing. This is in part because many maritime NGOs have their origins in environmental protection work, but also due to the opportunities that new technologies provide. In addition to the Sea Shepherd case discussed above, Global Fishing Watch (GFW) is a paradigmatic example of contemporary NGO work in this area.[65] GFW is a collaboration between Oceana, a nonprofit ocean conservation organization, and SkyTruth, an NGO that specializes in using satellite and aerial images. Its goal is to support states in monitoring fishing activities by providing them with big datasets, machine learning capabilities, and cloud computing technologies to identify suspicious behavior at sea. Several state organizations, including the United States Coast Guard and the Ghana Navy, collaborate closely with GFW and draw on its data, algorithms, and analytical tools in their fisheries protection activities. A number of other NGOs also work in the fisheries sector, including the Environmental Justice Foundation, Human Rights at Sea, Ocean Conservancy, and Spyglass, to name but a few.

The other area of maritime security where NGOs have been especially active is in people smuggling and irregular migration. The work of civil society organizations on this issue has a long history, including through the work of the International Red Cross and Red Crescent Movement during the two world

---

[64] "Maritime Security Index," Stable Seas, accessed June 7, 2023, https://www.stableseas.org/services.

[65] Lauren Drakopulos, Jennifer J. Silver, Eric Nost, Noella Gray, and Roberta Hawkins, "Making Global Oceans Governance in/Visible with Smart Earth: The Case of Global Fishing Watch," *Environment and Planning E: Nature and Space* 6, no. 2 (June 2023): 1098–1113.

wars and in later humanitarian crises such as that of the Vietnamese boat people in the 1970s. In the contemporary context, the Mediterranean has emerged as a flashpoint for NGO activities, largely in response to the European migration crisis and its legacy (see Chapter 5, Section 5.5). Groups such as Médecins Sans Frontières, Sea-Watch, and SOS Mediterranee operate vessels in the region that recover people traveling on the dangerous sea route from North Africa to Europe.

For the NGOs, these are important rescue operations guided by humanitarian imperatives and the duty to save life at sea.[66] They argue that their services are necessary because coastal states and the EU do not provide sufficient resources to meet humanitarian needs, and too often approach the issue as one of border protection and immigration control rather than protection of vulnerable people at sea. This contrasts with the position of some governments in the region, who argue that proactive rescue operations lessens the risks of such journeys and thus incentivize migrants to undertake them. The case is telling because it shows the way in which NGOs can sometimes fulfil state functions in maritime security, but also that they may do so in a way that undermines the political priorities of governments.

Illicit fishing and irregular migration will continue to be focus areas for NGOs. Another movement is forming around concepts of blue justice.[67] Blue justice activists are primarily concerned about the effects of marine conservation, resource exploitation, and maritime security initiatives on coastal communities and disadvantaged states and groups. Poorly designed illicit fishing laws, for example, can undermine the livelihoods of local subsistence fishers without providing viable alternatives. Marine spatial planning initiatives and blue economy policies can risk excluding local populations in favor of large-scale economic actors. The concerns raised by blue justice activists are important for maritime security, because socioeconomic exclusion and perceptions of injustice are often key drivers of blue crime (see Chapter 3, Section 3.5).

Summary

NGOs are important but often underappreciated actors in maritime security. They function as critical watchdogs measuring compliance with legal obligations, identifying problems and raising awareness of them. However, they can also be vital partners for state agencies in addressing seablindness and improving information sharing and maritime domain awareness. They can provide important

---

[66] Itamar Mann and Julia Mour, "Floating Sanctuaries: The Ethics of Search and Rescue at Sea," *Migration Studies* 10, no. 3 (2022): 442–463.

[67] For a discussion of the concept and related initiatives see Bueger and Mallin, "Blue Paradigms."

assistance to states by producing knowledge and expertise, acting as facilitators, or even through direct operational support at sea. NGOs operating at the local level also have an important role in addressing the root causes of blue crimes. While state agencies, private actors, and NGOs often have competing priorities or diverging interpretations of the situation at sea, maritime security can be significantly strengthened through constructive engagement and collaboration with the NGO sector.

6.6 Integrating Maritime Security Actors

To gain a holistic understanding of maritime security, it is important for the analyst and professional to grasp the different types of actors involved in providing security at sea, and the different rationales and agendas they may be working to. Reconciling conflicts and ensuring coordination between these disparate rationales is one of the key challenges of maritime security.

States are the most important actors in maritime security and provide the capabilities and material necessary to combat maritime threats through their navies, coast guards, and other agencies. The maritime security sectors of most states are quite complex, comprising multiple agencies, each with their own priorities, interests, and ways of working. Coordination between these actors is a common challenge for state-level maritime security operations. This issue is even more pronounced in multinational contexts. Here, different states with their own complex structures not only encounter each other, but also the growing number of international and regional organizations dealing with maritime security issues. IOs play an important role in facilitating joint action on transnational maritime threats, but also face challenges of fragmentation, duplication, and coordination in their activities.

Commercial actors are key players in the maritime domain, including shipping and port companies and extractive industries such as fisheries and oil and gas, as well as insurance companies and private maritime security providers. They are also critical to blue economy initiatives in many parts of the world. Their maritime security concerns focus on those issues that threaten their activities and profits, such as piracy. They have tended to show less interest in problems such as illicit fishing or pollution, and in some cases may even be implicated in these activities. Finally, the nongovernmental sector has emerged as an important, though often underrecognized, player in maritime security. NGOs are often critical of states, for example in relation to marine environmental protection or irregular migration at sea. However, they make an important contribution to maritime security, whether at a local community level or through the provision of capabilities such as data analysis or search and rescue at sea.

In our next chapter, we explore the tools that these various actors have developed to address maritime security challenges. We discuss the role that informal governance arrangements have played in maritime security, continue our analysis of interagency and multinational coordination, explore information sharing and maritime domain awareness, and examine the growing importance of maritime security strategy-making. We also turn to the problem of weak state capacity in maritime security and consider how international capacity-building assistance programs have attempted to address this issue.

7

The Toolbox of Maritime Security Solutions

7.1 Identifying Solutions

A key element in the evolution of the maritime security agenda has been the development of a dedicated set of solutions. Response mechanisms and practices geared at coping with and preventing threats, handling complexity, and assisting states have gradually consolidated along the four waves of maritime security we discussed in Chapter 2. These solutions are in many ways specific to maritime security and innovative, though also often have their origins in similar practices that are used in other domains, such as land or cyber space. Some, such as informal governance and maritime domain awareness, began as experimental responses to problems with which existing solutions were struggling to cope, such as maritime terrorism and contemporary piracy. Others were adaptations of practices in common use elsewhere, such as strategy writing and capacity-building, but had not been widely deployed in the maritime sector before.

In this chapter, we introduce the toolbox of maritime security solutions that every analyst and professional should be familiar with. We start out with a discussion of informal and experimental coordination mechanisms which have been vital in addressing issues on the agenda, before turning to maritime security operations at sea. We investigate the spectrum of tasks of these operations and how they draw on innovative instruments, such as ship-rider agreements or legal transfer systems. We then discuss maritime security strategies as a tool for sense-making and coordination that has become widely used by states and regional organizations.

From there, we discuss information sharing and surveillance initiatives, known as maritime domain awareness (MDA). These aim at providing the knowledge on the patterns of activities at sea, including spotting incidents and identifying anomalous or suspicious behavior. Finally, we consider the attempts to promote these tools globally through capacity-building. We point to the strengths and the challenges associated with each of these solutions.

7.2 Informality and Experimentalism

Maritime security was a novel challenge when it first became an issue on the international security agenda. It quickly became apparent that existing national and international institutions were struggling to deal with problems such as maritime terrorism or piracy. The characteristics of maritime security—especially its multiagency, transnational, and cross-jurisdictional nature (see Chapters 1 and 2)—meant that political and security actors had to identify new ways of dealing with these problems. Since many of the challenges that shaped the early agenda were urgent in nature, such as piracy off the coast of Somalia, political actors resorted to informal and experimental governance approaches to facilitate swift responses.

What Is Informality and Experimentalism?

Informal governance approaches are attempts to coordinate and align activities outside of formal organizations (such as UN agencies and their assemblies), with minimal reliance on explicit rules or legal treaties.[1] Informal governance offers a flexible way of addressing issues outside institutional procedures which impose limits on participation or constrain how quickly an issue can be addressed. Informality can help in depoliticizing an issue by addressing it at a primarily technical or operational level. Larger political conflicts can be avoided, and the focus becomes more immediately on what is feasible and can be implemented in a given context. Meeting in such formats can strengthen interpersonal networks, which can enhance the speed and quality of information sharing as well as the levels of trust between actors.

These formats can be seen as experimental when they develop and test new ways of dealing with a problem and do not work toward institutionalization or rule formation.[2] Experimentalism has the advantage of fostering an environment for brainstorming, developing new and unconventional ideas, and bringing in new forms of expertise. It can also strengthen the willingness of actors to take

---

[1] Vincent Pouliot and Jean-Philippe Thérien, "Global Governance in Practice," *Global Policy* 9, no. 2 (2018): 163–172.

[2] Gráinne De Búrca, Robert O. Keohane, and Charles Sabel, "Global Experimentalist Governance," *British Journal of Political Science* 44, no. 3 (July 2014): 477–486.

risks in adopting new methods to deal with an issue, and encourage mutual learning.[3] Over time, experimental ideas might become settled if successful, and codified in formats such as best-practice manuals. Ultimately, they may even open the way for the creation of new formal rules and institutions, even if this was not the original intention.

Maritime Security Formats

It is quite remarkable how significant informality and experimentation have been in the responses to maritime security issues. Several different formats can be distinguished: navy-to-navy cooperation, industry-state cooperation, diplomatic forums, and capacity-building formats. These formats often partially overlap, for example when different activities or working groups are incorporated into a single initiative.

Navy-to-Navy Cooperation

Naval forces have a long-standing tradition of informal cooperation, for example through joint education at international naval academies, exercises, or symposia where matters of shared interest are discussed. In this sense, it is not surprising that many of the early responses to maritime security were driven by informal navy-to-navy cooperation. A good example is naval coordination in the Western Indian Ocean.

Two formats were developed in this region that are widely considered to be pathbreaking and innovative.[4] The Combined Maritime Forces (CMF) was an initiative by the United States to coordinate voluntary naval contributions to maritime security operations in the Western Indian Ocean.[5] Originally the main purpose was counterterrorism, but with the outbreak of Somali piracy the focus turned quickly to counterpiracy. With the decline of piracy, the focus of CMF has shifted to smuggling and the deterrence of blue crimes. CMF is organized in a way that the United States provides basic operational infrastructure, while the leadership of task forces rotates among participating navies. Naval forces are free to join or leave CMF operations in a short time span according to their mandates and operational needs.

---

[3] Christian Bueger and Timothy Edmunds, "Pragmatic Ordering: Informality, Experimentation, and the Maritime Security Agenda," *Review of International Studies* 47, no. 2 (April 2021): 7–8.

[4] Christian Bueger and Timothy Edmunds, "Beyond Seablindness: A New Agenda for Maritime Security Studies," *International Affairs* 93, no. 6 (November 2017): 1304–1305.

[5] Combined Maritime Forces (CMF), accessed June 8, 2023, https://combinedmaritimeforces.com/.

Another format that originated in this region is the so-called Shared Awareness and Deconfliction meeting, known as SHADE.[6] SHADE was established in 2008 to conduct informal discussions and de-conflict the activities of the diverse nations and organizations involved in counterpiracy operations off the Horn of Africa. Initially, SHADE included only the CMF, European Union (EU), and NATO, but it rapidly expanded to incorporate all navies active in the area, including those of China, India, Japan, Russia, South Korea, and Ukraine. One of the most successful measures developed by SHADE was the Internationally Recommended Transit Corridor—a demarcated patrol area in which coverage by naval vessels was maximized through computer modeling and joint planning. SHADE also facilitated the creation of a neutral communication channel. The platform, called MERCURY, allowed various actors—including national navies, civil information sharing centers, and law enforcement agencies—to communicate with each other through synchronous text-based chat, with a live feed on naval operations and piracy incidents providing real time data to all participants.

The SHADE concept has been replicated in other regions, with analogues in the Mediterranean to coordinate the response to irregular migration (known as SHADE Med), and in the Gulf of Guinea (known as GoG-MCF SHADE) in relation to multinational counterpiracy operations.

CMF and SHADE are two important formats that were created to deal with maritime security issues. In addition, more traditional naval cooperation formats have come to address maritime security challenges too. For instance, the Indian Ocean Naval Symposium has working groups that focus on interoperability, standards for information sharing, and coordinating the response to blue crimes in the region.[7]

Navy-Industry Cooperation

A second set of informal formats have developed to coordinate between navies and the shipping industry. Several navies operate dedicated liaison offices for this purpose. Examples include the NATO Shipping Centre, the United Kingdom Royal Navy's UK Maritime Trade Operations (UKMTO) center, and the United States Naval Forces Central Command's Naval Cooperation and Guidance for Shipping unit. Some of these initiatives are linked to specific operations. For example, the EU operates the Maritime Security Centre Horn of Africa (MSCHoA) to facilitate contact between its counterpiracy operation in the region and the shipping industry.

---

[6] Sarah Percy, "Counter-Piracy in the Indian Ocean: A New Form of Military Cooperation," *Journal of Global Security Studies* 1, no. 4 (2016): 270–284.

[7] Indian Ocean Naval Symposium, accessed June 8, 2023, https://www.ions.global/.

These formats were established to facilitate information sharing between navy and industry actors. Navies issue alerts and guidance for the shipping industry. The industry can report their routes and ask for protection in high-risk areas or inform naval forces about incidents and suspicious behavior. The centers also provide platforms for high-level meetings and communications. For example, the NATO Shipping Centre organizes an annual dialogue between the shipping industry and NATO to foster mutual understanding and cooperation.

Informal cooperation between naval and industry actors is a critical component of many maritime security operations. For example, naval staff produce threat assessments which are used by the industry to inform their own risk assessment processes. Shipping industry associations also collaborated closely with the centers described above in the fight against piracy off the coast of Somalia. These activities included joint work to draw up a best management practices guidance document,[8] which laid out self-protection recommendations for vessels transiting the region, as well as establishing procedures for how to liaise with naval forces through UKMTO and MSCHoA. Another example is the Maritime Security Construct in the Middle East. This is a multinational naval coalition that works closely with the shipping industry in response to attacks and grey-zone incidents in the Strait of Hormuz (see Chapter 4, Section 4.4).

Diplomatic Fora

Informal formats are a conventional tool in diplomacy.[9] They include more institutionalized arrangements such as the Group of 7 (G7), the Group of 20 (G20), the BRICS, and the Quad (see Chapter 6, Section 6.3), but also diplomatic dialogues or problem driven contact groups on specific issues. The purpose and functions of these formats differ, but such groupings have been key to developing maritime security responses between multiple actors.

Meetings of the G groups take place at a relatively high level, and have the purpose of crafting joint declarations, sending diplomatic signals or making funding announcements. For example, in 2015 the G7 Foreign Ministers issued a joint declaration on maritime security, which was followed by a series of expert meetings on the topic, leading to the announcement of new funding for capacity-building initiatives.[10] Since then, the G7 have frequently issued

---

[8] Christian Bueger, "Territory, Authority, Expertise: Global Governance and the Counter-Piracy Assemblage," *European Journal of International Relations* 24, no. 3 (2018): 614–637. See also Chapter 7, Section 6.4.

[9] Jochen Prantl, "Informal Groups of States and the UN Security Council," *International Organization* 59, no. 3 (July 2005): 559–592.

[10] "G7 Foreign Ministers' Declaration on Maritime Security" (Lübeck, April 2015), https://www.mofa.go.jp/files/000076378.pdf.

statements on maritime security incidents and events. An example is the grey-zone attack on the *MV Mercer Street* in 2021.[11] Meetings in these forums can also be important for preparing decisions in more formalized settings such as the UN Security Council, and for aligning policies between members at a national level.

A considerable number of diplomatic dialogues on maritime security have also been developed. These tend to take place at a lower level of representation and involve technical experts. The European Union, for example, runs several dialogues on maritime security, including with India and with the Association of Southeast Asian Nations (ASEAN). The main purpose of these meetings is to strengthen mutual understanding and exchange information and interpretations of current developments, such as new strategies. They can also lead to ideas that might translate into more concrete policies or projects, such as capacity-building initiatives.

Another set of formats are issue specific. Two groupings of this sort have been especially significant in the fight against piracy. The Contact Group on Piracy off the Coast of Somalia (CGPCS) was established as a diplomatic forum in 2009 to coordinate counterpiracy activities.[12] The CGPCS provided a flexible solution to the challenge of bringing together the substantial number of actors involved in or affected by piracy, including the major trading powers, flag states, states in the region, the shipping industry, and international and regional organizations. At the peak of the piracy crisis more than 80 states, IOs, industry associations, and NGOs were represented at the group's meetings.

The purpose of the CGPCS was to identify cooperative solutions to piracy in the region, and to function as an overarching structure to coordinate work conducted in the more technical formats, such as the SHADE mechanism discussed above. The group served as the key vehicle through which to exchange views on the situation at sea and to introduce novel proposals and initiatives, for example in developing a new system to transfer arrested pirates for trial in regional states. The CGPCS also produced joint communiques on the piracy problem that had a significant influence on subsequent UN Security Council resolutions and IMO debates on this issue.

---

[11] See Chapter 4, Section 4.4 and HMG, "MV Mercer Street Attack: G7 Foreign Ministers' Statement," Press Release, August 2021, https://www.gov.uk/government/news/mv-mercer-street-attack-g7-foreign-ministers-statement.

[12] Henk Swarttouw and Donna L. Hopkins, "The CGPCS: The Evolution of Multilateralism to Multi-Stakeholder Collaboration," in *Fighting Piracy off the Coast of Somalia: Lessons Learned from the Contact Group*, ed. Thierry Tardy (Paris: EU Institute for Security Studies, 2014), 11–17.

A similar mechanism was also created for the Gulf of Guinea region, this time under G7 leadership. Known as the G7++ Friends of the Gulf of Guinea group, it was directly modeled on the experience of the CGPCS. It operates in a similar fashion, through differs in the sense that regional countries are more strongly involved.

Interagency Coordination

Informal and experimental formats are also utilized by governments and regional organizations. As we discuss in more detail in the chapter on national actors (Chapter 6, Section 6.2) and maritime security operations (Chapter 7, Section 7.3), maritime security involves a high number of actors. Many countries have established coordination committees and operational and maritime domain awareness centers to address this issue. These arrangements can be organized at different levels ranging from ministerial to agency focused initiatives, and have various degrees of formalization in relation to the frequency of their meetings, the flexibility of their agendas, or their expected outputs. Often interagency coordination mechanisms within states are informal in nature and based on interpersonal networks rather than formal information exchanges. Within many governments, social media apps, such as WhatsApp, are used for informal coordination.

Summary

The key advantages of informal governance are speed, flexibility, and inclusivity. Joint strategies, declarations, or statements can be developed quickly because there are few institutional procedures in place to slow down the process. Matters are in the hands of the actors concerned and largely dependent only on their willingness to proceed with them. Coordination tends to be more flexible and problem-driven, rather than determined by rules and procedures. Multiple relevant actors can also be more easily included because accreditation processes are avoided.

These formats can have disadvantages too. Because they do not rely on formal agreements, there is no automatic right to be heard. This can easily lead to exclusion, if, for example, the chair of a group is not aware of the importance of including a particular actor. Another key problem is that in informal and experimental set ups no one is formally in charge. This can make it difficult to hold actors accountable for their actions or inactions. Informal formats also run the risk of becoming talking shops, particularly if the purpose of the grouping is unclear or if it continues to meet after its original purpose has been achieved.

7.3 Operations at Sea

Operations at sea are the backbone of maritime security. They serve a number of key purposes, including enhancing maritime domain awareness through patrols, hailing and inspection of vessels, the deterrence of threats, and interdictions, as well arrest and evidence collection to enable prosecutions. Maritime security operations (MSOs) are usually limited to specific areas of interest or concern. While all MSOs aim to contribute to maritime security and maritime domain awareness in that area, they are usually targeted at one or two threats and rarely have cross-cutting mandates.

Due to their regional and issue-specific focus, the characters, composition, mandates, and organizational structures of MSOs differ considerably. They tend to blend elements of naval constabulary operations and coast guard functions, as we discussed in Chapter 6, Section 6.1. Navies tend to be prominent participants because of their seagoing capacities, deployability, and planning and logistical capabilities. MSOs hence often overlap with naval operations. Yet the majority of MSOs involve multiagency collaborations, and some have no military component at all. Indeed, the routine involvement of civil and nonstate actors is one of the defining features of such operations, with a key challenge being the question of how much or how little such operations should rely on military forces and command structures.

A useful general definition of MSOs is to understand these as coordinated activities by state agencies and/or regional organizations that combine civil and military measures to reduce insecurity at sea through surveillance, deterrence, and interception.

A Review of Important Maritime Security Operations

Since MSOs are a key instrument, their evolution reflects the waves of maritime security thinking that we outlined in Chapter 2. There has been a quite remarkable growth in the number of multinational MSOs over the years.

The first generation of MSOs were established in the 2000s to combat maritime terrorism and counter the proliferation of weapons of mass destruction. Important MSOs were the Proliferation Security Initiative, established in 2003 to coordinate counterproliferation activities at sea and in ports; the CMF, which was created in 2001, initially to undertake counterterrorism operations in the Western Indian Ocean; and NATO's Operation Active Endeavour (2001–2016) in the Mediterranean.

A second generation of MSOs can be linked to counterpiracy (see Chapter 5, Section 5.3). The CMF, for example, broadened its focus from terrorism to piracy, operating alongside dedicated missions from NATO (Operation Ocean Shield, 2009–2016) and the European Union (EUNAVFOR Atalanta, 2008–present). Earlier, in 2004, Indonesia, Malaysia, Singapore, and Thailand had established the joint Malacca Straits Patrol and in 2005 the Eyes in the Sky initiative to combat piracy in the Straits of Malacca and Singapore. In 2021, the EU deployed multinational naval forces to counterpiracy operation in the Gulf of Guinea under its Coordinated Maritime Presence format. Another example is the Trilateral Sea Patrol established in 2017 by the Philippines, Indonesia, and Malaysia to combat piracy in the Sulu and Celeb Seas. Many of these counterpiracy operations have subsequently evolved to focus on a wider range of maritime challenges, such as illegal fishing or narcotics smuggling.

MSOs often involve crossovers between mission mandates, as can for instance be seen in the Mediterranean. NATOs Sea Guardian (2016–present) for example conducts sanctions enforcement, search and rescue and interdiction operations against people smuggling in the Mediterranean. The EU runs its own dedicated MSO, Operation IRINI, which is focused on the disruption of people smuggling and the enforcement of the UN arms embargo on Libya. IRINI in turn succeeded the EUs Operation Sophia mission which ran from 2015 to 2020.

Another set of operations is directed at grey-zone threats (see Chapter 4, Section 4.4). The International Maritime Security Construct and European Maritime Awareness in the Strait of Hormuz missions were formed in in 2019 and 2020 to protect shipping in the Persian Gulf and its environs, following attacks on tankers in the region's waters, allegedly by Iran.

These operations are illustrative of the way in which multinational MSOs have expanded in the period since 2000 and the range of different issues and challenges they address, from counterpiracy and counterterrorism operations to the fight against various forms of blue crime. However, it is also striking that many MSOs have endured beyond the term of their original mandates (or been replaced by successor missions) and expanded their activities into other areas of maritime security. The CMF is a good example of this phenomenon, beginning as a counterterrorism operation before shifting to counterpiracy and later to maritime security more widely defined, including a focus on small arms and narcotics. This in turn indicates the flexibility of these structures, and their utility in assembling broad coalitions of actors to combat various forms of insecurity at sea.

Operating in Multiagency Environments

Maritime security challenges often require multiagency responses, even when they are undertaken by individual states in their own waters (see section 6.2).

Multinational MSOs add further complexity to this picture. Accordingly, a key question is how to coordinate operations across multiple different national and agency actors.

There is no one single model of how to organize multiagency MSOs, with states and organizations employing a variety of command-and-control models. The EU, for example, draws on several organizational models, each established on a bespoke basis for specific operations.[13] The EU's first naval operation, EUNAVFOR Atalanta, established a common headquarters with unique features, in which each participating nation would assign a liaison officer. Given the longevity of Atalanta, which by 2022 had been active for more than 12 years, it bequeathed the EU a de facto standing naval headquarters. Yet for its Sophia and IRINI operations in the Mediterranean, the EU opted for a separate structure. In 2021 the EU introduced another new concept, the Coordinated Maritime Presence , for which the Gulf of Guinea was the pilot case. Under this concept, naval forces remain fully under national command and coordination takes place on a voluntary basis, organized through a Maritime Area of Interest Coordination Cell based in Brussels.

A major trend in MSO coordination at a national level is the development of formal coordination bodies and policies to manage relations between agencies and across the civil-military spectrum. The interagency coordination structures that we discussed in detail in Chapter 6, Section 6.2 are reflections of this trend. Centers such as the Australian Maritime Security Operations Centre, the United Kingdom's Joint Maritime Security Centre, or the United States' Global Maritime Operational Threat Response Coordination Center function to coordinate operations, and deliver maritime domain awareness, and are important mechanisms for organizing and commanding MSOs.

Small states have drawn on similar models to pool and coordinate their national capacities for MSOs at a regional level. An example is the Regional Centre for Operational Coordination based in Seychelles, operative since 2019.[14] Run under the auspices of the Indian Ocean Commission, the center plans and coordinates MSOs at sea with a focus on blue crimes and environmental protection.

---

[13] Christian Bueger and Timothy Edmunds, "The European Union's Quest to Become a Global Maritime Security Provider," US Naval War College Review 76, no. 2 (Spring 2023): article 6, 9–10.

[14] Indian Ocean Commission, "The Seychelles Regional Centre for Operational Coordination Is Now Operational 24 Hours a Day, 7 Days a Week," Press Release, September 2019, https://www.commissionoceanindien.org/wp-content/uploads/2019/10/Final-communiqu%C3%A9-CRCO_H24_7j_Eng.pdf.

Interoperability

MSOs often involve participants with very different capabilities. This might be at the agency level, where some agencies have specialist skills (such as crime scene investigation, narcotics detection, or fisheries inspection) and jurisdiction, but not necessarily the required seagoing capabilities. This also applies to multinational operations, where contributors may have widely differing capabilities or jurisdictional mandates.

This situation creates the need for agreements to allow for capacity, expertise, and juridical responsibility sharing between states and agencies. One common solution is to use so-called ship-rider agreements. At a national level it is quite common for law enforcement officers such as coast guards, fisheries enforcement, or border officials to join naval vessels to facilitate the arrest of suspects in jurisdictions where naval officers do not have that power.

At an international level, the United States and Canada have spearheaded the development of this approach. Both countries have maintained jointly crewed vessels since 2000 to fight border crimes.[15] The United States has also established various bilateral ship-rider agreements with partner states in the in the Caribbean and South Pacific, which allow for state officials from a partner state to embark on a United States law enforcement vessel to counternarcotics smuggling, irregular migration or illicit fishing.[16] In this way larger states can lend capacity to smaller partners, while the latter retain jurisdictional authority in their own territorial waters and EEZs. In other cases, these agreements can enable burden sharing in areas of common interests.

At an interstate level, states also share resources and capacities through formal alliance arrangements such as NATO or joint maritime security assurance agreements, such as in relation to information sharing, joint search and rescue, or disaster relief operations. Often these latter programs are established to assist smaller states with relatively weak maritime security capacities to police their maritime territories. The United States has agreements with island states such as the Marshall Islands, and both China and India have pursued such arrangements with partner states, including Djibouti, Mauritius, and the Seychelles.

Another noteworthy example of this kind of capacity sharing was established for the counterpiracy operations in the Western Indian Ocean. To avoid costly trials in their home countries, international navies signed memoranda of

---

[15] Anna C. Pratt and Jessica Templeman, "Jurisdiction, Sovereignties and Akwesasne: Shiprider and the Re-Crafting of Canada-US Cross-Border Maritime Law Enforcement," *Canadian Journal of Law and Society / La Revue Canadienne Droit et Société* 33, no. 3 (December 2018): 335–357.

[16] UNODC, *Maritime Crime: A Manual for Criminal Justice Practitioners, Third Edition* (UNODC, 2020), 187–197, https://www.unodc.org/documents/Maritime_crime/GMCP_Maritime_3rd_edition_Ebook.pdf.

understanding with regional states, including Kenya and Seychelles to transfer piracy suspects for prosecution in their jurisdiction.[17] In this system, known as arrest, transfer, and prosecution, regional states would then take over the responsibility for trials and incarceration, while convicts were given the option of transferring to a prison in their homeland Somalia, if conditions allowed.

Challenges

MSOs can be challenging due to their multiagency character. One common problem is the potential for civil-military tensions.[18] With a few exceptions, such as the globally deployed United States Coast Guard, it is naval forces that are generally best prepared and equipped to conduct sustained MSOs at distance from home waters. This pattern is apparent in most of the MSOs discussed above, in which naval vessels and personnel have often been the main participants. This is potentially problematic because of the cost and wider organizational demands of such deployments, especially given that many states have deployed powerful vessels such as frigates and destroyers. These kinds of ships are more expensive to operate than smaller craft such as offshore patrol vessels, and arguably overspecified for what are at heart law enforcement operations. Moreover, the commitment of any single ship generally has implications for at least two others due to the replacement cycle of maintenance, training, deployment, and leave that is required to sustain a consistent operational presence at sea. Participation in MSOs can thus divert significant naval capability from other tasks.

Another issue is that navies can be drawn into what are ostensibly domestic law enforcement operations in ways that disrupt established norms and divisions of responsibility between civil and military actors in their home countries.

The strong reliance on military forces in MSOs also means that they carry the potential for militarization and to increase strategic competition at sea.[19] Several states, for example, have used counterpiracy operations off the coast of Somalia to establish or increase their geopolitical presence in the Western Indian Ocean region.[20] China established its first overseas naval base in Djibouti in 2017, consolidating what began as a counterpiracy deployment in 2008, and has

---

[17] Douglas Guilfoyle, "Counter-Piracy Law Enforcement and Human Rights," *International & Comparative Law Quarterly* 59, no. 1 (January 2010): 141–169.

[18] Ian Bowers and Swee Lean Collin Koh, "Introduction," in *Grey and White Hulls: An International Analysis of the Navy-Coastguard Nexus*, ed. Ian Bowers and Swee Lean Collin Koh (Singapore: Springer, 2019), 7–11.

[19] Lee Willett, "Pirates and Power Politics," *The RUSI Journal* 156, no. 6 (December 2011): 20–25.

[20] Christian Bueger and Jan Stockbruegger, "Maritime Security and the Western Indian Ocean's Militarisation Dilemma," *African Security Review* 31, no. 2 (April 2022): 195–210.

conducted joint naval operations in the region with Russia and Iran. Countries including the United States, India, United Kingdom, France, and others have engaged in geopolitical countermaneuvers of their own, for example by conducting joint exercises and developing security cooperation mechanisms such as the AUKUS and Quadrilateral Security Dialogue initiatives (see Chapter 8, Section 8.5).

Finally, MSOs face the challenge that the threats that they are addressing often have their origins on land (see Chapter 3, Section 3.5). Whether this is the panning and organization of blue crimes, or factors such as economic dislocation or spillovers from civil wars, the ability of MSOs to successfully prevent maritime threats emerging in the first place is limited, and requires additional measures carried out on land.

Summary

The rise of the maritime security agenda has led to a significant growth in the number and scope of MSOs. These contribute to enhanced maritime domain awareness and target specific threats at sea. Most MSOs incorporate several agencies, while many are multinational in nature. In consequence, institutional arrangements and coordination mechanisms, whether informal or formal in character, are generally important components of these operations. The growth in MSOs raises concerns over whether increased external naval presence in regions creates new lines of maritime strategic competition and geopolitical tension between states. MSOs moreover are only a temporary fix, and generally need to be supported by accompanying initiatives on land.

7.4 Maritime Security Strategies

Dedicated maritime security strategies are a key solution in the toolbox of maritime security. They have been an important element in the evolution of holistic maritime security thinking that does not focus on single issues but attempts to recognize interlinkages and grasp the maritime domain as an integrated space of insecurity and risk. Maritime security strategies identify and prioritize threats and risks, streamline responses across the complexity of intragovernmental actors, identify gaps, plan investments, and make other adjustments to security policy. In this sense, their primary purpose is to outline a coherent, forward-looking plan for the maritime security structures of a country or regional organization.

In most cases strategy-making is carried out by the drafting of a single document. There are different interpretations of how such a strategy differs from other security documents, such as a policy, plan, or doctrine.[21] While policies are most often more generic and political in nature, plans or doctrines are usually agency specific. Some strategic analysts contend that a strategy must rationally match ends, ways, and means, but this is by no means the only way to understand them.[22] Because the definition of strategy is contested, it is more useful to address the question in a pragmatic way, by asking what strategies do.

When approached in this way, we can see that maritime security strategies commonly serve several purposes. These include:

- To collate information and take stock of maritime security structures, including existing capacities (in equipment, human resources, assets), current mandates and responsibilities of agencies, and relevant legal provisions and obligations under international treaties.
- To agree on a shared assessment of the maritime security context and the threats, risks, and opportunities it presents. This often includes an assessment of the potential impact of different threats and how they should be prioritized.
- To agree on the state or regional organization's goals and ambitions in relation to maritime security and the capacities and actions necessary to deliver these.
- To lay out a governance structure for maritime security, including the responsibilities and obligations of ministries, agencies, and other governmental actors, and the principles underlying cooperation and coordination between them.
- To agree a plan for restructuring, if required, or investments in capacity development.
- To signal national or organizational priorities, plans, and intentions to domestic and international audiences.

Maritime security strategies vary significantly in the emphasis they place on these purposes. Below, we first provide an overview of key recent maritime security strategies before going on to consider variations between them, and their various strengths and weaknesses.

---

[21] See for example Hew Strachan, "The Lost Meaning of Strategy," *Survival* 47, no. 3 (October 2005): 33–54.

[22] Colin S. Gray, *Strategy and Defence Planning: Meeting the Challenge of Uncertainty* (Oxford: Oxford University Press, 2014), 53–58; For a treatment of the history of strategy and strategy-making see Lawrence Freedman, *Strategy: A History* (Oxford: Oxford University Press, 2013).

An Overview of Maritime Strategy-Making

The first dedicated maritime security strategy, in the sense that it used the concept prominently, was the 2005 National Strategy for Maritime Security by the United States Government. Since then many other countries and regional organizations have initiated their own maritime security strategy processes, making this an increasingly common global phenomenon. Examples include NATO (2011), the EU (2014, 2023), and African Union(2014), as well as individual states such as Spain (2013), the UK (2014, 2022), France (2015), India (2015), New Zealand (2020), and Australia (2021). Numerous other states, especially in Africa, have initiated maritime security strategy processes, including Ghana, Kenya, Nigeria, Seychelles, South Africa, and Tanzania. In these settings, strategy writing often forms a key component of capacity-building work.

This brief survey indicates the growing significance of strategy writing as maritime security solution. Taken together, the strategies are distinguished by their breadth and ambition. They aim to connect different maritime threats and risks and offer a comprehensive or holistic account of the challenges to be faced at sea. Thus, the 2014 EU strategy conceptualized maritime security as "a state of affairs of the global maritime domain, in which international law and national law are enforced, freedom of navigation is guaranteed and citizens, infrastructure, transport, the environment and marine resources are protected."[23] Similarly, the 2022 strategy of the United Kingdom outlines five wide ranging strategic objectives, comprising "protecting our home land," "responding to threats," "ensuring prosperity," "championing our values," and "supporting a security and resilient ocean."[24] The Spanish strategy likewise foregrounds "a comprehensive vision of maritime security."[25]

Each of the strategies has a different mix of emphases, inclusions, and exclusions. The NATO strategy, for example, prioritizes deterrence and collective defense, alongside issues such as crisis management and cooperative security, and thus continues to emphasize "hard" naval power alongside more diffuse maritime security tasks. By contrast, the 2021 Australian strategy is explicit in its emphasis on "civil" maritime security and the management of "non-military risk

---

[23] "European Union Maritime Security Strategy" (Brussels: Council of the European Union, June 2014), https://data.consilium.europa.eu/doc/document/ST%2011205%202014%20INIT/EN/pdf, 3.

[24] HMG, "National Strategy for Maritime Security, CP 724" (HMG, August 2022), https://www.gov.uk/government/publications/national-maritime-security-strategy, 19–20.

[25] Gobierno de España, "National Maritime Security Strategy," 2013, https://www.dsn.gob.es/gl/file/329/download?token=9Y92D968, 11.

to Australia."[26] The African Union's 2050 African Integrated Maritime Strategy emphasizes the importance of maritime resources and trade to economic security and development in the continent, with a focus on capacity-building including coast guard capabilities and port facilities. Both the 2020 New Zealand and 2022 UK strategies place considerable emphasis on marine environmental and sustainability themes.

Most of the strategies include discussions of maritime security governance arrangements between departments and across agencies. Some also introduce new structures and coordination bodies as well as mechanisms for regular measurement and review. The Australian strategy, for example, foregrounds a "whole-of-government approach to civil maritime security," establishes a new governance committee to provide "oversight and strategic direction for civil maritime security policy issues" and introduces an annual review process.[27] The 2022 United Kingdom strategy calls for a "whole system" response, establishes a cross-governmental governance structure and strengthens the coordinating role of the joint agency Joint Maritime Security Centre across United Kingdom maritime security operations.[28]

Maritime security strategies thus represent an attempt to understand and engage with the maritime environment as an interlinked security complex, rather than a series of discrete threats and challenges. They also play an important symbolic role in demonstrating the significance each actor attaches to the maritime domain.

Relation to Other Documents

The holistic emphasis of most maritime security strategies raises a dilemma of how they should be linked to or nested in other related strategies and policy documents. Some actors, such as the United States, the United Kingdom, or the EU, have a strong culture of producing written strategies. In these contexts, strategy production is a more routine affair, and a maritime security strategy usually sits in an established hierarchy of documents. This is generally capped by a top-level national security strategy under which various other thematic strategies are housed—such as defense, cyber security, counterterrorism, or organized crime—as well as specific organizational guidelines such as naval doctrine. In

---

[26] Government of Australia, "Australian Government Civil Maritime Security Strategy," 2021, https://www.homeaffairs.gov.au/nat-security/files/australian-government-civil-maritime-security-strategy.pdf, 3.
[27] Government of Australia, "Australian Government Civil Maritime Security Strategy," 32–38.
[28] HMG, "NSMS," 46–48.

other contexts, where these clear hierarchical relationships and assumptions are less established, the question of how a maritime security strategy relates to other documents, such as national security or counterterrorism strategy, can be more difficult to resolve.

The situation is complicated since many countries also have other strategic documents that deal with the maritime domain, for example ocean policies, blue economy strategies, fisheries policies, or even region-specific strategies. A key challenge is how to connect and cohere these various official papers in ways that harmonize priorities and minimize the potential for contradiction. For this reason, some countries and organizations, such as Ghana and the African Union, for example, have opted not to produce a dedicated maritime security strategy but to instead incorporate maritime security considerations into an overarching maritime strategy that deals with more general economic and environmental issues alongside specific maritime security concerns.

Strategy-Making

Because drafting a strategy implies assessments, evaluations, and interpretations of the nature of threats, goals, and the role of different agencies, strategy-making functions as an important collective sense-making exercise with the potential to grow a community of maritime security actors. The extent to which different agencies and departments are involved in the process can make a major difference to how much they commit to a strategy, in the sense of implementing its provisions and drawing on it as a guidance document.

There are three common models of how strategy writing is organized. The first is a top-down model, where one actor is put in charge of the process at the highest level of government. A second approach is collaborative, where the production of the document is a collective process carried out through multiple consultations, sometimes even drawing on co-authoring by different departments and agencies. Finally, there is an external model, where an outside consultancy is brought in to produce a strategy for a country of region.

Of these approaches, both the top-down and external models share a common challenge of securing departmental and agency buy-in. If the participation of key stakeholders in the drafting process is limited, there is a risk—whether perceived or substantive—that their priorities, concerns, and interpretations are not well considered, which in turn can create implementation challenges. This is especially so in contexts where multiple different thematic strategies are in place, creating a situation in which stakeholders have a menu of different strategic guidance to choose from, depending on their own interests and priorities: a practice sometimes known as "forum shopping."[29]

The collaborative model aims to ameliorate these problems by ensuring all key stakeholders have a voice in the process. However, it can lead to delay and complication. Many collaborative strategy-making process draw on consultation workshops with agencies and stakeholders, devolved writing processes, and multiple rounds of negotiation and contestation between actors. These approaches require clear leadership, coordination, and dispute resolution mechanisms if they are to retain coherence and achieve success. An additional challenge for both collaborative and external models is that they can be biased toward technical solutions and may struggle to engage with the political considerations and implications of the maritime security response.

Effects of Maritime Security Strategies

The effects of maritime security strategies are difficult to measure directly. Most strategies do not include benchmarks or other measurements against which success can be gauged. In practice much depends on the nature of the drafting process, but also on the purpose of the strategy overall, the ambitions that are linked to it, and resources that are allocated to support these goals.

The drafting process is a key variable because it is likely to influence the extent to which key stakeholders buy into the document or not, and particularly whether the competing priorities and interests of different actors are accommodated under a common narrative and vision. This in turn is likely to impact on how far relevant stakeholders implement the strategy in everyday routine and draw on it to coordinate their activities with others.

Almost all strategies are informative documents in that they contain interpretations of the maritime environment; take stock of the current maritime security structures; outline threats, risks, and challenges; offer guidance for future actions; and clarify stakeholder roles and responsibilities. In this sense, maritime security strategies have the potential to act as a common reference point for agencies within a country, as well as for external partners. This is important to signal to other states and international organizations about their plans and intentions, as well as to identify key points of contact. They also have an important role in informing the wider public about maritime issues and can be used as resources for staff training and in education.

---

[29] See for example Stephanie C. Hofmann, "The Politics of Overlapping Organizations: Hostage-Taking, Forum-Shopping and Brokering," *Journal of European Public Policy* 26, no. 6 (June 2019): 883–905.

Many maritime security strategies are self-consciously presented as "living documents," in the sense that they are expected to evolve and adapt as circumstances dictate. However, the extent to which this is the case after publication is often questionable. Some strategies do not indicate clear pathways to implementation, while matching resources to ambition is often a significant political challenge.

Other strategies incorporate specific reform proposals, such as the creation of new governmental structures, coordination committees, or information sharing mechanisms. These provide the most direct lines of action against which the implementation of strategy can be judged. Others are accompanied by dedicated action plans or review processes. The EU strategy of 2014, for example, was followed by an action plan that outlined concrete projects to implement the strategy's goals and identified lead agencies and relational hierarchies to accomplish this.[30] Action plans and review processes provide flexible ways to ensure that a strategy is followed up over time, as well as benchmarks against which success can be judged. Given the evolving maritime security environment, it is important that strategies are designed in a way that they can adapt to changing circumstances.

Summary

Maritime security strategies have emerged as an important mechanism through which states and regional organizations orchestrate their maritime security responses. They serve to consolidate the meaning of maritime security across government and agencies and offer a way to manage the problem of actor complexity, formalize interagency coordination, and introduce lines of accountability into maritime security governance. However, they require political commitment, stakeholder buy-in, and proper resourcing if they are to be effective, as well as review processes to ensure their adaptability and relevance over time.

7.5 Maritime Domain Awareness

Effective security responses depend on knowledge. One of the key tools to produce knowledge for maritime security is through initiatives known as maritime domain awareness (MDA) or maritime situational awareness (MSA). MDA focuses on the broader picture, while MSA is generally concerned with concrete

---

[30] European Commission, "The EU Maritime Security Strategy and Its Action Plan," 2023, https://eur-lex.europa.eu/legal-content/EN/TXT/?uri=CELEX:52023JC0008.

situations at sea and operational requirements. However, the two terms are often used interchangeably, and here we refer to MDA throughout.

MDA deals with questions, such as: What are the main threats that need attention? How do they manifest in a particular area? Can suspicious behavior be observed? How can the effectiveness of MSOs and patrols be enhanced to prevent and deter threats?

Producing knowledge that speaks to these questions is not an easy task. It is more difficult than on land, not only because the sea is a vast and fluid space, but also because far fewer people are at sea to observe what is going on. Established technologies such as radar and satellite imagery and increasingly affordable new sensor technologies, such as floating buoys or uncrewed vessels can assist in the surveillance of the oceans. Broadly, MDA inputs fall into two categories. First, they can be cooperative, in the sense that users of the sea agree to participate in them. Examples include AIS systems on board vessels or incident reporting systems. Second, there are also noncooperative methods—such as radar, visual sightings, or Radio Frequency intercepts—that function with or without the agreement of those being surveilled. A good understanding of maritime activity also requires the sharing and fusing of information among state agencies, with nonstate actors such as the shipping industry, and among regional and international partners.

Substantial investments have been made in MDA at national and regional levels, and improving MDA is often a cornerstone of capacity-building work (see Chapter 7, Section 7.6). MDA is a technological challenge in terms of how to collect better data on maritime activities through surveillance, how to fuse data from different sources, and how to analyze that data to identify hot spots and suspicious activities. However, since MDA depends on the quality of the collaboration between the full range of maritime security actors, and in particular their willingness to report and share information, it faces substantial sociopolitical challenges too.

In this section we provide a short introduction to the idea of MDA and its evolution at a regional level. We then discuss the technological and sociopolitical challenges of MDA that need to be overcome if it is to be effective.

What Is MDA?

MDA discussions originate in what we have called the first wave of maritime security thinking (see Chapter 2, Section 2.3). While navies have long collected intelligence at sea, the aftermath of the 9/11 attacks led to a range of new assumptions that paved the way for current approaches to MDA.[31] A key lesson was that the prevention of terrorist acts required collaboration and information

---

[31] See for a more detailed discussion Christian Bueger, "A Glue That Withstands Heat? The Promise and Perils of Maritime Domain Awareness," in *Maritime Security: Counter-Terrorism Lessons*

sharing across agencies and countries. Information sharing and data analyses was also seen as enhancing the effectiveness of policing and deterrence under conditions of limited capacity—in a practice known as "intelligence-led policing."[32] The events of 9/11 also expanded the understanding of what could be a threat and an object of attack. Transport systems in particular were seen as vulnerable and interpreted as both means as well as targets of future attacks (see Chapter 4, Section 4.3) This final assumption implied that any kind of maritime activity, whether it be shipping or fishing has a potential relevance for security.

The United States government was the first to outline a definition of MDA and described it as "the effective understanding of anything associated with the maritime domain that could impact the security, safety, economy, or environment of the United States."[33] Since then this definition has been widely adopted by other actors, including the IMO and the EU. The definition is remarkable because it stresses that MDA is not simply about information or knowledge. It is also about "understanding"—that is, making sense of activities related to the maritime domain. It is also wide-ranging, with the maritime domain being understood to comprise "all areas and things of, on, under, relating to, adjacent to, or bordering on a sea, ocean, or other navigable waterway, including all maritime-related activities, infrastructure, people, cargo, and vessels and other conveyances."[34] This conceptualization extends the notion of the maritime to the land, including supply chains, and almost any conceivable maritime or maritime-related activity.

When this ambition was initially outlined it focused on maritime terrorism but has since come to reflect a broader maritime security vision. This wider perspective was also apparent in another influential United States Navy initiative. The Council on the 1000 Ship Navy laid out a vision of how maritime security forces around the world could work together, comprising what has been described as "a self-organizing, self-governing, come-as-you-are cooperative global maritime security network [to] coordinate the activities of volunteer nations' navies, coastguards and constabulary units."[35] While the 1000

---

from *Maritime Piracy and Narcotics Interdiction*, ed. Edward R. Lucas (Amsterdam: IOS Press, 2020), 235–245.

[32] Edmund F. McGarrell, Joshua D. Freilich, and Steven Chermak, "Intelligence-Led Policing As a Framework for Responding to Terrorism," *Journal of Contemporary Criminal Justice* 23, no. 2 (May 2007): 142–158.

[33] United States Government. *National Maritime Domain Awareness Plan* (Washington, DC: The White House, 2005), n. p.

[34] United States Government. National Maritime Domain Awareness Plan (Washington, DC: The White House, 2005), n. p.

[35] Peter D. Haynes, *Toward a New Maritime Strategy: American Naval Thinking in the Post-Cold War Era* (Annapolis MD: US Naval Institute, 2015), https://www.usni.org/press/books/toward-new-maritime-strategy, 197.

Ship Navy concept ultimately foundered and was later reformulated more loosely as setting up a global network of navies,[36] it was important for the way in which it highlighted MDA as a key enabling structure for coordinating action, enhancing interoperability, and building trust between maritime security actors.

Narrow and Wider Understandings of MDA

Two different understandings of MDA are prominent in maritime security debates today. In its narrow version, MDA is conceived as an operational tool, the purpose of which is to direct patrolling and interdiction activities, to facilitate a swift response to incidents when they occur, and to issue early warnings for users of the sea. In this narrow operational sense, discussions often favor the notion of MSA.

The broad version, by contrast, highlights the wider functions of MDA-generated knowledge, as outlined in figure 7.1. In this respect, MDA is the engine room of national and regional maritime security. It enables policy integration, interagency coordination, and MSOs by building a common understanding of maritime security and building everyday relations of trust between agencies and states. Monthly or annual incident reports allow political decision-makers to better understand the maritime domain, including the threats and risks it presents and the capability requirements it demands. MDA analyses are a basis for the assessments that maritime security strategies draw on. The knowledge produced in MDA activities can also help the public more broadly to recognize the importance of the sea and the vulnerabilities that are associated with it. Reports from MDA also are vital teaching and training material. In this broader understanding, MDA is at the heart of maritime security governance, supporting and supported by the informal governance arrangements and maritime security strategy processes we discuss above.

The Evolution of MDA

There has been a substantial evolution of MDA activities at national and regional levels since the mid-2000s. Many states have developed national MDA centers, often as part of their maritime security strategy processes. The United Kingdom's National Maritime Information Centre, France's Maritime

---

[36] Jason Dittmer, "The State, All at Sea: Interoperability and the Global Network of Navies," Environment and Planning C: Politics and Space 39, no. 7 (November 2021): 1389–1406.

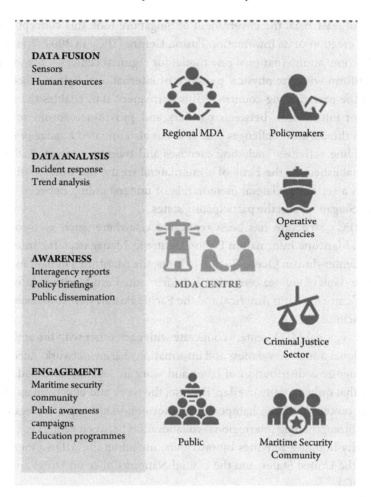

Figure 7.1 The extended understanding of maritime domain awareness. Source: Christian Bueger and Timothy Edmunds, "Mastering Maritime Security: Reflexive Capacity Building and the Western Indian Ocean Experience," *SafeSeas* (February 2018): 26–27.

Information Cooperation and Awareness Center and the Australian Maritime Security Operations Centre are good examples of this phenomenon.

A growth in regional centers has taken place alongside these national level developments, to the point where in many parts of the world, such as Southeast Asia and the Western Indian Ocean, regional initiatives have preceded or even replaced national arrangements. The idea of regional MDA was spearheaded by the Italian Navy for counterterrorism purposes in the Mediterranean, when it established what became known as the Virtual Regional Maritime Traffic Centre in 2006. Over 20 national navies joined the initiative. It was then expanded through the Trans-Regional Maritime Network, which aimed at sharing information across regions.

In Southeast Asia, the government of Singapore took this concept forward with the creation of its Information Fusion Centre (IFC) in 2009. The IFC has since become an international role model for regional centers.[37] It combines a data platform with the physical presence of international liaison officers from each of the participating countries. This permanent staff enables the swift exchange of information between partners and provides a forum to discuss common threats and challenges. The IFC has also initiated a range of community building activities, including exercises and training courses. Rather than being established on the basis of a multilateral treaty, the work of the IFC is based on a series of bilateral memoranda of understanding between the host country Singapore and the participating states.

The IFC's structure has been replicated elsewhere, such as through the Regional Maritime Information Fusion Centre in Madagascar, the Information Fusion Center–Indian Ocean Region in India, the Maritime Domain Awareness for Trade–Gulf of Guinea center in West Africa, the Peru Maritime Information Fusion Centre for Latin America, and the Pacific Fusion Center focusing on the South Pacific.

These regional MDA centers cooperate with each other with the ambition to form a global domain awareness and information sharing network. Accordingly, they recognize a distribution of labor and work in separate so-called areas of interest that only partially overlap. Even so, the work and effectiveness of some regional centers has been hampered by information sharing challenges across regions. Strengthening interregional collaboration between centers is a key goal of capacity-building activities by providers, including the MDA pioneer Italy, the EU, the United States, and the United Nations Office on Drugs and Crime (UNODC).

In Europe, the European Commission's European Maritime Safety Agency leads on the civilian Common Information Sharing Environment, while the European Defense Agency advances the Maritime Surveillance platform MARSUR focused on military information sharing. These projects work to coordinate activities and share information between EU states, and also support MDA in other regions.

Issue-specific initiatives complement this general MDA work in some cases. The problem of piracy, for example, gave rise to dedicated information sharing networks such as the ReCAAP mechanism in Southeast Asia, the Djibouti Code of Conduct in the Western Indian Ocean, and the Yaoundé Code of Conduct in the Gulf of Guinea. Other important examples are the Maritime Analysis and

---

[37] See the contributions in Christian Bueger and Jane Chan, eds., *Paving the Way for Regional Maritime Domain Awareness* (Singapore: S. Rajaratnam School of International Studies, 2019).

Operation Centre–Narcotics in Lisbon, which has facilitated counternarcotics operations in the Atlantic since 2017, and regional fisheries-focused centers such as the Pacific Islands Forum Fisheries Agency or the European Fisheries Control Agency.

Technical Challenges of MDA

The goal of most MDA systems is to provide a real-time picture and a historical record of all maritime activities in their area of interest. This leads to what is sometimes called a "common operational picture": that is, "a geographic display that contains position and amplifying information about contacts."[38] To develop this picture MDA platforms have two major layers of information: first, data from sensors,[39] and second, data from human sources. The Long Range Identification and Tracking (known as LRIT) and Automatic Identification System (AIS) technologies that track shipping vessels globally in real time and provide basic data (position, course, speed, owner, flag state) form the backbone of most MDA systems. These data are commercially available and collected through satellites and coastal radar systems. However, they can be manipulated by cyberattacks (see Chapter 8, Section 8.2), and while trackers are legally required under IMO regulations and flag state jurisdictions, vessels can turn their transponders off. Most countries also trace fishing fleets in their EEZs via a dedicated vessel monitoring system.

In addition, data are collected by patrolling ships, submersibles, and aircraft. Increasingly, uncrewed vehicles and remote sensors such as floating buoys are also used in MDA. Satellites provide an increasing range of data sources, including images, but also tracks of light and electromagnetic emissions. A growing industry is developing drones, remote sensors, and satellite technologies for maritime security, environmental protection, and scientific purposes, but also for the maritime industries to enhance their own surveillance and self-protection capabilities.

The most important data from human sources are distress calls and incident reports by users of the sea. Many MDA centers actively foster communications with marine users such as the shipping community to ensure that incidents are reported when they occur. Some even operate mobile phone

---

[38] Robert Hannah, "The Common Operational Picture: The Coast Guard's Window on the World," *The Coastguard Journal of Safety and Security at Sea* 63, no. 3 (2006): 65–68.

[39] Gregory Poling, "From Orbit to Ocean—Fixing Southeast Asia's Remote-Sensing Blind Spots," *Naval War College Review* 74, no. 1 (February 2021), https://www.enisa.europa.eu/publications/cyber-security-aspects-in-the-maritime-sector-1.

apps through which respondents can report incidents or suspicious activities. ReCAAP, for example, maintains an anti-piracy app to provide real-time data to seafarers and encourage the easy submission of incident reports. Others run dedicated engagement schemes with coastal communities and ocean users to encourage incident reporting. Since reporting can imply significant administrative costs or economic consequences, such as reputational damage or increased insurance costs, a significant level of unreported incidents can be expected.

One key technical challenge for MDA is how to fuse these different kinds of data from sensors and human sources in a coherent system that can be used across agencies and countries. These data can come in very different formats and draw on varied classification standards. Fusing such data not only requires considerable computing powers and data storage facilities, but also implies the risk of information loss in the fusion process. Another is the challenge of tracking so-called dark targets, which commonly feature in all types of blue crime. These are vessels that employ techniques to hide or obfuscate the positions or identities, for example by turning off their AIS or VMS systems, transmitting false positions, or using duplicate IMO numbers.

Most MDA centers develop their own proprietary fusion platform to store and provide access to the data, as well as analyses and visualizations for operations and reports. The United States offers countries use of its Seavision platform for MDA, while NGOs such as Global Fishing Watch (see Chapter 7, Section 6.5) and a range of private companies also offer MDA fusion tools. Outside of AIS and LRIT tracks, there are no commonly agreed-upon data standards or classifications of incidents and suspicious behavior. Systems differ in terms of how they conceptualize threats, and what kind of maritime issues they monitor at all. This is a problem because it means that national and regional MDA systems are often unable to transfer data between each other. In extreme cases, MDA reports might produce conflicting information on regional patterns and trends. Southeast Asia, for instance, saw a debate over whether piracy incidents were on the rise or in decline because of the different classification standards in use.[40]

The volume of data that MDA analysts deal with is substantial. Indeed, and perhaps ironically, one of the major problems of MDA is not too little, but too much data. The question then becomes one of how to find the needle in the haystack. Analysts commonly address this challenge with the help of algorithms which are programmed to identify suspicious behavior at sea. For

---

[40] Bateman, By Sam. 2015. "Piracy Monitoring Wars: Responsibilities for Countering Piracy," RSIS Commentary, No. 115—May 13, 2015 (S. Rjaratnam School of international Studies, Nanyang Technological University, Singapore).

instance, if two vessels anchor in the same position for a longer time than is usually the case it might indicate illicit transshipment activities; a loitering vessel might indicate involvement in smuggling activities. Algorithms then can trigger an operational response. Statistical analysis is also used to identify regional patterns, such as clusters and hotspots of criminal activity or major smuggling routes.

Sociopolitical Challenges of MDA

While the technological challenges of MDA are considerable, most analysts agree that they are solvable in one way or another. Sociopolitical issues present a more enduring problem. These relate to the human and organizational components of the MDA data chain.

One common sociopolitical challenge concerns the lack of willingness of agencies and countries to share information with each other. There are numerous reasons for why this might be the case. An agency might be protective of its data because it is classified as secret or confidential, or protected under national privacy laws. For example, evidence that is part of a criminal investigation by the police often cannot be disclosed. Military organizations sometimes tend to overclassify information as secret. Data emphases, inclusions, and exclusions are also often shaped by organizational mandates, values, and traditions, or may be cast in bespoke metrics, which makes them difficult to share.

An agency might also come under unwanted public attention when sharing its data, for example if it reveals how many incidents took place under its watch. Information sharing might also be perceived as a threat to organizational autonomy or national sovereignty. At an individual level, there may be few career incentives for information sharing. In most cases, careers are made in enhancing the success and reputation of a particular agency or organization, and rarely through collaborating with others.

Maritime security agencies as well as ocean users, such as the shipping industry, may also be wary of the organizational costs of information sharing, for instance through the allocation of staff or changing institutional procedures, especially if such costs are not linked to direct outcomes and benefits are not obvious or straightforward.

Another challenge for making MDA effective is how the knowledge produced translates to action. MDA systems need to be connected to decision-makers or risk being sidelined or lost in organizational hierarchies. Alerts or trend analyses are only useful if they trigger operational responses and if resources are allocated to them. If MDA analysis are not followed up, this might also decrease the willingness to share information in the future. Competing national political or economic priorities might also hinder what action is taken, for instance when funding is an issue, or if political decision-makers allocate resources and capacities to other priorities.

A noteworthy additional hurdle at the regional or global level is an increasing competition between systems. Because there is no common global standard for MDA, few systems are easily compatible or interoperable with each other. While this is partially a technical challenge, it is also a reflection of political priorities. For instance, the United States and the EU proactively advocate for their proprietary systems (the global US platform Seavision and the EU's Indo Pacific Regional Information Sharing platform) and provide training and exercises for them. This not only risks undermining efforts to develop national platforms, but also might to lead to reluctance to engage in MDA for political reasons. In some regions, such as the Western Indian Ocean, the sheer number of overlapping MDA projects, initiatives, and support activities risks a significant fragmentation of effort. This can drain the resources available for MDA activities and undermine the effectiveness of regional information sharing.

Summary

MDA offers a promising route to enhance the efficiency of maritime security operations and to inform decision-makers about what happens at sea. New technologies such as sensors, satellites, and algorithms will increasingly make surveillance of ocean space more effective and enhance data quality. However, sociopolitical barriers to information interpretation and sharing continue to be an issue for all MDA systems. For this reason, it is important that MDA is placed in its proper perspective. It is a helpful and increasingly important component of the maritime security toolbox, but one that is as much dependent on human resources and relationships as it is on technological advancements and innovations.

7.6 Capacity-Building

Many countries have responsibility for large territorial waters and EEZs but lack the kinds of capacities needed to ensure maritime security. There is therefore a high demand for external support from other states and international organizations. Variously known as "capacity-building," "technical assistance," "security assistance," or "security sector reform," these programs have emerged as one of the most important solutions in the maritime security toolbox.

While there is no one clear and agreed definition of what maritime security capacity-building entails, here we consider it to comprise of activities which are directed at the empowerment of governments and coastal communities to efficiently and efficaciously govern and sustainably exploit the maritime domain, including territorial waters and EEZs.

This definition first stresses that capacity-building is not only about governments and the state and its agencies, but also about communities. Second, it emphasizes that the overall goal of capacity-building is to work toward the efficient and efficacious governance of maritime spaces and the sustainable use of marine resources. This is a goal that goes beyond the immediate priorities of the maritime security sector alone. It emphasizes the importance of understanding maritime security as being nested within a wider set of ocean governance concerns.

Consequently, a broad range of relevant capacities need to be considered.[41] Coast guards, navies, and other agencies need material resources and personnel to do their jobs. Ships and boats are required patrol and police the waters for which they are responsible, and supporting infrastructures are needed to sustain them. MDA systems require sensors and computers, and people able to use them. Personnel require appropriate training to conduct law enforcement operations at sea, including skills such as boat handling, navigation, boarding, and evidence collection.

Day to day operations are made possible by wider governance and administrative structures including coordination bodies, budgetary and finance systems, training programs, and personnel and career management processes. They also require frameworks of laws and regulations to delimit responsibilities and define the range of legitimate actions available to maritime security providers. A whole range of more mundane items are also necessary to support these activities, including equipment such as radios and information technology, and consumables such as fuel and spare parts. More widely, coastal communities require capacities such as dock infrastructures and processing facilities if the benefits of the blue economy are to be maximized.

Major Capacity-Building Providers

Several international and regional organizations as well as individual states are active in maritime security capacity-building. These capacity builders rely on different approaches and methods, but also have divergent underlying priorities and interests. International organizations and major economic powers have an overarching interest in maintaining good order at sea and assisting states to monitor their waters and EEZs. However, capacity-building engagements might also

---

[41] Christian Bueger, Timothy Edmunds, and Robert McCabe, "Into the Sea: Capacity-Building Innovations and the Maritime Security Challenge," *Third World Quarterly* 41, no. 2 (February 2020): 228–246.

stem from geopolitical and geostrategic priorities, such as concerns over spheres of influence and competition with adversary states. Activities might also be motivated by an intention to improve trade and economic relations, to create a favorable investment climate for a provider's companies or linked to plans to sell dedicated maritime security equipment and maintenance contracts.

At the level of international organizations, UN agencies such as the IMO and UNODC are key maritime security capacity-building providers. Because they work under UN auspices and member state mandates, these programs are generally understood to operate in a less politically motivated manner than comparable activities by states. For example, the IMO provides capacity-building to assist countries to comply with IMO regulations and standards and to strengthen their human and institutional capacities. IMO capacity-building takes place through its Integrated Technical Cooperation Programme, with global projects covering themes ranging from marine environmental protection and maritime livelihoods as well as maritime security specifically. This program is vital in particular in port security capacity-building, marine safety, and search and rescue, and to facilitate regional informal cooperation initiatives, such as the Djibouti Code of Conduct in the Western Indian Ocean (see Chapter 6, Section 6.3).

The UNODC's Maritime Crime Programme (GMCP) provides capacity-building programs to states across the world with a focus on maritime law enforcement and criminal justice. GMCP works across the spectrum of coast guard functions, with a particular focus on arrest and evidence collection and prosecution procedures, as well as on broader institutional support in terms of the drafting of legislations, management of detention facilities, and training of lawyers and courts, but also maritime domain awareness and maritime security strategy development.

Many states and regional organizations prefer to financially support the work of IMO and UNODC through trust funds or direct project funding given their proven expertise, methods, and political neutrality. Yet many also operate their own capacity-building initiatives in areas of strategic, political, or economic concern. The EU, for example, is a major maritime security capacity-building provider running a series of large-scale capacity-building programs in several regions of the world.[42] In the Western Indian Ocean in 2022, for example, it was operating four initiatives: the EUCAP Somalia program, which focuses on strengthening law enforcement, institutions, and legal and prison systems in Somalia; the MASE 2 program, which addresses legal reform, coastal community development, and regional coordination in information sharing and law

---

[42] Bueger and Edmunds, "The European Union's Quest to Become a Global Maritime Security Provider."

enforcement across the region as a whole; the CRIMARIO 2 program, which is focused on information sharing; and a dedicated port security program. The EU also has a range of similar capacity-building initiatives in the Gulf of Guinea region, as well as a border assistance program with Libya in the Mediterranean.

A significant number of states also conduct capacity-building activities either on a bilateral basis with regional states or through donations to projects implemented by others. The United States, for instance, operates a rich set of programs organized by different vehicles within the defense budget, including a series of larger scale maritime security exercises and extensive training programs. Smaller international donors that run a strong portfolio of bilateral capacity-building initiatives include Australia, Germany, Denmark, France, Norway, Japan, the United Kingdom and Türkiye.

These initiatives often follow the geostrategic interests of countries or may be driven by commercial interests or shared historical relations. Australia, for example, provides significant support to the island states of the Pacific Islands in part because it views this region as part of its sphere of influence. Türkiye has become an important capacity-building provider to Somalia as part of its own wider strategic reorientation to Africa and Asia. Denmark is especially active in Ghana, a former Danish colony, and where the largest Danish shipping company, Maersk, has commercial interests.

Forms of Delivery

Capacity-building activities use different forms of delivery that can be distinguished by the type of capacity being supported.[43] Often these are straightforwardly material in nature, comprising the donation of items ranging from evidence-collection kits to computers, cars, patrol vessels, buildings (such as prisons or courts), or even entire installations such as port facilities. Other activities focus on the development of human capacities through education or training. Capacity-building can also be institutional in nature, including projects designed to strengthen organizational structures, legal provisions, or administrative procedures.

As we show next, capacity-building draws on particular techniques that differ in terms of time horizons and resource demands and entail specific strengths and weaknesses.

Maritime security capacity-building often incorporates training courses and education programs of various sorts. These aim to inculcate specific operational

---

[43] Christian Bueger and Timothy Edmunds, "Mastering Maritime Security: Reflexive Capacity Building and the Western Indian Ocean Experience" (SafeSeas, February 2018), 26–27.

skills, such as boat handling, navigation, evidence collection, or learning how to swim, or institutional procedures such as handovers, information sharing, or norms compliance. Education programs develop deeper expertise in issue areas, such as maritime law or management and may even include university programs that run over one or more years. Education programs and training courses can strengthen the capacity of agencies to understand, plan for, and carry out maritime security tasks. They may also take place with the aim of "training the trainer," in the sense of embedding knowledge and expertise at a local level that can then be passed on through indigenous training structures over the long term.

These activities can sometimes have the disadvantage of focusing only on a narrow cadre of recipients such as English speakers or political appointees, rather than the maritime security sector as a whole. They may also represent a poor use of resources if recipients later leave their posts or are sidelined by their superiors. Matching training with existing resources is also important. Training coast guards in boat handling and maintenance skills, for example, will have little impact if they have no boats available to use, or no fuel to put them to sea.

Technical workshops can facilitate knowledge-transfer and exchange between donors, experts, and recipients. They are the most frequently used tool, since they can also encourage relationship and network-building and are relatively inexpensive and straightforward to organize. However, and as with training and education, they can often focus on a small group of English speakers who attend multiple events at the expense of engaging organizations more widely. Their short-term nature—sometimes lasting only a day or an afternoon—means they risk being overly generic and insufficiently sensitive to needs. The relative ease with which they are organized can also lead to duplication when different donors organize events on very similar subjects. This in turn can saturate the local environment with activity and become a drain on resources, with personnel attending workshops rather than going to work. It can also lead to fatigue and cynicism on the part of the recipients themselves.

Exercises are an important instrument to test how well current maritime security solutions work and are able to cope with threat scenarios. They are also an important tool to enhance interoperability between agencies and regional countries, and useful to increase awareness within governments and identify gaps in capacities. Exercises come in two formats. In tabletop exercises, smaller groups of agency representatives come together to play through scenarios and game how they would respond to them. Exercises at sea often involve the employment of vessels and other maritime security forces and tend to imply substantial organizational efforts. The major challenge in running exercises is to identify the appropriate scenarios and threats for which to train. Exercises at sea can also be very costly, especially in terms of fuel consumption, and if they are carried out over several days might distract maritime security forces from their everyday tasks.

Mentoring involves the pairing of external advisors and agencies with the aim of offering support, advice, and expertise, particularly at leadership level. Mentoring is a long-term activity and requires a relationship of trust between mentors and mentees. To succeed, the mentor requires a good understanding of organizational routines and an awareness of their potential to change. When done well, it can provide an ongoing channel for knowledge exchange between mentors and mentees, often focused on practical problems as they arise. Mentoring can be a demanding activity. It requires a lasting commitment from donors, and the identification and secondment of suitable expert mentors with the ability and commitment to engage substantively with their mentees. Mentors also require more than technical expertise, to be successful they will need specialist language and cultural skills.

Some capacity-building activities entail the provision of equipment and infrastructure. Equipment provision has a number of advantages. It tends to be readily appreciated by recipients. Equipment provides a concrete capacity that can be left behind when the donor leaves and thus represents a relatively uncomplicated deliverable. Infrastructure provision can be a concrete and visible commitment to capacity-building on the part of donors. It can also provide important facilities—such as prisons, courts, or ports—that a country may be unable to build or resource themselves. However, the provision of equipment or infrastructure may have little substantive impact if agencies do not have the resources, skills, or available personnel to utilize or maintain it. Consequently, such donations are rarely enough on their own. For this reason, the most impactful capacity-building programs of this type tend to be those that are accompanied by integrated maintenance and repair contracts, as well as training activities.

Institution-building is a more diffuse but often very important component of capacity-building. The goal is to create legislation, policies, strategies, processes, administrative and operational structures, and training and education structures that can maintain capacity in the long run, and provide more effective frameworks for future capacity-building. A priority area is often the drafting of criminal laws that allow for the prosecution of blue crimes and ensure a "legal finish" in particular to deter future crimes. Writing maritime security strategies can provide an important mechanism for improving administrative and operational procedures. Other work aims at creating or supporting dedicated centers, such as in the field of MSOs or MDA, as well as support to the management of agencies performing coast guard functions. Since these forms of assistance are very direct interferences into the workings of the government and state, they can be met with considerable political resistance by receiving countries, even if welcomed in principle. Navigating national politics, parliaments, party politics, and interagency rivalries can be a difficult affair and implies in-depth knowledge of the political system and constellation. If it is to be successful at all, institution-building requires a long-term horizon.

Challenges

Maritime security capacity-building requires careful planning and preparatory work if it is to be successful. There are a series of common challenges that capacity-building projects need to overcome to ensure that programs meet the needs of their partners and have lasting effects.[44]

The sheer number of actors engaged in capacity-building, often working with the same partner states, means that an enduring challenge is how to coordinate projects between donors and with recipients. There is often a lack of strategic oversight of these activities that can lead to duplication and even contradiction between programs. Sometimes this lack of oversight can even be deliberate on the part of the recipient, who might benefit if it allows them to gain benefits from multiple sources, or on the part of donors, who may be in competition with each other for influence or resources.

Since there is no universal model for how to organize and carry out maritime security, contradiction can also occur if donors introduce conflicting best-practice models or organizational procedures based on their own national experiences and approaches. For these reasons, the coordination problem can be difficult to resolve. Actors have sought to ameliorate it through coordination meetings in informal settings, by mapping ongoing capacity-building work in shared databases, and by empowering recipients to determine their own requirements more clearly. However, these measures often fail because they tend to provide static and incomplete pictures, due to a lack of willingness or capacity to share information in a timely manner.

A related challenge is how to determine what the gaps and needs in a region, country, or organization actually are. Donors and receivers do not necessarily share the same priorities, and since there is a lack of accepted capacity standards, beyond general understandings of coast guard functions (see Chapter 6, Section 6.2), gap assessments risk to be based on models and experiences that do not fit the context of the recipient state. Addressing this challenge requires preparatory work to understand the local context and recipient needs, including existing resource constraints, roles and responsibilities of agencies, and organizational ways of working. In many cases, locally specific understandings and related

---

[44] Bueger and Edmunds, "Mastering Maritime Security."

expertise are weak, which creates the problem of trying to apply a one-size-fits-all model to diverse national circumstances.

Different priorities also lead to the challenge of whether capacity-building should be issue-based, for example focused on piracy or narcotics smuggling or whether a holistic approach should be pursued. The latter requires a settled national prioritization, which is often not in place. An overemphasis on one issue can lead to displacement effects, in that the strength of a capacity in one area can lead to criminals or other disruptive actors exploiting weaknesses elsewhere (see Chapter 5, Section 5.2). Holistic approaches also face the challenge of balancing a sector wide focus with the specific, often very technical and specialized tasks and skill requirements of agencies, such as in the field of fisheries inspection, or narcotics detection.

These challenges can be exacerbated by the fact that many capacity-building projects are organized and funded in a way that favors short-term, easily measurable impacts. The focus of many programs is on outcomes that are tangible and quantifiable and can be achieved in a project life span that usually last two to five years. Critically important but less tangible or longer-term outcomes—such as staff retention, organizational expertise propagation, or even the ability to retain equipment in service once external support is withdrawn—often receive much less attention. This can undermine the impact of capacity-building over time and mean that any positive benefits are quickly lost once a specific project comes to an end.

Other challenges arise at the project level. Often there is a lack of communication between headquarters level programming and administration bodies and implementers on the ground. This can mean that projects can lack the flexibility to adopt to changing needs and priorities, especially if they are working to specifications and criteria that become outpaced by changing circumstances or events on the ground.

It is also important to recognize that while most capacity-building projects are technical in nature—in the sense that they aim to inculcate skills and best practices or provide new material capabilities to recipient states—they are also interventions into a political context.[45] Accordingly, even seemingly technical changes such as the introduction of a professionalized career progression structure or the strengthening of one ministry, department, or agency over another can impact individual, organizational, and political interests and create winners and losers. These political consequences are to some degree inescapable in any intervention that aspires to change how governments work and how agencies

---

[45] Timothy Edmunds and Ana E Juncos, "Constructing the Capable State: Contested Discourses and Practices in EU Capacity Building," *Cooperation and Conflict* 55, no. 1 (March 2020): 3–21.

relate to each other, even if in principle this takes place with the apparently straightforward aim of strengthening capacity and improving effectiveness. This makes it all the more important that the analysis of political context, recipient voices, and requirements are properly integrated into the planning, implementation, and evaluation stages of capacity-building activities.

Summary

Capacity-building has emerged as an important element in the toolbox of maritime security solutions. It aims to strengthen the capacity of regional states to police and protect their own maritime zones, to meet their responsibilities under international conventions, and to contribute to maritime security operations. Maritime security capacity-building comprises a wide range of different activities focused on the material, organizational and human resource requirements of policing at sea. However, if these are to be successful and sustainable over the long term it requires that projects are designed with sufficient attention to local circumstances, requirements, and needs. Coordination between donors and with recipients is also important to minimize the chances of duplication and even contradiction in project delivery.

7.7 Using and Improving the Toolbox

The rise of maritime security as concept and agenda has led to the development of a distinct set of solutions. Given the novelty of many maritime security issues, their complexity, and the urgency linked to them, many of these solutions were initially informal and experimental in nature. Yet with the agenda maturing, the toolbox of solutions has become established and settled. In this chapter we have focused on informal governance, operations at sea, maritime security strategies, and capacity-building as the main responses to maritime security.

The toolbox of maritime security solutions has become commonplace across different regions of the world, as experience has been shared and best practices developed in one region have been tested and applied in other contexts too. It is notable, for example, that regional maritime domain awareness and information sharing mechanisms developed initially in Southeast Asia—ReCAAP and the Singapore IFC—have been emulated in the Western Indian Ocean, Gulf of Guinea and elsewhere. Similarly, the SHADE deconfliction mechanism has been adapted for operations in the Mediterranean and Gulf of Guinea, while strategy writing has become an integral part of maritime security governance and reform process in many countries and regions.

Even so, these are not one-size-fits-all solutions. Context matters in maritime security, both in relation to the causes and structure of specific maritime insecurities themselves, but also because countries and regions are in different situations and positions when it comes to government systems, political economy, geopolitical relations, and geography. In consequence, what works or is appropriate in one country or region may not always be directly applicable to another. It is important that maritime security analysts and professionals are aware of and sensitive to local needs and conditions when experiences and practices are transferred across countries and regions.

Moreover, the maritime security environment is not static. New threats and challenges emerge, and existing insecurities change over time, as do the capacities required to deal with them. This may be because of changing political or environmental circumstances or the rise of new strategic or criminal threats at sea. In our last chapter we discuss how the context in which the maritime security toolbox operates is changing and consider what new challenges may be on the horizon.

8

New Challenges and a Look to the Future

8.1 The Evolving Maritime Security Environment

Maritime security is constantly evolving as new issues gain importance or appear on the horizon. The maritime security agenda is also influenced by wider dynamics in global ocean politics and international political order. The maritime security analyst and professional not only needs to understand the lessons and experiences of the past, but also maintain a forward-looking gaze, spot trends, and recognize new challenges. In this chapter we reflect on current trends and developments in the maritime security landscape.

We start with three issues that are impacting on maritime security thinking today: automation and cyber security, critical infrastructure protection, and climate change and biodiversity loss. These are agendas that are already having visible influence in the maritime security debate and will continue to do so in the future, not least since their relation to maritime security is not fully established and solutions not settled.

We then reflect on two wider trends in global ocean politics and consider their impact on the maritime security agenda: 1) the new momentum in global ocean governance, especially around multilateral environmental protection; and 2) the resurgence of geopolitical thinking and strategic competition, implying a militarization of maritime security. Taken together, these two trends provide a paradoxical outlook for the future of maritime security: on the one hand we can expect a continuing rise of planetary thinking and an increased drive for international cooperation to address shared problems, and on the other anticipate growing tensions, confrontation, and competition between states and diminishing opportunities for common solutions. We end with an investigation of whether these trends imply that maritime security is now entering a fifth wave of thinking and practice, or if we are entering a new era entirely.

Understanding Maritime Security. Christian Bueger and Timothy Edmunds, Oxford University Press.
© Oxford University Press 2024. DOI: 10.1093/oso/9780197767146.003.0008

8.2 Automation and Cyber Security

There is a growing trend toward automation in the maritime domain. Modern ports are highly automated and networked, allowing them to operate with fewer staff and significantly lower labor costs than was the case in the past. On board ship, most captains rely on electronic charts and use autopilots and other navigational aids. Many routine tasks—such engine management, cargo processing, or fire control systems—are also mechanized and digitized.

Increasingly prototypes are tested that go one step further, and the first fully automated ships are now available. In 2022, the first fully autonomous cargo vessels, the Norwegian *Barka Yara Birkeland* and the Chinese *Zhi Fei*, departed on their maiden voyages. These efforts remain essentially experimental in nature and limited to short distance shipping and passenger routes. Automation seems unlikely to replace the traditionally crewed ship across large distances any time soon. However, technology is constantly advancing, and it is likely that ever greater automation will be a common feature in future maritime activities.

The trend toward automation is also visible in maritime security agencies, where a substantial technological transformation is underway. Uncrewed underwater, surface, and aerial drones are now common in the inventories of many navies and coast guards. Most are used for surveillance purposes and are remote controlled. With artificial intelligence research rapidly progressing, these drones are likely to become more autonomous and potentially capable of working independently, for example by setting their own course, avoiding collisions, or identifying targets. This development has the potential to substantially increase the data quality of maritime domain awareness, and, given these assets can cover wider areas, will create new opportunities for cheaper and more effective maritime security operations.

Remote controlled and automated vehicles, however, also open a new spectrum of threats if these technologies are used by extremists, criminals, or state adversaries for hostile or illicit purposes. This includes the potential to carry out drone attacks as part of grey-zone operations (see Chapter 4, Section 4.4), but also to facilitate criminal activities such as narcotics smuggling. Drones not only pose a new set of legal questions, but will require new countermeasures.[1]

Automation implies that cyber threats to marine systems will become a more pressing concern, including attacks where perpetrators take over, manipulate, or

---

[1] Anna Petrig, "The Commission of Maritime Crimes with Unmanned Systems: An Interpretive Challenge for the United Nations Convention on the Law of the Sea," in *Maritime Security and the Law of the Sea*, ed. Malcolm D. Evans and Sofia Galani (Cheltenham: Edward Elgar Publishing, 2020), 104–131.

disrupt automated systems. These scenarios have become increasingly common in maritime security threat planning. For example, as early as 2011, the European Union Agency for Cyber Security published a report that documented the severity and range of cyber threats and vulnerabilities in the maritime domain.[2] Major efforts are underway by international organizations and industry associations, including the International Maritime Organization (IMO) and the Baltic and International Maritime Council (BIMCO), to prepare ports and shipping to meet these threats. In the following section we investigate some key maritime cyber threat scenarios and as well as known vulnerabilities and potential countermeasures.

NotPetya: A Harbinger of Things to Come?

In June 2017, a major cyber event took place which played a critical role in raising the importance of cyber issues on the maritime security agenda. Following a cyberattack on Ukrainian energy infrastructures by a group of Russia-related hackers, a malware code called NotPetya infected the IT systems of A. P. Møller–Mærsk, one of the largest global shipping companies. This resulted in 574 of its offices in 130 countries around the world being impacted, with all communications systems, including all telephones, paralyzed. "76 ports on all sides of the earth" were affected, "and nearly 800 seafaring vessels carrying tens of millions of tons of cargo, representing close to a fifth of the entire world's shipping capacity, was dead in the water."[3] Seventeen of Mærsk's port terminals were shut down, with gates frozen and cranes inoperative. Ships could not be unloaded and tens of thousands of trucks had to be turned away, causing major traffic disruption. It took the company 10 days to rebuild its IT system and caused a reported USD 300 million in damage.[4]

The NotPetya malware did not target the maritime industry or Mærsk specifically. However, it demonstrated the vulnerabilities of interconnected digital systems and infrastructure. It was a wake-up call for the maritime industry and security agencies to take cyber security seriously.

---

[2] ENISA, "Analysis of Cyber Security Aspects in the Maritime Sector" (Brussels: European Network and Information Security Agency, November 2011), https://www.enisa.europa.eu/publications/cyber-security-aspects-in-the-maritime-sector-1.

[3] Andy Greenberg, "The Untold Story of NotPetya, the Most Devastating Cyberattack in History," *Wired*, accessed June 19, 2023, https://www.wired.com/story/notpetya-cyberattack-ukraine-russia-code-crashed-the-world/.

[4] Afenyo and Caesar, "Maritime Cybersecurity Threats," 1.

Types of Maritime Cyber Threats

Cyber threats in the maritime sector broadly fall into three categories.[5] The first are attacks which aim to cause disruption, for example to commercial operations or to global manufacturing or supply chains, for strategic, extremist, criminal, or activist purposes. A second category are those that exploit vulnerabilities in systems for the purposes of state or corporate espionage, or to create opportunities for criminality such as extortion, identifying ships for piracy attacks, or facilitating the movement of smuggled goods through ports. A final category comprises the collateral damage caused by such attacks, as in the case of NotPetya. These include the knock-on effects of disruption to a major port to wider supply chains, or the indirect impact on the maritime sector of a cyberattack directed elsewhere.

Cyberthreats in the maritime domain can also be distinguished by whether they take place at sea or onshore.[6] Attacks at sea are likely to be relatively localized, in that while modern ships are highly automated with integrated on-board systems, their links to wider IT networks are disconnected while at sea. In contrast, modern port systems are highly networked, often at a global scale. Port logistics are complex, involving multiple different processes and activities including the loading and unloading of cargo, security scanning, data and inventory management, and the onward movement of goods through the supply chain.[7] These activities are managed through interconnected software and communication systems, database infrastructures, and IT processes. The multinational nature of many port and shipping companies means that these systems are often shared across many ports in different parts of the world. Similar observations can be made in regard to offshore installations such as oil and gas fields or windfarms, which are highly interconnected systems at a regional or global scale. In consequence, a cyberattack on one component of the system can have cascading impacts at global scale.

---

[5] Chris Bronk and Paula deWitte, "Maritime Cybersecurity: Meeting Threats to Globalization's Great Conveyor," in *Cyber Security: Critical Infrastructure Protection*, ed. Martti Lehto and Pekka Neittaanmäki (Cham: Springer International Publishing, 2022), 10.

[6] Bronk and deWitte, "Maritime Cybersecurity," 10.

[7] Jenna Ahokas et al., "Cybersecurity in Ports: A Conceptual Approach," in *Digitalization in Supply Chain Management and Logistics: Smart and Digital Solutions for an Industry 4.0 Environment*, ed. Wolfgang Blecker Kersten and Christian M. Thorsten Ringle, *Proceedings of the Hamburg International Conference of Logistics (HICL)*, n.d., accessed January 11, 2023, https://doi.org/10.15480/882.1448, 353.

Maritime Cyber Threat Scenarios

Major ports around the world were the subject of around 12 attempted cyberattacks a day in 2017, with this figure increasing by 900% in 2023.[8] Of these, the most common type of incident are ransomware attacks. These block access to key systems or threaten to publish sensitive data unless a ransom is paid to the perpetrator. However, since NotPetya, several other scenarios have been suggested for how cyberattacks might impact maritime security.

One is the potential for an attack targeted at vessel navigation or propulsion systems. The signals from the automated identification (AIS) or the global positioning (GPS) systems used by ships, for example, are not encrypted and can be manipulated and interfered through a practice known as "spoofing." Other communication and navigation systems, such as the Electronic Chart Display and Information System that is widely used to replace paper charts, can be manipulated remotely. Demonstrations from research groups have shown how easy it might be to hack into such systems. For example, college students showed in 2013 how to spoof the GPS signal of a yacht. Without detection, they transmitted a fake signal that caused the vessel to go off course.[9] A suspected spoofing incident involving over 20 vessels also took place in the Black Sea in 2017.[10]

A spoofing attack could be used by malign actors looking to cause chaos and disruption to shipping, while similar techniques could also be used to hide the real position of a vessel. This might be to distract maritime security forces from criminal activities such as illicit transshipment, or it could form part of a piracy operation, with a ship being misdirected to a location suitable for attack.

Another cyber risk is directed at port automation systems. Gaining access to or even control over port systems could offer numerous advantages to criminals. It might be possible to hide a particular cargo for a smuggling operation, for example, or to locate cargo to steal it. Similar methods could also be used to facilitate the movement of illicit weapons for criminal or terrorist purposes.

Regulatory Responses and Other Countermeasures

The IMO has issued guidelines and a resolution to address maritime cyber security for the shipping industry. Its Guidelines on Maritime Cyber Risk

---

[8] Mawuli Afenyo and Livingstone D. Caesar, "Maritime Cybersecurity Threats: Gaps and Directions for Future Research," *Ocean & Coastal Management* 236 (April 2023): 1.

[9] Maritime Executive, "Hacker Demonstrates Attack on Superyacht IT Systems," May 17, 2017, https://maritime-executive.com/article/hacker-demonstrates-attack-on-superyacht-it-systems

[10] Maritime Executive, "Hacker Demonstrates Attack on Superyacht IT Systems."

Management provide high-level recommendations for how to make maritime systems more resilient to cyberattack.[11] In June 2017, the IMO's Maritime Safety Committee also adopted a resolution on Maritime Cyber Risk Management in Safety Management Systems with the aim of making these procedures compulsory from 2021.[12] Shipping industry associations such as BIMCO also provide guidance on how to implement cyber security measures on board ships, while organizations such as the International Association of Ports and Harbors do so for ports. The industry has also created an International Maritime Cyber Emergency Response Team, which provides a tool for information sharing alerts and assistance in attack situations.

Other actors have also established maritime cyber security regulations, guidelines, or task forces. The European Coast Guard Functions Forum, for example, created a Cyber Security Working Group in 2023 focused on knowledge exchange between members, while the European Maritime Safety Agency has a cyber task force that provides training for maritime inspectors.[13] At a national level, many states have dedicated cyber security strategies and response infrastructures, and cyber concerns are an increasingly prominent feature of maritime security strategies as well.[14]

Incidents reported in public news outlets suggest an increasing cat and mouse game between cyber attackers and cyber resilience measures. They also point to the growing role of state-sponsored attacks in maritime grey-zone activities (see Chapter 4, Section 4.4). Increasingly, therefore, cyber security is now an integral part of maritime security. However, the sector still faces considerable obstacles in this area.

In a review conducted in 2023, researchers identified four particular challenges.[15] First, there is a lack of real time data on maritime attacks, and a reluctance to share data. This is in large part due to concerns around reputation management among affected organizations. However, it makes it difficult to model future attack scenarios and countermeasures and hampers lesson

---

[11] IMO, "Guidelines on Maritime Cyber Risk Management, MSC-FAL.1/Circ.3," June 2021, https://wwwcdn.imo.org/localresources/en/OurWork/Facilitation/Facilitation/MSC-FAL.1-Circ.3-Rev.1.pdf.

[12] IMO, "Maritime Cyber Risk Management in Safety Management Systems, MSC.428(98)," June 2017, https://wwwcdn.imo.org/localresources/en/OurWork/Security/Documents/Resolution%20MSC.428(98).pdf.

[13] "Cyber Threats in the Maritime Sector: Cybersecurity Working Group," mobility, accessed July 1, 2023, http://mobilit.belgium.be/en/news/cyber-threats-maritime-sector-cybersecurity-working-group.

[14] See for example HMG, "National Strategy for Maritime Security, CP 724," August 2022, https://www.gov.uk/government/publications/national-maritime-security-strategy, 36–39.

[15] Afenyo and Caesar, "Maritime Cybersecurity Threats."

learning between actors. Second, the wider economic impacts on a large-scale cyberattack are poorly understood, with implications for supply chain resilience and preparedness. Third, there is often a lack of training and awareness of cyberthreats among maritime professionals, which can increase vulnerabilities in the sector. For example, an industry report found that most shipowners significantly underinvest in cyber security management, with more than half spending less than USD 100,000 a year.[16] Finally, national and international legal and insurance frameworks may be inadequate to deal with the maritime cyber space. This is especially so given the potentially globally distributed nature of any cyberattack in terms of both perpetrators and victims.

In addition, cyber security responses are often in the hands of specialist government agencies, or private consultant and response teams some of which might have only narrow understanding of the maritime sector and its laws. This adds further to actor complexity in the maritime security sector.[17]

Summary

As automation in the maritime sector advances, these trends are expected to gain further momentum. Cyber security is already a high priority issue for governments and commercial actors around the world, as illustrated by the publication of dedicated cyber security strategies and the institutionalization of wide-ranging cyber resilience measures. In the maritime sector, cyber security has become an increasingly high priority for states and industry, though significant vulnerabilities and preparedness gaps remain. Both cyber and maritime domains are notable for their globalized and transnational character. However, there is a need for greater harmonization between the two regimes, and the potential for significant mutual learning and cross-fertilization of the debate in terms of the toolbox of responses and resilience measures. This is especially so given the critical role that IT systems, ports, and shipping play in the infrastructure of the global economy.

In the following section, we explore the critical infrastructures of the maritime domain in more detail and consider the growing importance of critical infrastructure protection to the maritime security agenda.

---

[16] CyberOwl, "CyberOwl, HFW Report: Maritime Industry Pays Average $3m Ransom In Cyberattacks," *Cyber Owl* (blog), March 2022, https://cyberowl.io/cyberowl-hfw-report-maritime-industry-pays-average-3m-ransom-in-cyberattacks/.

[17] Diego Edison Cabuya Padilla and Carlos Castaneda-Marroquin, "Maritime Cyberdefense Actors Taxonomy for Command and Control," in *Developments and Advances in Defense and Security*, ed. Álvaro Rocha, Carlos Hernan Fajardo-Toro, and José María Riola Rodríguez (Singapore: Springer, 2022), 37–46.

8.3 Critical Infrastructure Protection: Ports, Cables, and Pipelines

The protection of critical infrastructure is an important element of both maritime and cyber security. Because of the technical nature of the issue area, but also the inherent vagueness of the concept of critical infrastructure, it is often approached as an independent issue by different academic and policy communities.[18] However, there are many important links to the maritime domain, and these are increasingly recognized and addressed.[19] In particular, the protection of offshore installations and underwater infrastructures such as data cables and pipelines has become an increasingly significant feature of maritime security debates, especially since the attack on the Nord Stream pipelines in the Baltic Sea in September 2022.

In this section we briefly reconstruct the general critical infrastructure protection debate, before examining ports, data cables, and energy infrastructures as examples of key maritime infrastructures. We end by reflecting on the relationship between critical maritime infrastructure protection and maritime security.

What Are Critical Infrastructures?

"Infrastructure" is a complicated and diffuse term.[20] In a general sense, it refers to those structures that underlie and enable societal, economic, and political activities. Roads and public transportation, electricity grids and power stations, communication cables and data centers, offshore platforms, wind and solar farms, shipping, ferries, airports, and ports can all be considered infrastructures in this sense.

A core feature of infrastructures is that they are designed to operate in the background without raising attention. In consequence, infrastructures are often invisible.[21] They only become a matter of public scrutiny when they fail or stop functioning as expected. It is when bridges are closed or there is a power cut

---

[18] Reidar Staupe-Delgado, Dina Abdel-Fattah, and Christer Pursiainen, "A Discipline without a Name? Contrasting Three Fields Dealing with Hazards and Disaster," *International Journal of Disaster Risk Reduction* 70 (February 2022): 102751.

[19] Christian Bueger and Tobias Liebetrau, "Critical Maritime Infrastructure Protection: What's the Trouble?," *Marine Policy*, 155 (2023): 105772.

[20] Christian Bueger, Tobias Liebetrau, and Jan Stockbruegger, "Theorizing Infrastructures in Global Politics," *International Studies Quarterly*, 67, no. 4 (2023): squad101.

[21] Christian Bueger and Tobias Liebetrau, "Protecting Hidden Infrastructure: The Security Politics of the Global Submarine Data Cable Network," *Contemporary Security Policy* 42, no. 3 (July 2021): 391–413.

that we become aware of their importance. A good illustration of both the importance and everyday invisibility of maritime infrastructure is the Suez Canal. A key point of passage for global shipping between Europe and Asia, its vital role in the world economy became highly visible in 2021 when the container ship *Ever Given* became stuck, blocking the Canal for weeks and causing the breakdown of global supply chains.[22]

The term "critical infrastructure" indicates that some infrastructures, such as the Suez Canal, are more essential for the functioning of society, economy, and security than others. Designating infrastructures as critical implies that they should receive special consideration and protection. However, the question of how to designate infrastructures as critical remains contested. While several methodologies have been proposed for identifying criticality,[23] in practice it tends to be a matter of political choice, often driven by changing securitizations and security practices (see Chapter 3, Section 3.4). Critical infrastructure protection is often challenging because different industrial sectors (e.g., transport, electricity, water, health) and their intersections need to be considered, and many infrastructures have complicated public-private ownership structures.

Changing Understandings of Critical Infrastructures

The concept of critical infrastructure protection has roots in debates on civilian protection in the Second World War but was first defined in American security discourses of the mid-1990s. It was extended and rose to global prominence in the wake of the 9/11 attacks of 2001, when many states published critical infrastructure policies as part of their counterterrorism response strategies.[24] The key question driving the debate was which infrastructures could become physical targets of terrorist groups. Primary attention was initially given to airports as security relevant sites, and, after the London attacks of July 2007, to public transportation. As we discuss in Chapter 4, Section 4.3 reviewing maritime terrorism, the focus in maritime security was mainly on ports.

---

[22] Jade Man-yin Lee and Eugene Yin-cheung Wong, "Suez Canal Blockage: An Analysis of Legal Impact, Risks and Liabilities to the Global Supply Chain," *MATEC Web of Conferences* 339 (2021): 01019.

[23] Jose M. Yusta, Gabriel J. Correa, and Roberto Lacal-Arántegui, "Methodologies and Applications for Critical Infrastructure Protection: State-of-the-Art," *Energy Policy* 39, no. 10 (October 2011): 6100–6119.

[24] Jens Ivo Engels, "Introduction," in *Key Concepts for Critical Infrastructure Research*, ed. Jens Ivo Engels (Wiesbaden: Springer Fachmedien, 2018), 443–462.

		On the sea	In the sea	On land
	Transport	Ships, shipping lanes	Emissions	Ports
	Energy	Platforms	Platforms, electricity cables, pipelines	Ports, landing stations, repair facilities
	Communication	Repair ships	Data cables	Landing stations, repair facilities
	Fisheries	Ships, fishing zones	Fishing gear, aquaculture	Ports, aquaculture
	Ecosystems	Biodiversity	Biodiversity, carbon sink, carbon storage	Coastal areas, beaches

Figure 8.1 Maritime infrastructures considered to be critical. Source: Christian Bueger and Tobias Liebetrau, "Critical Maritime Infrastructure Protection: What's the Trouble?," *Marine Policy* 155 (2023): 105772, 3.

With the rise of cyber security concerns, attention has gradually shifted to the data infrastructures used by governments in areas such as health services, finance, air traffic control, electricity, water, and public transportation. The relevance for the maritime domain was only recognized relatively late, with the NotPetya incident serving as the main wake-up call.

Since the late 2010s, and in the light of the growing tensions between NATO members and Russia, attention has increasingly turned toward underwater infrastructures.[25] The initial focus was on the potential vulnerability of submarine data cables. As we show later in this chapter, after the sabotage of the Nord Stream pipelines in the Baltic Sea in 2022, there was also a new focus on underwater energy infrastructures such as oil and gas pipelines and electricity cables. A key concern now is how hostile states might exploit the vulnerability of such infrastructures through grey-zone operations (see Chapter 4, Section 4.4). Figure 8.1 provides an outline of maritime infrastructures considered to be critical.

Ports

Ports were at the focus of the critical infrastructure debate early on, because of their role at heart of the global economy and trade. They are vulnerable to cyberthreats, as discussed above, but also to attacks on their physical infrastructures and operations. Their importance was highlighted when concerns over terrorism led

---

[25] Bueger and Liebetrau, "Critical Maritime Infrastructure Protection."

states to consider how to protect their most critical infrastructures, leading to a new emphasis on physical security at port facilities.[26] The potential for disruption caused by a port incident is considerable. The shutdown of a major port, for example, could have major implications for national supply chains and energy supplies. The fact that many ports are located close to population centers or even within urban environments has the potential to intensify these impacts. This was tragically demonstrated by the 2020 Beirut port disaster, when a large store of ammonium nitrate exploded, causing at least 200 deaths and 7,000 injuries.[27]

Key port security responses include the IMO's International Ship and Port Facility (ISPS) Code, and the Proliferation Security Initiative, all of which aim to make ports more resilient in face of threats posed by terrorism and organized crime (see Chapter 4, Section 4.4). The growing importance of cyber security issues for the maritime sector has also led to significantly greater investments in the digital security of port infrastructures.

Underwater Communication Cables

The protection of underwater infrastructures became an increasingly important priority for many states in the 2010s. In Europe, this was mainly due to two factors. First, European states observed increased naval activities by the Russian navy in the vicinity of their underwater infrastructures, especially subsea data cables.[28] Second, security analysts noted that while the socioeconomic importance of these cables had increased exponentially with the rise of the internet and information technologies, they had largely been absent from the mainstream security agenda.[29]

Underwater cables have been critical to global communications since the late nineteenth century.[30] Transoceanic and transcontinental telegraph cables allowed for swift communication across time zones for the first time. This communications infrastructure created new possibilities for diplomacy, but also for managing empires and providing instructions to military forces

---

[26] James A. Malcolm, "Responding to International Terrorism: The Securitisation of the United Kingdom's Ports," *British Journal of Politics and International Relations* 18, no. 2 (May 2016): 443–462.

[27] Christian Bueger and Scott Edwards, "Beirut Explosion: The Disaster Was Exceptional but Events Leading up to It Were Not—Researchers," *The Conversation*, August 2020, http://theconversation.com/beirut-explosion-the-disaster-was-exceptional-but-events-leading-up-to-it-were-not-researchers-144011.

[28] Bueger and Liebetrau, "Protecting Hidden Infrastructure."

[29] Robert Martinage, "Under the Sea," *Foreign Affairs*, January 2015, https://www.foreignaffairs.com/articles/commons/under-sea.

[30] Simone M. Müller, *Wiring the World: The Social and Cultural Creation of Global Telegraph Networks* (New York: Columbia University Press, 2016).

abroad. In consequence, control over telegraphic cable infrastructures was a key issue in the early twentieth century, including during the two world wars where attention focused on intercepting messages from cables or disrupting them. Telegraphic cables were replaced by more efficient coaxial cables in the postwar period and became a target of spying operations during the Cold War.

Today's internet runs through a global system of underwater optic fiber cables. This infrastructure has the capacity to transport high volumes of data and almost all intercontinental transfers, including emails, telephone communications, and financial transactions, run through them. The technology differs radically from old cable systems, since data is split into and travels in packages. This makes the direct interception of data flows in cables as part of intelligence operations more difficult than was the case in the past.

Accidental failures in cable systems happen quite frequently.[31] These are mainly caused by natural events such as submarine earthquakes or tsunamis, or accidents caused by regular marine activities such as bottom trawling. However, the potential remains for undersea cables to be deliberately damaged by terrorist groups, criminals, or hostile states. By 2023, no incident of deliberate sabotage on a subsea data cable had been publicly recorded, though several incidents were seen as suspicious However, the vulnerabilities of the global cable system are a growing concern. While full information blackouts remain unlikely scenarios for those countries with multiple cable connections, the issue is more critical for small islands or weakly connected states where single cable cuts could cause major damage.

Maritime Energy Infrastructures

Energy infrastructures, particularly offshore oil and gas platforms and pipelines, have featured prominently as geopolitical and national security priorities since they were first constructed.[32] Indeed, discussion over the protection of energy infrastructures was one of the key features of the widening of security debates beyond military issues alone (see Chapter 3, Section 3.4). Since then, offshore oil and gas production has expanded considerably. The industry is dependent

---

[31] Christian Bueger, Tobias Liebetrau, and Jonas Franken, "Security Threats to Undersea Communications Cables and Infrastructure—Consequences for the EU," In-Depth Analysis for the European Parliament Requested by the SEDE Sub-Committee (European Union, June 2022), https://www.europarl.europa.eu/RegData/etudes/IDAN/2022/702557/EXPO_IDA(2022)702557_EN.pdf.

[32] Roland Dannreuther, *Energy Security* (Cambridge: Polity, 2017).

on a complex network of pipelines and shipping routes to transport its products to land.[33]

With the turn to green energy, oil and gas infrastructures have been joined by other facilities such as offshore wind farms. As part of the green energy transition offshore wind farms are being continuously expanded worldwide.[34] Since not all waters lend themselves equally to wind farming, regions with significant potential such as the North Sea are gaining in strategic importance.

Windfarms connect to the land via undersea electricity cables. These underwater power cables also increasingly run between countries and regions. For example, Norway and Scotland are linked through an underwater cable system that allows them to trade green energy. Major underwater power cable grids are planned, such as in the Mediterranean to deliver solar energy from North Africa to Europe, and there are even plans in place to build a connection between Australia and Singapore. Future initiatives include the construction of artificial islands to become new offshore green energy hubs, the use of wind power to produce hydrogen from the sea, and the colocation of floating wind and solar farms. Another set of expanding green energy infrastructures are projects that aim to store carbon dioxide under the sea to reduce carbon emissions.

While recognized as important critical infrastructures, offshore energy facilities and underwater pipelines and cables did not feature prominently in maritime security debates, until recently.[35] Instead, they were discussed within specialized and quite technical energy security, homeland security, or resilience debates focused on engineering solutions and system analysis.

This situation changed in 2022 when two major pipelines connecting Russia to Germany—known as Nord Stream 1 and 2—were attacked in the Baltic Sea.[36] Four explosions just outside the territorial waters of Sweden and Denmark demonstrated the vulnerability of maritime infrastructures, and the difficulties of detecting and deterring such attacks. How the sabotage was carried out and who

---

[33] Jean-Baptiste Jouffray, Robert Blasiak, Albert V. Norström, Henrik Österblom, and Magnus Nyström, "The Blue Acceleration: The Trajectory of Human Expansion into the Ocean," *One Earth* 2, no. 1 (January 2020): 43–54.

[34] GWEC, "Global Offshore Wind Report 2022" (Global Wind Energy Council, 2021), https://gwec.net/gwecs-global-offshore-wind-report/.

[35] Christian Bueger and Timothy Edmunds, "Maritime Security and the Wind: Threats and Risks to Offshore Renewable Energy Infrastructures," *Ocean Yearbook* 38 (2024), https://brill.com/view/journals/ocyo/ocyo-overview.xml?language=en.

[36] Christian Bueger, "Nord Stream Pipeline Sabotage: How an Attack Could Have Been Carried out and Why Europe Was Defenceless," *The Conversation*, October 2022, http://theconversation.com/nord-stream-pipeline-sabotage-how-an-attack-could-have-been-carried-out-and-why-europe-was-defenceless-191895.

the culprits were remained under investigation at the time of writing. However, the attacks have triggered ongoing speculation and concern in maritime security circles.[37] The 2022 Nord Stream incidents were a significant event that triggered a substantial response among North Sea and Baltic Sea coastal states, including the procurement of additional naval vessels with a primary role of seabed infrastructure protection. They also brought both energy infrastructures and data cables into the heart of the maritime security agenda, with a growing number of analysts focusing on infrastructure and the most recent maritime security strategies such as those of the United Kingdom and the European Union incorporating them too.

Summary

Critical infrastructure protection and maritime security are two increasingly convergent debates. While the specificities of the maritime domain were for a long time absent in the critical infrastructure discussions, cross-fertilization has led to a growing awareness of their importance in maritime security. The question of how the maritime security toolbox (see Chapter 7) can contribute to national and regional resilience in this area has thus become vital. Maritime domain awareness (see Chapter 7, Section 7.5), for example, can play a key role in the detection and prevention of suspicious or hostile activities and crimes in the vicinity of critical maritime infrastructures. Even so, given the sheer scale of these infrastructures, including thousands of kilometers of cables on the sea floor, this means that it will continue to be a challenging task and significant risks and vulnerabilities are likely to remain for the foreseeable future.

As the debate on critical maritime security infrastructures matures, and given the rising investments in offshore infrastructures, in particular wind energy, it is likely that it will be a key driver of future maritime security debates. The pursuit of this agenda will lead to new linkages between cyber security, maritime security, and energy security and new interest in regions, such as the North Sea or Baltic Sea, that have not featured prominently in maritime security debates to date. Insofar as ecosystems and fisheries can be interpreted as critical infrastructures, it also paves the way for a new holistic agenda for infrastructure protection.

---

[37] Christian Bueger, "Ukraine War: Kremlin's Threat to Interfere with Undersea Data Cables May Be Bluster, but Must Be Taken Seriously," *The Conversation*, June 2023, http://theconversation.com/ukraine-war-kremlins-threat-to-interfere-with-undersea-data-cables-may-be-bluster-but-must-be-taken-seriously-208125.

8.4 Climate Change and Biodiversity Loss

One of the major global developments of the past few decades has been an increasing recognition of the dramatic impact of climate change and biodiversity loss. These issues also have consequences for maritime security. The link between the environmental politics and maritime security agenda is increasingly important and has started to influence strategic thinking. Changes to the marine environment are linked to maritime security in at least three ways. First, they will put new operational pressures on maritime security capabilities. Second, they are likely to lead to new forms of maritime insecurity and patterns of blue crime. Third, maritime security forces are confronted with a new spectrum of tasks. In this section we briefly summarize the key transformations caused by climate change and biodiversity loss in the maritime domain, and then discuss each of these challenges in turn.

Climate Change and Biodiversity Loss

It is an established fact that human induced climate change is leading to a rapid process of global warming, with severe impacts on the marine environment. This is already having dramatic effects, with significant implications for maritime security.

The first of these concerns sea-level rise. While predictions vary, the latest report by the UN Inter-Governmental Panel on Climate Change estimates that sea levels are likely to rise by up to 0.3 meters by 2050, and to as much as 1.1 meters by the end of the century.[38] Under these scenarios, some coastal zones and islands are expected to become uninhabitable. The physical existence and viability of some small island states will also be threatened. Climate change contributes to an increase in the frequency of severe weather events at sea. This might mean more frequent and severe storms, but it will also impact on wind patterns, tides, storm surges, and average wave heights. This will make the maritime domain a harsher environment for seafarers of all types, but also put pressures on coastal zones and islands.

---

[38] Michael Oppenheimer, Bruce C. Glavovic, Jochen Hinkel, Roderik van de Wal, Alexandre K. Magnan, Amro Abd-Elgawad, Rongshou Cai, Miguel Cifuentes-Jara, Robert M. DeConto, Tuhin Ghosh, John Hay, Federico Isla, Ben Marzeion, Benoit Meyssignac, and Zita Sebesvari, "2019: Sea Level Rise and Implications for Low-Lying Islands, Coasts and Communities," in *IPCC Special Report on the Ocean and Cryosphere in a Changing Climate*, ed. Hans-Otto Pörtner, Deborah C. Roberts, Valerie Masson-Delmotte, Panmao Zhai, Melinda Tignor, Elvira Poloczanska, Katja Mintenbeck, Anders Alegría, Maike Nicolai, Andrew Okem, Jan Petzold, Bardhyl Rama, and Norma M. Weyer (Cambridge and New York: Cambridge University Press), 327, accessed February 4, 2024, https://www.ipcc.ch/site/assets/uploads/sites/3/2022/03/06_SROCC_Ch04_FINAL.pdf.

These changes have worrying implications for marine biodiversity.[39] This might be because warmer waters mean that some species, such as corals and the flora and fauna that depend on them, will no longer be able to survive and may even become extinct, or it might be because fish and other animals are forced to migrate to new areas. These changes will impact on food security and the potential of blue economies world-wide, but also have implications for the vulnerability and resilience of coastal zones and islands to extreme weather events. Given the importance of the ocean floor and kelp and mangrove forests as carbon sinks, marine biodiversity has a fundamental role in mitigating climate change, since the destruction of ecosystems enhances global carbon release.[40]

Much of the decline in marine biodiversity does not result directly from climate change, and the oceans face many of other critical environmental stressors.[41] Unsustainable fishing practices, whether legal or illegal, harm fish populations and threaten the extinction of some species. Pollution from plastics, chemicals, and the shipping industry puts pressure on marine ecosystems. These are outcomes of underregulation and crimes on land or of environmental crimes at sea, such as the deliberate release of waste, oil, chemicals, or ballast water (see Chapter 5, Section 5.5). They are also related to marine disasters and accidents, such as oil spills, container loss, on-board fires, ship collisions, or other failures that lead to the abandonment of vessels at sea. Given the anticipated increase of extreme weather events, such accidents are expected to increase and lead to further pollution in the future.[42]

Operational Challenges for Maritime Security Forces

These developments will pose challenges for maritime security forces on a practical and operational level, with the most direct and immediate impact taking place at the level of infrastructure and seagoing capabilities.

Sea-level rise and more frequent severe weather events increase the risk of flooding in coastal regions. This threatens the viability of many bases, ports,

---

[39] Andrew S. Brierley and Michael J. Kingsford, "Impacts of Climate Change on Marine Organisms and Ecosystems," *Current Biology* 19, no. 14 (July 2009): R602–R614.

[40] C. Heinze, S. Meyer, N. Goris, L. Anderson, R. Steinfeldt, N. Chang, C. Le Quére, and D. C. E. Bakker, "The Ocean Carbon Sink—Impacts, Vulnerabilities and Challenges," *Earth System Dynamics* 6, no. 1 (June 2015): 327–358.

[41] Martin R. Stuchtey, Adrien Vincent, Andreas Merkl, Maximilian Bucher, Peter M. Haugan, Jane Lubchenco, and Mari Elka Pangestu, "Ocean Solutions That Benefit People, Nature and the Economy" (Washington, DC: World Resources Institute, 2020), https://oceanpanel.org/publication/ocean-solutions-that-benefit-people-nature-and-the-economy/.

[42] AGCS, "Safety and Shipping Review 2023" (Allianz Global and Corporate Speciality, May 2023), https://www.agcs.allianz.com/news-and-insights/reports/shipping-safety.html.

and harbor infrastructures, whether due to their potential for inundation or because of damage to their power and water supplies or physical structures. The US Navy, which conducted a thorough assessment of the impact of climate change on its operations, concluded that a significant majority of facilities were at risk. In a report published in 2011, the navy noted that "utilities such as electrical substations, sewage treatment facilities, and communications nodes, as well as other important and critical infrastructures on the base, may be destroyed or seriously degraded by flooding caused by sea-level rise."[43]

Changing weather conditions, including higher wave heights will also place more severe demands on vessels, implying that hardening measures, or new ship designs will be needed. The training of skills such as navigation and boarding also have to adapt to a harsher maritime environment. Sea-level rise and coastal erosion may also lead to the creation of new marine areas, including shallow waters and intertidal zones, which in turn may provide new areas of operation for maritime criminals and raise the need of dedicated operational capabilities.

The decarbonization of societies and industries required to address climate change, will also lead to public demands for "green" navies and coast guards.[44] Decarbonizing seagoing maritime security forces, for instance, by using hydrogen as fuel, wind power, or electrifying components, implies new investments in infrastructures, engine, and ship design as well as repair and maintenance.

New Patterns of Maritime Insecurity and Blue Crime

These changes to the operating environment are largely physical in nature and directly predicable from what we know about the effects of climate change. A second challenge is more speculative. Will climate change and biodiversity loss lead to new maritime insecurities and patterns of blue crime? Taking account of the debate on root causes introduced in Chapter 3, Section 3.5, there are good reasons to think that they will.

Climate change and biodiversity loss will lead to economic pressures and threaten coastal economies and livelihoods across the world.[45] The severe impact that declines in fish stocks can have on artisanal fishers is already apparent, but

---

[43] National Research Council, *National Security Implications of Climate Change for U.S. Naval Forces* (Washington, DC: The National Academies Press, 2011), 74, https://nap.nationalacademies.org/download/12914; see also Chris Rahman, "The Implications of Climate Change for Maritime Security Forces," *Climate Change and the Oceans*, November 2012, 170–172.

[44] Neta C. Crawford, *The Pentagon, Climate Change, and War: Charting the Rise and Fall of U.S. Military Emissions* (Cambridge, MA: MIT Press, 2022).

[45] Basil Germond and Antonios D. Mazaris, "Climate Change and Maritime Security," *Marine Policy* 99 (January 2019): 263.

environmental pressures will threaten other areas of the blue economy such as tourism as well. A loss of inhabitable land, flooding, an increase of severe weather events, or shortages of fresh water will damage coastal economies against the backdrop of growing populations. This creates the potential for increased economic marginalization and dislocation in coastal regions, which could lead to new motivations for irregular migration and incentives for engaging in criminal activities at sea. This is not only a potential issue for poorer nations, or the Global South. Aggrieved and marginalized fishers, for instance, might feel motivated to support crimes, such as smuggling illicit goods and narcotics, across regions.

Climate change has impacts on land far beyond coastal regions. Desertification or changing weather patterns on land are likely to threaten traditional agricultural regions and practices in many parts of the world, forcing more people to leave their homes.[46] This is turn is likely to lead to more irregular migration, with its associated problems of people smuggling and human trafficking, including by sea. These changes may also exacerbate political instabilities on land, with implications both for the spill over of civil conflicts into the maritime domain, but also the capacity of states to manage and police blue crimes.

Environmental changes might also lead to the emergence of new geographic hotspots for blue crime.[47] This is most obvious for the case of illicit fishing, as fish stocks come under new pressures or migrate to new regions. However, the abandonment of formerly inhabited areas due to sea-level rise might also create new opportunities for smugglers or pirates, particularly if they are lightly policed.

Moreover, sea-level rise and resource scarcity have the potential to create new interstate tensions and boundary disputes at sea.[48] Sea-level rise presents a significant challenge to the United Nations Convention on the Law of the Sea (UNCLOS) rules for maritime border delimitation because of the way in which it will alter coastlines and may even lead to the total immersion of island territories to which sizable exclusive economic zones (EEZs) are attached. This could lead to new tensions over already settled boundaries, or new difficulties in the arbitration of ongoing border disputes. It could also create new patterns of blue crime, which often thrives in contested and ambiguous jurisdictional zones. Climate change also has the potential to open new arenas of geopolitical contestation at sea, most notably in the Arctic, where ice-melt seems likely to open new sea routes between Asia and Europe but also allow easier access to—and potentially competition over—marine resources such as oil and gas.

---

[46] Stuart Kaye, "Climate Change and Maritime Security," *Climate Change and the Oceans*, November 2012, 157–159.

[47] Kaye, "Climate Change and Maritime Security," 159–162.

[48] Rahman, "The Implications of Climate Change for Maritime Security Forces," 168–170.

New Tasks for Maritime Security Forces

Environmental pressures in the maritime domain imply that the demands on maritime security forces will increase. New expressions of maritime insecurity will intensify existing law enforcement tasks, for example around policing blue crimes or managing new patterns of irregular migration. An increase in severe weather events will create a high risk of accidents at sea, leading to more frequent search and rescue operations and salvage responses, including potentially in remote areas or regions with low capacities. An increase in weather-induced catastrophes implies that humanitarian and disaster relief operations will become more frequent, with maritime security forces being called upon to support these operations from the sea.[49] More work can be expected across the entire spectrum of established coast guard functions and constabulary roles.

The task spectrum of these operations will also widen substantially, with new environmental laws, standards, and regulations coming into force as part of the response to climate change and biodiversity loss. This is perhaps most apparent in relation to marine protected areas, which place vast new areas of the ocean under special protections which need to be monitored and policed.[50] But it also relates to marine environmental regulations more widely. These are likely to become stricter over time, with the criminalization of previously permitted activities, for example around vessel emissions, pollution restrictions, or fish catch standards. This in turn will create new capacity demands in relation to environmental policing and compliance, as well as criminal investigation and prosecution.

These new tasks will also include critical maritime infrastructure protection. The expansion of green offshore energy infrastructures, including windfarms, energy islands, electricity cables, and hydrogen pipelines, has become a political priority to mitigate climate change, but also creates new vulnerabilities. The destruction of the Nord Stream pipelines discussed in the prior section illustrates the risk that hostile actors potentially pose to maritime critical infrastructures, and expansions of these installations will need to be accompanied by new protective measures.

Finally, the role that maritime security forces can play in climate change adaptation will receive further attention. For instance, coastal restoration, such as the reforestation of kelp and mangroves—vital for both carbon storage and coastal protection—is labor-intensive and requires significant capabilities. An example of the contribution that agencies can make in this regard is the Pakistan Navy Mangroves Plantation Campaign of 2017, in which the navy in collaboration

---

[49] Rahman, "The Implications of Climate Change for Maritime Security Forces," 172–176.
[50] Noella J. Gray, "Sea Change: Exploring the International Effort to Promote Marine Protected Areas," *Conservation and Society* 8, no. 4 (2010): 331–338.

with the International Union for Conservation and Nature agreed to plant one million mangrove saplings.[51]

Summary

Climate change and biodiversity loss induce substantial transformations both in terms of the meaning of maritime security in particular with regard to environmental crimes, but also a widened spectrum of tasks for maritime law enforcement. While a new generation of maritime security strategies acknowledges the importance of the environmental agenda at a general level,[52] the impacts of environmental degradation at sea continue to be poorly understood among policymakers, maritime security practitioners, and analysts alike. This raises the need for research and new planning methodologies, as well as revised capacity-building and training approaches. The intersections between climate change, biodiversity loss, and maritime security, and also the crossover to the critical (green) maritime infrastructure agenda, will become a key driver in future maritime security debates.

8.5 Between Planetary Thinking and Geopolitics

Automation, cyber security, critical infrastructure protection, climate change, and biodiversity loss are all developments that are influencing the maritime security agenda today and are likely to do so more strongly in the future. They not only transform the issues that are relevant to maritime security; they also widen the spectrum of actors involved and the kind of capacities and coordination instruments that are required to address them.

In this section we investigate how two other master trends in world politics are influencing the maritime security agenda. These are more diffuse and take place at a grander political and diplomatic scale. Since they are not issues that can be straightforwardly addressed at an operational level, their impact on maritime security is less tangible. However, they set the parameters for future discussion as they present major transformations in global political order.

In our short history of maritime security (see Chapter 2) we discussed how important strategic developments such as the end of the Cold War and the war

---

[51] "Pakistan Naval Chief Pledges to Plant a Million Mangrove Saplings During 2017" (IUCN, August 2017), https://www.iucn.org/news/pakistan/201708/pakistan-naval-chief-pledges-plant-million-mangrove-saplings-during-2017.

[52] European Commission, "The EU Maritime Security Strategy and Its Action Plan," 2023, https://eur-lex.europa.eu/legal-content/EN/TXT/?uri=CELEX:52023JC0008; HMG, "NSMS."

against terrorism were for the development of the maritime security agenda. In the 2020s new master trends are unfolding, which we introduce in more depth here. First we look at a new multilateral momentum in global ocean governance, before turning to a renaissance of geopolitical thinking and strategic competition.

Planetary Thinking and the New Momentum in Global Ocean Governance

In parallel to the evolution of the maritime security agenda, a significant re-evaluation of the oceans as a social, economic, and environmental space has taken place in global politics.[53] This process has in many ways been closely linked to the climate change and biodiversity agenda and has progressed as the substantial decline in ocean health has become better documented. It is also a product of a recognition that the oceans could be a new economic frontier if managed in a sustainable and environmentally friendly manner. This assumption is at the heart of "blue economy" thinking. The blue economy in this respect represents an ambition to enhance environmentally sustainable economic growth in the maritime sector through new ocean business models and practices, of which wind farms, aquaculture, or ecotourism are often seen as paradigmatic examples.

Discussions of blue health and the blue economy form part of a substantial and growing array of informal ocean governance mechanisms, including UN Sustainable Development Goal 14: Life Below Water, advisory bodies, such as the High Level Panel for a Sustainable Ocean Economy, and regular intergovernmental forums, such as the UN Ocean Conference, Our Ocean Conference, or the Economist's World Ocean Summit.

Many of the key solutions being sought to protect and restore ocean health and provide for sustainable maritime economic development lie in integrated ocean management approaches, also known as marine spatial planning. Marine spatial planning aims to better organize and harmonize the many uses of ocean space and resources, while identifying the most critical zones for the marine ecosystem and turning these into marine protected areas. This is a global trend, with around 8% of the global oceans already designated as protected areas by 2022, and the Conference of the Parties (COP15) to the UN Convention on Biological Diversity agreeing in December 2022 to protect 30% of the oceans by 2030 (known as the 30x30 target).

---

[53] Christian Bueger and Felix Mallin, "Blue Paradigms: Understanding the Intellectual Revolution in Global Ocean Politics," *International Affairs*, 99, no. 4 (2023): 1719–1739.

The year 2023 also saw the successful conclusion of negotiations on an international treaty that will allow for the creation of protected areas in international waters. This is known as the Biodiversity Beyond Areas of National Jurisdiction (BBNJ) or High Seas Treaty.[54] The treaty, once ratified, will provide an institutional framework for designating protected areas and specifying rules within them. It also deals with the question of the use and distribution of income from genetic maritime resources and technical assistance. Concluded against the backdrop of the war in Ukraine and the heightened geopolitical tensions we discuss in the next section, observers have hailed the treaty to be a significant new symbol for planetary thinking and commitment to multilateral solutions.[55]

The international agreement on 30x30 and the conclusion of the BBNJ negotiations are indicative of new forms of global thinking that emphasize the oceans as a planetary common and shared heritage of humankind (see Chapter 2, Section 2.2). Other measures and treaties are also underway and further feed this observation. Negotiations on an effective climate change regime for shipping have gathered pace, as have efforts to negotiate an international treaty regulating the problem of plastic waste pollution in the oceans.[56] These developments show how the maritime space is increasingly conceived of as a globally integrated ecosystem that must be carefully managed and restored.

Sceptics point out that this turn to planetary thinking and notions of a globally integrated ocean ecosystem have not so far led to more coordinated action between states, nor to the establishment of an integrated global governance mechanism to oversee these measures in practice. In part, this is because the global governance arrangements that deal with oceans as a whole are even more complex than the picture we painted in our discussion of the international organizations of maritime security in Chapter 6, Section 6.3. This situation is often described as one of institutional "fragmentation."[57] Fragmentation implies that

---

[54] Stewart Patrick, "The High Seas Treaty Is an Extraordinary Diplomatic Achievement," Carnegie Endowment for International Peace, accessed June 28, 2023, https://carnegieendowment.org/2023/03/08/high-seas-treaty-is-extraordinary-diplomatic-achievement-pub-89228.

[55] Elizabeth Mendenhall, Rachel Tiller, and Elizabeth Nyman, "The Ship Has Reached the Shore: The Final Session of the "Biodiversity Beyond National Jurisdiction' Negotiations," *Marine Policy* 155 (September 2023): 105686.

[56] Jan Stockbruegger and Christian Bueger, "From Mitigation to Adaptation: Addressing Climate Change in the Maritime Shipping Industry" (WIRE Climate Change forthcoming 2024); UNEP, International Negotiating Committee on Plastic Pollution, accessed January 11, 2024, https://www.unep.org/about-un-environment/inc-plastic-pollution.

[57] See the contributions in *Regime Interaction in Ocean Governance: Problems, Theories and Methods*, edited by Seline Trevisanut, Nikolaos Giannopoulos, and Rozemarijn Roland Holst (Leiden: Brill Nijhoff, 2020), as well as Robin Mahon and Lucia Fanning, "Regional Ocean Governance: Polycentric Arrangements and Their Role in Global Ocean Governance," *Marine Policy* 107 (May 2019): 103590.

the growing number of international and regional ocean initiatives has added significantly to the complexity of global ocean governance, and led to a lack of coordination, the risk of duplication, and weaknesses of practical response.

The problem of fragmentation is particularly apparent if we consider the question of how maritime security relates to these new ocean governance initiatives. So, for example, it is generally the case that the agendas of the governance forums discussed above, such as the UN Ocean Conference or the BBNJ treaty, pay only scant attention to maritime security concerns. They do not address how maritime insecurities may impact the ocean or exacerbate marine environmental challenges. Neither do they address what kinds of security measures, such as maritime policing and surveillance, may be necessary to ensure that initiatives such as MPAs are meaningfully enforceable in the future. Indeed, MPA initiatives have been criticized as being "paper parks"[58] or reflecting ambitions of territorial control by states, rather than effectively contributing to marine environmental protection.[59]

This creates a paradoxical situation. On the one hand, planetary thinking is on the rise and the range and number of marine environmental protection initiatives increasing. However, on the other, institutional fragmentation and an insufficient link to the maritime security demands they imply raises doubts about the viability and sustainability of these measures in practice.

The difficulties of establishing new institutions at a global scale also suggest that it is doubtful whether marine environmental security responses will become more institutionalized or centralized in the future. It is more likely that maritime security will continue to be handled primarily through informal cooperative security solutions (see Chapter 7, Section 7.2) or through regional arrangements such as the EU and ASEAN. The tools that we discussed in Chapter 7 are thus unlikely to fall out of fashion any time soon, but will need to be improved and strengthened if they are to meet the challenges of marine environmental security going forward.

The Renaissance of Geopolitics and Strategic Competition

The rise of planetary thinking and the paradoxical fragmentation spurred by the new momentum in ocean governance is the first of the two master trends that will

---

[58] Alexis N. Rife, Brad Erisman, Alexandra Sanchez, and Octavio Aburto-Oropeza, "When Good Intentions Are Not Enough . . . Insights on Networks of 'Paper Park' Marine Protected Areas," *Conservation Letters* 6, no. 3 (2013): 200–212.

[59] Elizabeth M. De Santo, "Militarized Marine Protected Areas in Overseas Territories: Conserving Biodiversity, Geopolitical Positioning, and Securing Resources in the 21st Century," *Ocean & Coastal Management* 184 (February 2020): 105006.

determine the future of the maritime security agenda. A second drives the maritime security agenda in a different direction. It concerns a resurgence of interstate competition at sea, and the return of ideas that see the oceans as being part of geopolitical spheres of influence or subject to the territorial control of states.

Geopolitical issues have always been a consideration in the maritime domain (see Chapter 2, Section 2.2 and Chapter 3, Section 3.3). The oceans encompass numerous spaces of critical strategic and economic importance, which have the potential to become vectors of geopolitical contention. These include major sea lanes, along which the bulk of international maritime trade passes; "choke points" such as the Panama Canal, Suez Canal, or Strait of Malacca, where the traffic on these sea lanes is compressed and concentrated in narrow geographic locations; and maritime territories that might hold untapped natural resources or have the potential to threaten or protect a state's national security interests.

The rise of China and other major powers such as India is leading to a new and vigorous wave of geopolitical competition at sea.[60] Maritime security is increasingly seen as an interstate problem to be addressed through military means, with many states strengthening their naval capabilities to enable them to project presence and power into waters far from their own borders. These tensions are expressed at a diplomatic level too. States enter alliances and defense partnerships with each other, and smaller states seek shelter in such forms of cooperation. Geopolitical competition also has an important economic dimension, such as when states seek to secure access to critical resources like offshore oil or gas, or to control important infrastructures such as ports.

The fulcrum of geopolitical competition in the maritime domain today can be found in what is now often termed the Indo-Pacific region.[61] This is an explicitly maritime regional construct, comprising the ocean space stretching from the coast of East Africa to the South Pacific islands and beyond. Tensions center on the East Asian subregion, with ongoing maritime disputes in the East and South China Seas (see Chapter 4, Sections 4.2 and 4.4).

However, geopolitics is also increasingly influencing interstate relations across the wider region too, including in the Western Indian Ocean and South Pacific. Both China and India have invested heavily in their naval capabilities, for example, and foster diplomatic and economic relations with regional states including the construction of overseas bases and other infrastructures.[62] In the

---

[60] See for example Kai He and Mingjiang Li, "Understanding the Dynamics of the Indo-Pacific: US–China Strategic Competition, Regional Actors, and Beyond," *International Affairs* 96, no. 1 (January 2020): 1–7.

[61] Ashok Kapur, *Geopolitics and the Indo-Pacific Region* (Abingdon: Routledge, 2020).

[62] Mohan Malik, "China and India: Maritime Maneuvers and Geopolitical Shifts in the Indo-Pacific," *Rising Powers Quarterly* 3, no. 2 (2018): 67–81.

case of China, these activities are part of a wider strategy of global infrastructure development under the auspices of its One Belt One Road Initiative.

For their part, western countries, including Australia, EU member states, Japan, and the United States, have also reorientated their foreign and security policies to reflect these geopolitical shifts. This has included the development of dedicated Indo-Pacific strategies, naval deployments, heightened diplomatic cooperation with partner states in the region, and the creation of mini-lateral agreements between groups of states. Formats such as the QUAD and AUKUS (see Chapter 6, Section 6.3) have been strengthened into tighter defense alliances. These have deepened maritime security cooperation between some states, but also led to concerns that they might exacerbate geopolitical divisions and tensions and undermine regional cooperation more widely.

These increasing tensions between global powers are leading to substantial changes in the political context for maritime security, in at least two ways. First, thinking in geopolitical terms to some degree runs counter to the cooperative dynamics that characterize much of the toolbox of maritime security solutions and the rise planetary thinking which requires cooperation and multilateral rule setting. This in turn risks undermining the quite remarkable unity of effort that has characterized many multinational maritime security operations since 2010. It is notable, for example, that two recent UN Security Council debates on maritime security issues (in 2019 and 2021) were unable to reach a shared conclusion, in part due to geopolitical frictions between China and the United States.

Second, the rise of geopolitics in the maritime domain exacerbates what has been termed the "militarization dilemma" in maritime security.[63] This refers to the fact that because many regional states lack the capacity to protect shipping lanes or their EEZs on their own, they must rely on external actors to assist them in doing so. Yet the involvement of external actors also leads to the growing presence of foreign military forces, in ways that have the potential to increase geopolitical tensions and strategic competition. This can draw small states into wider geopolitical struggles, increase more localized regional tensions, and make developing a collective response to shared challenges of maritime security more difficult to achieve.

The war in Ukraine following the Russian invasion of 2022 has exacerbated these developments. The direct consequence of the war, at least in Europe, has been a turn to substantial military investments, potentially at the price of civilian and law enforcement efforts, as well as strengthening security thinking in terms of state threats and geopolitics. This has also caused regional organizations such as the EU to look more inwardly toward their home waters rather than working

---

[63] Christian Bueger and Jan Stockbruegger, "Maritime Security and the Western Indian Ocean's Militarisation Dilemma," *African Security Review* 31, no. 2 (April 2022): 195–210.

toward global and cooperative maritime security abroad, a trend that is reflected in the 2023 EU Maritime Security Strategy. Support for the sanctions against Russia has, moreover, created a new dividing line, with several states, including Türkiye, India, Brazil, and a range of African states, taking a critical or unsupportive stance toward some Western measures.

Taking a broader outlook, these trends fall together with what is sometimes discussed as a decline of the "liberal world order" or "rules-based order" that is characterized by multilateralism, effective international organizations, and universal principles of sovereignty, law, human rights, and democracy.[64] This is perhaps best visible in the maritime sector in the increasing contestation of the universality of UNCLOS, where China in particular has started to argue that UNCLOS should not be taken as universally applicable to all maritime activities but instead should be read as a specific treaty with more narrow scope.[65]

Summary

The future of maritime security is likely to be influenced by these two conflicting master trends. On the one hand, we can expect the oceans to receive more international attention and see stronger multilateral cooperation than ever before because of the rise of what we have called planetary thinking about ocean governance and environmental challenges. On the other hand, however, increasing geopolitical competition and tensions between major powers makes cooperation between states more difficult and risks exacerbating the militarization dilemma, whereby international naval deployments ostensibly for the purposes of maritime security operations import dynamics of geopolitical competition and militarization from outside.

8.6 Fifth Wave or New Era?

In this chapter, we have identified a series of new and emerging trends in global ocean politics. When discussing how the maritime security agenda historically

---

[64] Rebecca Strating, "The Rules-Based Order as Rhetorical Entrapment: Comparing Maritime Dispute Resolution in the Indo-Pacific," *Contemporary Security Policy* 44, no. 3 (July 2023): 372–409. See also the contributions in "Challenges to the Liberal International Order: International Organization at 75," *International Organization* 75, Special Issue no. 2 (Spring 2021); and "Ordering the World: Liberal Internationalism in Theory and Practice," *International Affairs*, 94, Special Issue no. 1 (January 2018).

[65] See for example Douglas Guilfoyle, "The Rule of Law and Maritime Security: Understanding Lawfare in the South China Sea," *International Affairs* 95, no. 5 (September 2019): 999–1017.

evolved over four waves in Chapter 2, we suggested that these developments might mean that a fifth wave of maritime security is on the horizon. However, if the changes between the first four waves were about incremental expansions of focus and the consolidation and spread of a common toolbox of solutions, the transition to a fifth wave is more profound and transformative in nature. Indeed, rather than constituting a further evolution of existing patterns, the fifth wave of maritime security might represent a more fundamental shift to a new era of security at sea—as significant as the shift from the Cold War to the post–Cold War period, or the unsettling of the maritime political order that occurred at the end of the 1990s (see Chapter 2).

The cornerstones of this new era are likely to be climate change, strategic competition, and critical maritime infrastructure protection. The new momentum in ocean governance and the renaissance of geopolitics drive the first two, while the critical maritime infrastructure debate might be on its way to becoming an encompassing umbrella to address the nexus between maritime terrorism, blue crime, cyber security, and energy security. These changes are already apparent in maritime security thinking. A telling example is the EU maritime security strategy of 2023, where, in stark contrast to its 2014 predecessor, the emphasis is on geopolitics, the environment, and infrastructures, rather than blue crime and maritime terrorism.[66]

It is not so much that the four waves of maritime security have been replaced; rather, they are now met with a set of more critical and politically urgent priorities of international security and global environmental sustainability. Consequently, these issues are bound to influence the response and approach to other aspects of maritime security as well.

One example is the risk of a growing militarization of maritime security responses. If the success story of counterpiracy off the coast of Somalia was one of international cooperation around a shared problem, its legacy may be one of increased military tensions as the naval deployments, relationships, and structures that were established to deal with the piracy problem turn their attention to a new era of strategic competition at sea. There is also the risk of new exclusions if cooperative efforts flounder, and the maritime security problems that most impact the coastal communities in the Global South—such as illicit fishing for example—become consumed by climate concerns and geopolitical tensions.

However, there are also important continuities and synergies between the first four waves of maritime security and the emerging new era. Indeed, in some ways, the recentering of maritime security as a core concern of international

---

[66] European Commission, "EUMSS."

politics is itself a product of the mainstreaming of the agenda and its institutionalization in strategy documents, coordination centers, and maritime domain awareness structures. The toolbox of maritime security solutions is likely to remain at the heart of the agenda in the new era, as will the nature of the actors and the character of the interactions between them. This is especially so in the case of the cooperative solutions that will be required in consequence of the turn to planetary thinking in global governance.

It is too early to say which of the two master trends in maritime security, planetary thinking or geopolitical competition, will dominate over the long term. Certainly there is a risk that international cooperation to tackle the environmental emergency at sea will be held hostage by the geopolitical concerns of states. However, it is equally the case that as the scale and impact of climate change and marine biodiversity loss become ever clearer, the imperative for states and other actors to work together will also increase. In this context, the future of maritime security will likely be one of uneasy and ongoing interaction between these two trends, with no one completely dominating the other, and ebbs and flows in the balance of influence of each over time. Either way, the maritime security agenda seems here to stay.

INDEX

For the benefit of digital users, indexed terms that span two pages (e.g., 52–53) may, on occasion, appear on only one of those pages.

Abu Sayaf, 3, 73, 75, 96
Achille Lauro, 71–72, 131
Africa, 26, 47, 101–103, 109, 156, 167–69
African Union, 132, 167–9
AIS (Automatic Identification System), 103, 177–78, 194
Al-Qaeda, 72, 74
Al-Shabaab, 3, 75
archipelagic sea lands (ASLs), 34
Arctic, 2, 7, 63, 207
armed guards, private, 24, 94, 142
AUKUS, 135, 214
Australia, 26, 40, 96, 103–5, 121, 128, 135, 167–68, 183, 202, 214
Australia Government Civil Maritime Security Strategy, 167–68
Australian Maritime Security Operations Centre, 128, 162, 174
Automatic Identification System. *See* AIS
automation, 9, 37, 190–91, 196, 209

Baltic and International Maritime Organization. *See* BIMCO
Baltic Sea, 133, 199, 202–3
Beirut Explosion, 74, 200
best management practices. *See* BMP
BIMCO (Baltic and International Maritime Organization), 139–40, 192, 195
Biodiversity, 88, 199, 211
biodiversity loss, 9, 12, 17, 27, 88, 117, 190, 204, 206, 208–9
blue acceleration, 16–17, 202
blue economy, 6–7, 26–27, 45–47, 130, 137–38, 144, 181, 205–6, 210
blue justice, 7, 27, 55–56, 148, 150
Blue Paradigms, 138, 150, 210

BMP (best management practices), 142, 157
Bob Baker, The, 116
Borgese, Elisabeth Mann, 14
Brazil, 102, 120, 135, 215
BRICS, 135, 157
Buzan, Barry, 1, 22, 47

Cabo Delgado, 109, 144
Canada, 62, 65–66, 75, 114, 163
capacity-building, 10, 134, 157–58, 182–83, 186–87
categories of blue crime, 87–91
CCG (China Coast Guard), 79–80
CGPCS (Contact Group on Piracy off the Coast of Somalia), 136, 158–59
Chagos Islands, 38, 63–64
China, 67–70, 78–80, 83–84, 113, 120, 122, 135, 139, 156, 163–64, 213–15
China Coast Guard. *See* CCG
Chinese fishing vessels, 79–80
climate change, 9, 12, 27, 37, 47, 70, 148, 190, 204–10, 216
climate change and biodiversity loss, 12, 190, 204, 206, 208–9
CMF (Combined Maritime Forces), 155–56, 160–61
CMP. *See* Coordinated Maritime Presence
coastal communities, 4–6, 56–57, 95, 144, 146, 150, 178, 180–82, 216
coast guard functions, 7, 124–25, 143, 160, 182, 186
cocaine trade, 75, 101–2, 104
Cold War, 15, 20, 201, 210, 216
Combined Maritime Forces. *See* CMF
commercial actors, 119, 138, 143–44, 151, 196
Comoros, 109–10

219

company security officer (CSO), 141
concept analysis, 45–46
Contact Group on Piracy off the Coast of Somalia.
   See CGPCS
Coordinated Maritime Presence (CMP),
   98, 161–62
coordination, 5, 9, 126, 128, 149, 151, 153, 159,
   162, 166, 170
counterpiracy operations, 98, 120, 126, 156,
   161, 163–64
counterterrorism operations, 134, 160–61
criminalization, 87, 89, 112, 144, 208
critical infrastructure protection, 9, 190, 193, 197–
   98, 203, 209
crystal meth, 104
CSO. *See* company security officer
cyber security, 9, 168, 190–93, 195–97, 199, 203,
   209, 216

data cables, 1, 9, 74, 82, 197, 199, 203
decolonization, 18–19, 55, 63–64
Denmark, 62, 82, 121–22, 139, 183, 202
DeSombre, Elizabeth R., 17, 65
Dittmer, Jason, 44, 174
doctrines, 124, 166

East Africa, 103, 213
East and South China Seas, 67, 78, 213
economic development, 6, 17, 26–27, 46–47, 51,
   55, 58, 130, 210
economic dislocation, 4, 52, 55–56, 144, 165
ecosystems, 9, 88–89, 114, 199, 203–5
EEZ (exclusive economic zone), 4, 32–35, 66, 68–
   70, 89, 120–22, 128, 177, 180–82, 207, 214
Egypt, 72, 75
EMASOH (European Maritime Awareness in the
   Strait of Hormuz), 161
energy, green, 144, 202
energy security, 201, 203, 216
environmental crimes, 87–89, 91, 110, 112, 117–
   18, 124, 133, 138, 145, 148, 205, 209
environmental protection, 6, 13, 32, 36, 122, 124,
   129, 133, 152, 177, 182
EUNAVFOR Atalanta, 161–62
European Commission, 28, 124, 134, 171,
   209, 216
European Maritime Awareness in the Strait of
   Hormuz. *See* EMASOH
European Migration Crisis, 25, 106–108, 150
European Union, 26, 43, 66, 121, 124, 129, 134,
   156, 158, 161–62, 167
exclusive economic zone. *See* EEZ

FAO (Food and Agriculture Organization), 16–19,
   111, 113, 115, 130–32
fisheries control, 4, 122–23, 127
Fisheries Crime, 112–116

fishing fleets, 2, 66, 69, 79–80
flags, 34, 62–63, 83, 117, 121–22
Food and Agriculture Organization. *See* FAO
France, 15, 25, 64, 67, 69, 139, 147, 165, 167, 183

G7, 135, 157–58
Germany, 82, 123, 183, 202
GFW (Global Fishing Watch), 148–50, 178
Ghana, 167, 169, 183
Global Fishing Watch. *See* GFW
Global Maritime Crime Programme. *See* GMCP
global ocean governance, 111, 121, 190, 210, 212
GMCP (Global Maritime Crime Programme), 26,
   132, 182
governance, informal, 55, 153–54, 159, 188
Greece, 81, 107, 121
Greenpeace, 147–48
grey-zone activities, 2, 59, 62, 77–78, 80, 82–85,
   123, 134, 195
Guilfoyle, Douglas, 35–37, 68, 164, 215

HADR (Humanitarian Assistance and Disaster
   Relief), 125
Hastings, Justin V., 55, 97
high-risk area. *See* HRA
Hormuz, Strait of, 2, 34, 80, 133, 157
Houthis, 76
HRA (high-risk area), 142, 157
human rights, 36, 46, 71, 106, 148, 150, 164, 215
human security, 6, 46–47, 130
human trafficking, 6, 88, 89, 106, 109–10
hybrid warfare, 8, 77, 81

Illegal, Unregulated and Underreported fishing
   (IUU), 3, 111, 114, 132
illicit fishing, 1, 54, 56, 59, 87–89, 91, 110, 112–
   17, 132–33, 138, 146, 148–49, 152
IMO (International Maritime Organization),
   18–19, 36, 42, 91, 130–31, 136, 139–43, 173,
   182, 192, 194–95
IMSC (International Maritime Security
   Construct), 161
India, 25, 69, 135, 156, 158, 163, 165, 167,
   176, 213–15
Indian Ocean, 27, 55, 93, 101, 103, 121, 129, 136–
   37, 144, 156
Indian Ocean Commission (IOC), viii, 134, 162
Indian Ocean Naval Symposium, 136, 156
Indonesia, 67–68, 95–96, 104, 121, 161
Indo-Pacific Region, 40, 213–14
installations, offshore, 143, 193, 197
interagency coordination, 5, 25, 159, 171, 174
International Maritime Organization. *See* IMO
international organizations (IOs), 18–19, 42, 44,
   113, 115, 119, 121, 129–30, 133–34, 137,
   142–43, 157–58, 180, 182, 215
international straits, 34, 89

INDEX

International Tribunal for the Law of the Sea. *See* ITLOS
interstate disputes, 4, 52, 62, 65, 83, 126
IORA (Indian Ocean Rim Association), 134
Iran, 35, 78, 80–81, 83–84, 102, 113, 161, 165
irregular migration, 105–6, 108, 124, 126, 133, 146, 148, 150, 152, 156, 163, 207–8
Islamic State group, The, 75
island building, 69, 79–80
islands, 4, 34, 53, 62–65, 68–70, 79, 116, 201, 204–5
Israel, 35, 72, 80–81
Italy, 72, 107, 176
ITLOS (International Tribunal for the Law of the Sea), 61, 64, 130, 132

Japan, 15, 26, 40, 79, 104, 120, 122–23, 135, 156, 183, 214

Kenya, 26, 103, 164, 167
kidnap for ransom, 89, 91
Klein, Natalie, 31, 35, 36, 73

law enforcement, 24, 35, 54, 58, 75, 89, 103, 118, 182–83
Liberation Tigers of Tamil Eelam (Tamil Tigers), 76
Libya, 102, 107, 161, 183
Libyan Coast Guard, 108

Malacca, Strait of, 13, 34, 91, 95–96, 161, 213
Malaysia, 67–68, 95–96, 104, 116, 161
Malta, vii–viii, 20, 121
marine pollution, 17, 88, 111–12, 136
marine protected areas. *See* MPA
maritime domain awareness. *See* MDA
Maritime Security Centre Horn of Africa (MSCHoA), 156–57
maritime security operations. *See* MSO
maritime security strategies, 25, 28, 165–66, 168, 170–71, 174, 185, 188, 195, 203, 209
MARPOL, 111–12, 120
Mauritius, 62–64, 147
MDA (maritime domain awareness), 25, 124, 127, 131, 133, 136, 151–53, 160, 162, 171–74, 176–80, 182, 185
MDA centers, 177–78
militarization dilemma, 214–15
military bases, 64, 79
mining, seabed, 31, 132, 138
Mongolia, 35, 121
Mozambique, 103, 109, 144
MPAs (Marine Protected Areas), 121, 208, 210–12
MSCHoA (Maritime Security Centre Horn of Africa), 156–57
MV Limburg, 71, 73

MV *SuperFerry*, 71, 73

NATO (North Atlantic Treaty Organization), 40, 43, 66, 134, 156–57, 161, 163, 167
NATO members, 62, 199
NATO Shipping Centre, 156–57
naval diplomacy, 83, 124–25
naval strategy, 5, 7, 124, 126
Netherlands, 15, 121
networks, 4, 38, 43–44, 54, 56–57, 104, 107, 146, 193, 212
Newport Manual, 36–37
New Zealand, 104–5, 147, 167–68
NGOs, 108, 116, 119, 145–52, 158, 178
Niger Delta, 97
Nigeria, 97, 117, 143–44, 167
North Africa, 24, 107, 150, 202
North Sea, 32, 129, 202–3
Norway, 82, 121, 139, 183, 202
NotPetya, 192–94

ocean governance, 7, 10, 13–14, 20, 31, 130, 133, 135, 211, 213, 215–16
oil tankers, 48, 80, 111
operations
    constabulary, 124–25
    grey-zone, 191, 199
    joint, 43, 127
Østhagen, Andreas, 40–41, 61
overfishing, 66, 111, 115, 144

Percy, Sarah, 23, 93, 156
Persian Gulf, 80, 161
Peters, Kimberley, 12–13
Philippines, 67–69, 96, 104, 161
piracy, 23, 53, 91–98
pollution crimes, 56, 133
Project Kraken, 146
Proliferation Security Initiative (PSI), 73, 160, 200

Rainbow Warrior, 148
ReCAAP, 95, 177, 188
Red Sea, 76, 109
regional organizations, 2, 5, 9, 25, 129–30, 132, 151, 153, 158–60, 165, 167, 181–82
RFMOs (Regional Fisheries Management Organizations), 111–13, 115
Russia, 15, 78, 81–83, 102, 120, 135, 156, 165, 199, 202, 215

sanctions, international, 35, 80–81
satellites, 149, 177, 180
sea power, 2, 5–8, 14, 39–40, 46, 130
Second World War, 15–16, 18–19, 41, 67, 198
Security Council, 23, 26, 81, 84, 86, 91, 97, 133, 157–58
Seychelles, 64, 103–4, 117, 139, 162–64, 167

SHADE, 156, 158, 188
shipping containers, 16, 75, 99, 102–3, 139
shipping industry, 23, 25, 91, 94, 111, 131, 138, 141–43, 156–58, 172, 179
Singapore, vii–viii, 20, 25, 92, 95–96, 121, 123, 161, 164, 176, 178, 196, 202
smuggling, 1, 3, 24, 28, 54, 59, 88–90, 96, 98–100, 106, 110, 148, 155
  arms, 75, 88, 99
  methods, 99–100
  narcotics, 1, 8, 35, 75, 87–89, 91, 98–99, 101–05, 114, 132
  people, 1, 3, 8, 24, 49, 75, 87, 88–89, 105–10 (*see also* human trafficking)
  varieties of, 99
SOLAS (Safety of Life at Sea), 18, 141
Somalia, 8, 23–24, 26, 28, 55, 57, 91, 93–95, 97, 109–10, 134, 136–38, 142–43, 157–58, 182–83
Somali Piracy, 24, 28, 55–56, 91, 94–95, 131, 146, 155
South Africa, 109, 113, 135, 167
South America, 15, 101–2
South China Sea, 2, 38, 47, 62, 65, 67–69, 78–79, 83, 213, 215
Southeast Asia, 3, 7–8, 22–23, 25–26, 67, 91, 93, 95–97, 101, 104–5, 128–29, 175–76, 178
Southern Africa, 15, 109, 136
South Pacific, 7, 105, 121, 147, 163, 213
sovereignty, 12, 14, 33, 39, 65, 68, 78, 96, 121, 145, 215
Spain, 13, 15, 25, 65–66, 107, 113–14, 167
Sri Lanka, 76, 109
Steinberg, Philip, 12–13
Strategic Studies, 23, 38, 93, 125, 144
Suez Canal, 13, 34, 74, 76, 198, 213
surveillance, 5, 7, 54, 122, 124, 147, 160, 172, 177, 180, 212
Sweden, 82, 202

Switzerland, 121
Syria, 72, 81, 102, 107

Tanzania, 103, 167
territorial disputes, 20, 63, 67
territorialization, 13, 19, 40
Thailand, 96, 104, 161
Thunder, 116–17
Titanic disaster, 18, 141
trade, global, 1, 13–14, 17, 89, 99, 101, 137, 145
trust, 128, 146, 154, 174, 185
Turkey, 35, 102, 107, 183, 215

UK Maritime Trade Operations. *See* UKMTO
UKMTO (UK Maritime Trade Operations), 156–57
Ukraine, 63, 82, 102, 156, 211, 215
UNCLOS (United Nations Convention on the Law of the Sea), 4, 7, 19–21, 31–32, 34–42, 66, 68–70, 92, 128, 132–33, 207, 215
UNCLOS III negotiations, 19–20
underwater infrastructures, 82, 197, 199–200
United Arab Emirates, 80, 121
United Kingdom, 14, 25–26, 28, 40, 63–64, 66, 69, 121–23, 135, 139, 147
United Nations, 17–18, 106, 129–31
US Navy, 72, 79, 127, 205
USS Cole, 22, 71–73

Vietnam, 67–69, 80, 113, 121

war in Ukraine, 63, 82, 211, 215
Western Indian Ocean, 22, 25, 73, 75, 107–9, 134, 136, 155, 160, 163–64, 175–76, 180, 182
Whisky War, 62–63
Wilson, Brian, 86, 126, 133
wind farms, 1, 74, 193, 202, 208, 210

Yemen, 3, 72–73, 76, 109–10

Printed in the USA/Agawam, MA
October 29, 2024

875264.001